AMO
PRIMITIVE
IN
BORN

A LOWLAND DUSUN ON A BUFFALO.

This ungainly looking brute is a favourite steed, and can keep up a jog-trot for hours, when it is not exposed to the full heat of the sun. The animal is " steered " by means of the cord attached to the nose-ring. A saddle with a high wooden peak is generally used in buffalo-riding.

AMONG PRIMITIVE PEOPLES IN BORNEO

A DESCRIPTION OF THE LIVES,
HABITS & CUSTOMS OF THE PIRATICAL
HEAD-HUNTERS OF NORTH BORNEO,
WITH AN ACCOUNT OF INTERESTING OBJECTS
OF PREHISTORIC ANTIQUITY DISCOVERED
IN THE ISLAND

BY
IVOR H. N. EVANS

With an Introduction by
BRIAN DURRANS

SINGAPORE
OXFORD UNIVERSITY PRESS
OXFORD NEW YORK
1990

Oxford University Press

Oxford New York Toronto
Delhi Bombay Calcutta Madras Karachi
Petaling Jaya Singapore Hong Kong Tokyo
Nairobi Dar es Salaam Cape Town
Melbourne Auckland
and associated companies in
Berlin Ibadan

Oxford is a trade mark of Oxford University Press

First published by
Seeley Service & Co. Ltd., London, 1922

First issued as an Oxford University Press paperback 1990

ISBN 0 19 588974 6

Printed in Malaysia by Peter Chong Printers Sdn. Bhd.
Published by Oxford University Press Pte. Ltd.,
Unit 221, Ubi Avenue 4, Singapore 1440

INTRODUCTION

IVOR EVANS was a pioneer in Malaysian ethnography and archaeology. Most of his career was spent as a museum curator in peninsular Malaya, which gave him access to the sites, communities, and collections around which he built his reputation. But it was in Borneo, specifically British North Borneo (now Sabah, part of Malaysia), that the happy idea of devoting his life to studying the cultures of this region first occurred to him. Visiting the country for less than a year between 1910 and 1911, he fell permanently under the spell of the land and its people.[1]

This book is based on that brief but profound experience, supplemented by a further two-month visit in 1915. Although hardly a full-fledged academic treatise, neither is it just an enthusiastic report. It encompasses ethnographic observation, culture history, and colonial and personal perspectives, but doubles as a vivid and enjoyable piece of travel writing. Since Evans himself permeates the book, often in the first person, this introduction begins with a biographical sketch of the author and tries to show connections between his background and achievements. The second part considers the book itself in terms of the conditions in which it was written and briefly compares it with more recent work on North Borneo.

* * *

Ivor Hugh Norman Evans was born in Cambridge on 6 October 1886, the only child of a University official. The family's background was respectable and conservative: Ivor's paternal grandfather was a minor cleric married to the daughter of a Bank of England administrator; his maternal grandfather was a Tory Member of Parliament.

Ivor's father was excluded from the dedication to his unpublished autobiography ('To my mother's memory and to Din bin Brahim, companion of my travels for so many years') probably for a more deeply felt reason than that he was, in his son's words, 'a man of little imagination, rather selfish, and much too dogmatic'. He is credited only with encouraging an interest in nature and collecting, but even in this respect, McKenney Hughes, Professor of Geology, was perhaps more influential (Evans, 1948, p. 13). Ivor admits that 'of my father I find some difficulty in writing; it is much less easy to form a just and correct estimate of those nearer to one than of strangers' (ibid., p. 6). He says so little of his mother that this probably also applies to her. Although his autobiography clearly confirms that Ivor was homosexual, it does so between the lines. His father's attitude must have been a major factor in the development of Ivor's character, and to assess his father justly and correctly would probably have meant referring to his own sexuality more explicitly than he wished. Ivor tries to blame his father's character defects, in part, on an unhappy childhood, spent 'with little intellectual company' (ibid., p. 8). His own, however, seems to have been scarcely more enjoyable.[2] But if his father's life was cramped and conventional, Ivor's response to the frustrations of his own youth lay in the very different direction of personal eccentricity.

Evans's character seems to have been not just quirkiness but a strategy for social survival, and probably underlay the enthusiasm for other ways of life which is revealed in both his career and writing. The autobiography indicates a refusal to let social prejudice about his sexuality intimidate him into either hypocrisy or a stereotyped role. On the evidence of his personal philosophy, which is eclectic and inconsistent even in the formal version he presents in his writing, this difficult and lifelong manoeuvre was not wholly successful.

If eccentricity was one way of handling, expressing, or avoiding his problems, his academic style gave it a suitable outlet. Evans preferred pottering in scattered fields rather than concentrated, integrative work. This is not to deny the documentary value of his specialized studies of Malayan Negritos or of Dusun religion; but they lack the theoretical integrity of the usual ethnographic monograph. More energy was channelled into notes and short papers on a variety of subjects: folk-tales, rituals, linguistics, economics, bronze drums, and prehistoric stone tools. Most of his books (including the present one) consist of largely self-contained chapters.

This eclecticism cannot be wholly blamed on the nature of museum work, for although he had to respond to unpredictable opportunities, he also enjoyed considerable scope to pursue his interests and could have specialized more had he wished.[3] Were he more closely linked to the individuals and universities through which anthropology underwent its functionalist revolution in the 1920s, his approach might be interpreted as an alternative to re-learning the subject. But the main factor seems to have been personal: a magpie's view of academic facts and ideas would especially suit someone already inclined to separate contradictory aspects of his life.

It was not only Evans's mental filing system that counteracted a tendency of his private experience towards a more comprehensive questioning of social convention: he is likely in any case to have been more conventional in one respect to compensate for being less so in another. Personal eccentricity was then both an expression of this double strategy and also a repair-kit for its occasional punctures.

Someone whose adaptation to the world is complex and shaky usually prefers to believe it is simple and secure. Evans states his personal philosophy as if it were a kind of Sermon on the Mount. He expresses an unsnobbish liking for 'agreeable and pleasant company—not necessarily highbrow' and for 'primitive and simple people', while dismissing 'intolerance', 'hide-bound conventions and those who follow them', 'persons who always conceal their opinions', and 'cruelty, including mental cruelty'. One wonders what personal experience prompted his hatred of those who 'take a perverse pleasure in preventing others from being happy'. His own ideal was that 'one should obtain as much pleasure out of life as is possible, but without doing harm to others'.[4] The significance of these precepts from the perspective of trying to understand Evans (and through him, his work) is not so much whether he lived up to them—his writing suggests considerable inconsistency[5]—as that he found it necessary to formulate them at all. He was sceptical of religion and detached from some of the most ingrained conventions of his own background. Finding established creeds inadequate, he therefore had to invent his own. But he should not be regarded as simply a man with problems. Evans owed much of his later scientific achievement to the spirit of independence and selective open-mindedness which his personal predicament engendered. A taste for protracted argument, such as he had with the missionary–ethnographer Paul Schebesta,[6] also seems rooted in his personal background.

After a distasteful time at King's College Choir School and as a boarder in Yorkshire, he enrolled at Charterhouse which was much more to his liking. Discipline was lax, and he learnt or developed a disrespect for the 'good and great'. Then a brief holiday gave Ivor his first taste of travel outside Europe when he accompanied his father to South Africa for a meeting of the British Association. With this came two experiences that were to influence him significantly: first, visiting Zulu villages during an excursion outside Durban kindled a passion for tribal and non-European cultures; and second, a direct encounter with the widespread practice of importing an outside work-force (in this case, Chinese) rather than developing the economy with local labour raised doubts about colonial policy. While this encounter bred criticism only of the practice rather than the principles of colonial policy, it seems to have made a lasting impact on the young man and helped give an international dimension to personal and social problems with which he had been grappling up till then.

From Charterhouse, Evans entered Clare College, where he confesses he spent his time in more pleasurable activities than studying. It was there, however, that his earlier interest in collecting turned towards ethnography, under the influence of William Ridgeway, Disney Professor of Archaeology, and especially of Baron von Hügel, the first Curator of the University Museum of Archaeology and Anthropology.[7] Equipped with an eccentric personality, a life-style judged aberrant by the standards of his time, a taste for adventure, a little anthropological knowledge and rather more enthusiasm, he joined the North Borneo Chartered Company as a junior civil servant and arrived in the territory in 1910, at the age of 24.

In this part of South-East Asia, Evans found peoples already inured to foreign interference (Chinese, Indians, and Malays had long preceded Europeans) and with proud traditions of their own. But Borneans were probably even more appealing to him because, in their environment, he could avoid the polite but oppressive conventions of English society. For British servants of the Empire, if Malaya was a backwater, Borneo was truly *ultima Thule*; the best-connected preferred India. Among those attracted to Borneo were therefore men who, for various reasons, did not see themselves primarily as civil servants at all. By contrast with the Indian service, the workload of officials here was more varied because there were so few of them; there were hardly any European women; and local administrative support was scant, especially upcountry where there was no previous bureaucracy to adapt for colonial purposes.[8]

But if Evans liked the country, the people, and the travelling, he hated being ordered from place to place (see pp. 74–5 of this book). He was enchanted with North Borneo but his career lay elsewhere and in a different type of work. He resigned in 1911, less than a year after his arrival, returned to Cambridge for anthropological training under Professor Haddon and others, and shortly after, in April 1912, was appointed assistant curator and ethnographer at the Perak Museum in Taiping. By this time, he was beginning to publish notes on the Dusun of North Borneo,[9] although it was another four years before more appeared and longer still before the present book began to take shape, each depending on additional observations from a second visit to North Borneo for two months in 1915.[10] Besides editing the *Journal* of the Federated Malay States Museums and becoming active in archaeological work,[11] he had already begun work on this book by around 1920.

In 1926, Evans was promoted Ethnographer in the Federated Malay States Museums, and a year later most of his papers were published in a separate volume (Evans, 1927). In 1932, due to economic recession, he took early retirement in Suffolk which he tolerated long enough to complete perhaps his most important book, *The Negritos of Malaya* (1937), and then returned to Borneo, where he remained except for occasional visits to England after the Second World War.

Like other expatriate Europeans, Evans was interned by the Japanese in April 1942; a fellow prisoner at Kuching recalls that he was known as 'Old Bangau'—a North Bornean term for the secretary bird—on account of his hair (which curled up at the neck); his tall, thin physique; and his 'donnish' gait (leaning slightly forward with his hands behind him).[12] Learning after the war that his manuscript on the Dusun had been destroyed in Labuan (where it had been stored with other material, also lost), he set about recreating it and adding fresh information. His autobiography, written and revised in Labuan by 1948 and rejected by at least one publisher, was originally to have been called *Mr Inquisitive*, but the author changed his mind. The completed book on Dusun religion was published in 1953, over four decades after his first encounter with these people.[13] Ivor Evans died in Labuan on 3 May 1957. His estate was divided between Din bin Brahim and Cambridge University, whose Evans Fund has since supported much significant work in the ethnography and archaeology of South-East Asia.

* * *

This book first appeared in 1922, which might claim to be the date of birth of modern ethnography. In that year were published Malinowski's *The Argonauts of the Western Pacific* and Radcliffe-Brown's *The Andaman Islanders*, two now-classic studies which established participant-observation field-work as the hallmark of professional anthropology.

These two monographs broke new ground in their theoretical approach, treating social and cultural systems as integrated wholes. On the other hand, they tapped into an existing (and continuing) tradition of what might loosely be called exotic travel writing. The serious academic and the entertaining travel writer are today two different people, or at least roles; but until the second half of this century, social anthropology was still establishing its intellectual credentials and the style in which academics (at least, anthropologists) presented their findings was more accessible than it usually is today. The growth of enquiry and the state of European empires created favourable conditions for both pathbreaking and more modestly descriptive ethnographies.

But to rescue the present book from the shadow of its illustrious contemporaries takes more than a claim that it is an expression of its times. It was intended neither as a contribution to anthropological theory nor (as the author himself acknowledged) as a definitive ethnography of North Borneo.[14]

In fact, the book belongs in a quite different category: that of cultural, historical, and environmental description written in an unpretentious and frankly subjective style. Another volume published in the same series (and advertised in the endpapers of the original edition of Evans's book) was Tyndale Biscoe's *Kashmir in Sunlight and Shade*, an account of imperialism with a human face, which *The Times* eulogized as 'the justification and embodiment of British rule in the East'. But although it is somewhat disjointed in composition and inconsistent in some of its arguments, the present book is quite different from that. It was also different from Owen Rutter's *British North Borneo* (1922). If Biscoe's book was an apologia, Rutter's, published the same year as Evans's and dealing with the same part of the world, was serious ethnography which studiously avoided political controversy. Not surprisingly, when Sir Joseph West Ridgeway, President of the British North Borneo Chartered Company, wrote an approving preface, it was for Rutter's book, not this one.

While revealing the predictable bias of an Englishman in his position and generation, Evans chose in this book to politely but devastatingly demolish the pretence of the Chartered Company, then the local agent of colonial power, to serve the best interests of the Bornean people. The force of his argument derives not from morality (of which, like religion, he is suspicious) but from property relations. The Company's shareholders, he argued, are generally bound to favour the best return on their investment; the cost to local people is no concern of theirs. For his predicament, Evans blames neither the shareholders nor the officers of the Company. A cynic might suspect he used this argument only to avoid antagonizing personal friends or colleagues more than absolutely necessary; while that may still have been a consideration, to exaggerate this motive would be to misinterpret both his main point and his character. In the Bornean context, he argued, investing for profit privileged economic interest over morality. To the directors of the Company and its apologists, however, Evans was essentially an insider, and his expression of familiar prejudices must have made his criticism look more like letting the team down rather than outright Bolshevism. If for that reason he got his points across, his personal eccentricity meant they need not be taken too seriously.[15] A loner rather than a spokesman, Evans could probably neither follow a leader nor integrate himself in a group, however far he might have agreed with its principles.[16]

While the present book deals mainly with a small part of North Borneo, a later book by Owen Rutter, *The Pagans of North Borneo* (1929), is not only broader in scope but also more thorough; and it carries a seal of anthropological approval in the form of an introduction by C. G. Seligman. As a general introduction to the ethnography of North Borneo, whether for the time in which it was written or for today, Rutter's book far surpasses Evans's. But the present book has the compensating merit of revealing far more clearly the interaction between the writer and his circumstances; it has the intimacy of a notebook. Nothing since published on North Borneo quite matches its good-humoured enthusiasm. The serious student will find a wealth of more detailed, and better-based, information in a range of specialist literature, especially the journals of the Sabah Society and of the Sarawak Museum. As he himself anticipated, this later work has corrected, amplified, or re-focused much of what Evans wrote; but it can never revise the infectious style of his writing. In the words of the former curator of the Raffles Museum in Singapore, 'A curator, to be efficient, should be versatile, and he will earn, as Evans has done, the enduring gratitude of future workers in his whole range of subjects if he bequeaths to them the benefit of his experience and learning instead of taking it with him to the grave.' (Tweedie, 1958, p. xx.) In this book, Evans bequeaths to us the experience of a human being, before he acquired the learning of a curator.

British Museum BRIAN DURRANS
March 1990

1. Through a dramatic first impression, North Borneo came to epitomize the entire region for him: 'I . . . was placed in charge of the Tempasuk sub-district, as it was then called, with which I fell in love immediately' (Evans, 1953, p. xv); '. . . it always seemed to me, in 1910 and 1911, that here, on turning a corner, one might suddenly come upon the Spirit of the East' (Evans, 1948, p. 451). From 1938 until his death nineteen years later, North Borneo became Evans's adopted home.

2. Among other disappointments and difficulties, 'I appeared . . . to have been circumcised in a very half-hearted manner, though I was never told so . . .' (Evans, 1948, p. 11).

3. He tried to rationalize this in terms of the special needs of museum work: 'It is no use appointing to the curatorship of a general ethnological museum, a man who is a specialist, shall we say, on some one corner of Africa, unless it appears that he is capable of, and will, take a world-wide interest in ethnographica' (Evans, 1948, p. 167). One could as easily argue the contrary, that detailed understanding of how a particular culture works is more useful in museum work than more general knowledge thinly spread; but in practice, these curatorial qualifications are complementary. The main point, however, is that Evans's attempt at self-justification may reflect resentment of specialists whose work drew more attention than his own. In the words of a colleague and friend: '. . . he craved recognition [and] . . . keenly resented

lack of appreciation . . .' (Cole, 1958, p. xix).

4. Evans, 1948, pp. 657–8.

5. For instance, it is clear from his autobiography (Evans, 1948) that his hedonism (ibid., p. 658) is tempered by a sense of responsibility towards the future, with regard to preserving artefact collections (ibid., p. 164); and for all his democratic pretensions (ibid., pp. 31, 657), he admitted 'to some admiration for historical name and inherited rank and breeding' (ibid., p. 336).

Evans's inconsistency also extends to his views of the peoples of South-East Asia. While stating that a man's background is irrelevant if his character is pleasant (ibid., p. 336), he also claims that 'the Chinese as a whole, for some reason, difficult to state, . . . fill me with feelings of revulsion' (this volume, p. 78). This suggests that when the Malays get the same treatment—'on the whole I prefer the Malays of the Malay Peninsula to the other peoples [of South-East Asia]' (Evans, 1948, p. 256); whereas 'altogether the Mohammedan native is not usually a very attractive personage' (this volume, p. 30)—this cannot be dismissed as wisdom overruling youthful impetuosity: the present book was published when Evans was already 36, and his remark about the Chinese was made when he was 62.

6. Differences between the two men on the Negritos of Malaya—pursued for a decade from the late 1920s in *Man*, the *Journal of the Royal Anthropological Institute*, and in Evans, 1937—concerned differences of research methodology as well as of interpretation. Evans's failure to see that Schebesta's work was flawed not just empirically, but also in some of its theoretical assumptions, stemmed from the narrow empiricism of his own work, perhaps tinged with anti-Catholic (or anti-clerical) prejudice; he cannot resist pointing out, for instance, that Schebesta's research was 'financed by Pope Pius XI' (Evans, 1937, p. v).

A useful account of the views of Evans and Schebesta on Negrito deities is given in Endicott, 1979, Ch. 7.

7. Ebin and Swallow, 1984.

8. A sketch of the life of a North Borneo District Officer is found in both Evans, 1922 and Rutter, 1922; but perhaps the shrewdest assessment, contrasting it with that of the District Commissioner in India, is in Bruce, 1924, Ch. IV.

9. Evans, 1912. Since the 1950s and 1960s (that is, after Evans's time), the term 'Dusun' has been used less, or less sweepingly, both by students of North Bornean ethnography and by the peoples themselves. Many formerly known as Dusun now regard themselves as Kadazan, while for ethnographers, 'Dusunic' is a linguistic rather than a cultural category.

10. Evans revisited North Borneo for two months in 1915 and on that basis wrote a second paper (Evans, 1917, see p. 151) to supplement his earlier one (Evans, 1912). In the present book, while describing a feature of Bajau coffins, he states that 'I write from memories of five years ago' (p. 227). From this it might reasonably be assumed that Evans was writing in 1920, a plausible two years before the book was published, about his observations of 1915—rather than in 1916, a less likely six years before the publication date, about his initial sojourn of 1910–11. In fact, not only did he probably revise his memories of 1910–11 in the light of what he learnt in 1915, but it is a surprising admission that even for observations made in 1915 (after he had received further training in anthropology), he relied on an uncertain memory rather than notes.

11. Sites Evans worked on in peninsular Malaya are listed in Matthews, 1961, while Harrisson and Harrisson (1971) give an account of the prehistory of Sabah to which Evans's work also contributed.

12. A. J. N. Richards, personal communication, 1989. Evans could also joke at his own expense: 'People with long legs should be careful when riding a buffalo in the plains . . .' (this volume, p. 63).

13. The 1953 book—his last—is now affectionately dedicated to Din alone ('companion of my travels for more than thirty years, whose care of me has made this work possible') but although its autobiographical preface refers to diaries and other matters, it is silent about the 1948 document.

14. Writing a year after the original publication of this book, Evans refers to his published work, especially that on Borneo (including the present volume), as being 'of a pioneering nature, forming a rough track, which later-comers will, I hope, develop into a fair highway' (Evans, 1923, p. vi). In this book, as in much else he wrote, Evans's empiricism allows him to report ethnographic facts without wrapping them in too much interpretation. If this makes his choice of facts seem haphazard, it can also bring the reader closer to at least some aspects of traditional life. For example, in the view of one colleague, Evans's recording of folk-tales is superior to 'mere ethnographical treatises' in giving insight into native thought (Tweedie, 1960, p. 110).

15. Nevertheless, the Company was still in a dilemma. In letters sent to both the publisher and Evans himself between September and December 1922, the Company objected to certain passages, among them the splendid questioning, on p. 23 of the present book, of the Company's moral and legal right to any of the territories which it then possessed. After consulting with the publisher, Evans, in a letter dated 9 January 1923, informed the Company Secretary, H. G. Forbes, that they 'advise me that, should there be a future edition of my book, they have no objection to the two paragraphs, specified in your former letter, being withdrawn. It is understood that this letter is without prejudice.'

Evans is here making the merest conciliatory gesture towards the Company, and in conceding its demands for the exclusion of the two passages to which it objected in its letter of 11 September 1922, leaves the fundamental criticism intact. To begin with, the Company did not even notice the offending passage, only objecting in its letter to the publisher dated 8 December 1922.

The Company preferred to threaten legal action rather than carry it out, probably because it was more in their interests to leave the awkward criticism undisturbed than to give it a wider airing in the courts.

For drawing my attention to this correspondence, I am indebted to the Director and Deputy Director of the Sabah Museum and State Archives, where it is held. For further background to the Chartered Company period of British colonialism in North Borneo, see Tregonning, 1958.

16. In his youth, Evans was invited by John Maynard Keynes ('the financial expert') to join his 'Agenda Society'—'the idea was that every member should take up something that ought to be done, and to do it . . , I thought to myself, "If I want to do a thing, I'll do it without belonging to any society, and should hate to 'take up' anything in which I'm not interested, just because it ought to be done, especially when I have so many things that I want to do already" ' (Evans, 1948).

References

Black, I. D., 'Interethnic Relations and Culture Change under Colonial Rule: A Study of Sabah', in G. N. Appell (ed.), *Studies in Borneo Societies: Social Process and Anthropological Explanation*, Center for Southeast Asian Studies, Northern Illinois University, Special Report No. 12, 1976, pp. 27–43.

Blagden, C. O., Review of Evans, *Among Primitive Peoples in Borneo* . . . (London, Seeley Service, 1922), *Man*, 1922, No. 81.

Bruce, Charles, *Twenty Years in Borneo*, London, Cassell, 1924.

Cole, Fay-Cooper, 'The Late Ivor Hugh Norman Evans, MA', *The Sarawak Museum Journal*, Vol. VIII, No. 11 (New Series), No. 26 (Old Series), June 1958, pp. xviii–xix.

Ebin, V. and Swallow, D. A., *'The Proper Study of Mankind . . .'—Great Anthropological Collections in Cambridge*, Cambridge University Museum of Archaeology and Anthropology, 1984.

Endicott, Kirk, *Batek Negrito Religion*, Oxford, Clarendon Press, 1979.

Evans, Ivor H. N., 'Notes on the Religious Beliefs, Superstitions, Ceremonies, and Tabus of the Dusuns of the Tuaran and Tempassuk Districts, British North Borneo', *Journal of the Royal Anthropological Institute*, Vol. XCLII, 1912, pp. 380–96.

——— 'Notes on Some Beliefs and Customs of the "Orang Dusun" of British North Borneo', *Journal of the Royal Anthropological Institute*, Vol. XLVII, 1917, pp. 151–9.

——— *Studies in Religion, Folk-Lore, and Custom in British North Borneo and the Malay Peninsula*, Cambridge, Cambridge University Press, 1923.

——— *Papers on the Ethnology and Archaeology of the Malay Peninsula*, Cambridge, Cambridge University Press, 1927.

——— *The Negritos of Malaya*, Cambridge, Cambridge University Press, 1937.

——— 'The Years Behind Me: An Autobiography', unpublished typescript in the Cambridge University Museum of Archaeology and Anthropology, 1948.

——— *The Religion of the Tempasuk Dusuns of North Borneo*, Cambridge, Cambridge University Press, 1953.

Harrisson, Tom and Harrisson, Barbara, *The Prehistory of Sabah*, Monograph of the Sabah Society Journal, Vol. IV (1969–70), 1971.

Matthews, John, *A Check-List of "Hoabinhian" Sites Excavated in Malaya 1860–1939*, Kuala Lumpur, University of Malaya, Department of History, Papers on Southeast Asian Subjects No. 3, 1961.

Rutter, Owen, *British North Borneo: An Account of Its History, Resources and Native Tribes*, London, Constable, 1922.

——— *The Pagans of North Borneo*, London, Hutchinson, 1929.

Tregonning, K. G., *Under Chartered Company Rule*, Singapore, University of Malaya Press, 1958.

Tweedie, M. W. E., 'The Late Ivor Hugh Norman Evans, MA', *The Sarawak Museum Journal*, Vol. VIII, No. 11 (New Series), No. 26 (Old Series), June 1958, pp. xix–xx.

——— 'Ivor Hugh Norman Evans, MA', *Journal of the Malayan Branch of the Royal Asiatic Society*, Vol. 33, No. 1, May 1960, pp. 109–10.

CONTENTS

Contents

CHAPTER XXV

CHAPTER XXVI

CHAPTER XXVII

CHAPTER XXVIII

CHAPTER XXIX

CHAPTER XXX

CHAPTER XXXI

APPENDICES

LIST OF ILLUSTRATIONS

Among Primitive Peoples in Borneo

CHAPTER I

BRITISH NORTH BORNEO—GENERAL DESCRIPTION—HISTORY—GOVERNMENT

THE country with which this book deals is the territory of the British North Borneo Company, and in particular the adjacent districts of the Tuaran and Tempassuk, called after two rivers that take their rise in Mount Kinabalu the magnificent, which towers up almost perpendicularly on its seaward face to a height of 13,400 feet.

Borneo, the second largest island in the world, which is hazily connected by the crowd with the existence of wild men, lies, roughly speaking, south of the Philippines, with Java to the south, Celebes to the east, Sumatra and the Malay Peninsula to the west, while the Equator cuts almost through the centre.

About two-thirds of the whole island, comprising the two Residencies of South-East and West Borneo, is under Dutch rule. The remainder is divided into three states: Sarawak, which occupies a long strip of territory on the west coast and has an English ruler (Raja Brooke); British North Borneo, governed by a Chartered Company, towards the northern end of the island; and the little native state of Brunei, wedged between these two, which have both enriched themselves at her expense. The last-named is now protected by Great Britain and administered by officers of the Straits Settlements Civil Service.

The first European traveller to give an account of the

manners and customs of any Bornean tribe was Antonio Pigafetta, who visited the city of Brunei in 1521. The name Bornei, by which he calls that old state, has now been further corrupted into the modern Borneo.

The credit of being the first Europeans to discover the island rests apparently with the Portuguese or the Spaniards, somewhere between 1518 and 1526, but it seems uncertain to which nationality the laurels should be awarded. Possibly the Italian traveller Varthema may have visited the country before either the Portuguese or the Spaniards. However, there is little doubt that the Chinese had been in the habit of visiting Borneo at least since the sixth century A.D., and possibly much earlier, as in the works of various of their historians we have accounts of embassies which were sent from China to the Royal Court of Brunei, and *vice versa.*

Trade followed, or perhaps preceded, the ambassadors; but, though old Chinese pottery and beads are found almost everywhere in Borneo, it is very doubtful if there was ever a resident Chinese population numerous enough to have introduced a serious amount of Chinese blood among the aboriginals, as has been supposed by some writers. But I shall have something more to say on this subject when I come to deal with the question of the races and tribes inhabiting the country.

The total area of Borneo is about 290,000 square miles. The island is very compact and has not many bays or inlets, though there are a few on its north-eastern coast. A belt of mangrove swamp of varying breadth fringes most of the shores, and behind this are plains—not necessarily open country—foot-hills and finally the mountainous regions of the interior. Among the plains and swamps wind the lower courses of the rivers, which take their rise in the mountains, and eventually empty themselves into the sea through deltas formed of detritus from the uplands.

No land is better provided with rivers than Borneo, but unfortunately the majority of them are not navigable for boats of any size owing to the formidable bars at their mouths.

The country is thickly covered with primeval jungle, except where there is, or has been, a considerable native population. In such districts virgin jungle is found chiefly on the highest of the lower hills, and on the mountains, while the valleys are filled with big secondary growth which has sprung up on the sites of old native clearings. Taking it as a whole, the west coast is far more thickly populated than the east, wherefore the east is much more given over to jungle.

The climate of Borneo very much resembles that of the Malay Peninsula, but the island is a good deal less healthy, the north-eastern coast in particular having a very bad reputation for fever. As is stated by Guillemard and Kean (*Compendium of the Geography of Australasia*), Borneo, being bisected by the Equator, "is exposed to the action of four Monsoons, in the northern portion to the N.E. and S.W., and in the southern to the S.E. and N.W., but these winds become considerably altered with the locality." The general climate may be described as hot and damp, and though severe droughts sometimes occur, there is no true dry season. Roughly speaking, the rainiest part of the year in British North Borneo is from October to February.

The total population of Borneo was estimated in 1905 to be about 1,820,000.

To turn now to British North Borneo. This state, with an area of 31,000 square miles and a population of 208,000, is governed by a Chartered Company, formed for the purpose of developing certain lands, concessions for which had been obtained from the Sultans of Sulu and Brunei in consideration of stipulated annual payments. The negotiations with these Sultans for the transfer of the territories to a Provisional Company were concluded by the late Sir Alfred Dent and Baron Overbeck in 1877.

The American Consul in Brunei had already obtained

concessions for some of the territories which are now under the flag of the British North Borneo Company, a trading Company had been formed, and, with a view to opening up the country, Chinese had been imported and settled at Kimanis. However, neither the settlement nor the Company flourished, and its rights were finally acquired by Baron Overbeck. Sir Alfred (then Mr) Dent visited various parts of the territories, accompanied by representatives of the Brunei and Sulu Governments, who were empowered to notify the inhabitants that the rights of both Sultans had been transferred to the Company; European officers in command of small bodies of police were left at Sandakan—now the capital—Tempassuk and Papar; the Dent house flag was hoisted at the stations opened, and the new territories came, at any rate in name, under the control of the lessees.

In 1881, in spite of bitter opposition on the part of the Dutch and the Spaniards, a Royal Charter was granted to the Provisional Company which had been formed to acquire the rights of the lessees. The Dutch, who had previously done everything in their power to hinder the affairs of Raja Brooke in Sarawak, naturally did not welcome the formation of yet another British state in Borneo; while the Spanish were displeased at the British obtaining any power in the northern portion of Borneo which they considered within their sphere of influence, as being in juxtaposition to the southern islands of the Philippines, and nominally under the Sultan of Sulu. Indeed the latter seem to have had some title to those districts over which the royal house of Sulu claimed to exercise power, since the Sultan of Sulu had for some time been subject to them. However, the concessions from the Sultan were obtained while he was in rebellion against the Spaniards, and, as he did not make his peace with them until later in the year, the moral rights of the Spaniards, whatever they might be worth, were not recognised.

The British North Borneo Provisional Association was dissolved on the formation of the Chartered Company in 1882, when Sir Rutherford Alcock, Mr A. Dent, Mr R. B. Martin, Admiral Mayne and Mr W. H. Read, who had formed the Board of the Provisional Association, became the first Directors. The nominal capital of the new Company was £2,000,000 in £20 shares; but only 4500 fully paid shares were issued to the vendors, while £12 per share was called up on the remainder. The actual cash, therefore, with which the Company started its existence, including £1000 received for forfeited shares, was only about £384,000.

The Charter granted to the Company stipulated for the proper treatment of the natives, and provided that whenever a new Governor was chosen his name should be submitted to the Secretary of State for the Colonies for approval before the appointment was confirmed. The Company was to have sovereign rights within its own territory, but all dealings with foreign powers were to be conducted with the sanction of the Home Government, while provision was also made for maintaining the British character of the body. The Company's flags were to be the Union Jack "defaced" with a lion passant in the centre, and the Blue and Red Ensigns with a lion in the fly.

Such, then, were the beginnings of the new Company: a few European officers holding insecure positions with the aid of small companies of police, a certain amount of cash, and absolute rights over a large territory leased to the Company by two Sultans who were practically without power to enforce their will in the portions of it claimed respectively by each. At first, however, things went fairly well; settlements were founded at Sandakan, Kudat, Gaya Island and elsewhere; while these three stations—the Gaya Island settlement having since been removed to the mainland and given the name of Jesselton—are still the most important towns in the Company's territory, though Kudat, the old capital, has lagged somewhat behind the other two.

Luckily for the Company, the natives of British North Borneo are neither so warlike nor so well organised as those of Sarawak; consequently there have been fewer wars. The two most troublesome tribes have been the Bajaus and Illanuns of the west coast, who are by nature and education undisciplined robbers, sea-rovers and freebooters. In the old days the Illanuns were the most notorious pirates in the Archipelago, and their very name was a terror even to people living so far away as the Malay Peninsula, to the inhabitants of which probably a good many piracies were credited, which were really the work of the former. The Illanuns are resident in the Tempassuk district, while the Bajaus are found on both coasts, those on the west having settled villages, while those on the east live the lives of sea-gipsies.

From among the Bajaus of Inanan in the Tuaran district arose one leader to withstand the rising power of the Chartered Company. Mat Saleh, a man of good birth, partly by appealing to the predatory instincts of the more disorderly tribes, partly by trading on the natives' mistrust of the Chartered Company, which was assuming control of large tracts of country without consulting the wishes of the inhabitants, was able to raise considerable forces, and for a number of years gave the Directors many uneasy moments. Among his chief exploits, or those of his lieutenants, were the plundering of Gaya Treasury, a march on Sandakan and the sacking and burning of Kudat "Arsenal."

By some Mat Saleh has been condemned as a treacherous and crafty enemy and a rebel against the government of the country; by others—the love-your-enemy-and-hate-your-neighbour party in Parliament—he has been canonised as a patriot saint, defending his country against the encroachments of a Company of chartered freebooters. Neither of these estimates is correct. He appears to have been a man of good presence, considerable activity and great courage, who, besides being a born leader, was possessed of considerable powers of persuasive eloquence. Patriotism, in the sense in which it is understood in Europe, or indeed in any sense, is unknown among the native tribes of Borneo; but Mat Saleh well represented the prevailing Bajau feeling with regard to the new government, which was both disliked and feared, since it threatened to put bounds to the Bajaus' immemorial right of doing exactly as they chose, and to their equally venerable custom of oppressing and cheating the natives of the interior.

On the other hand, it cannot be said that the Chartered Company had morally—even supposing that its legal rights were above suspicion—any right to possess itself of its present territories. Except in the case of a few small districts acquired at a later date, which were taken over from minor chiefs in consideration of annual payments, the titles to the country were obtained from the Sultans of Sulu and Brunei. These Sultans were claimants to nearly all the territory which is now under the rule of the Chartered Company; but, except perhaps for one or two valleys not far from the present border of the state of Brunei, their claims were of the most shadowy description, neither potentate being able to enforce his orders even in the coastal regions, while practically the only tangible sign of the Sultan of Sulu's existence, as far as Borneo was concerned, were raids by Sulu pirates and the settlements formed, chiefly on the east coast, by his somewhat undesirable subjects.

The Sultan of Brunei seems to have been occasionally able to exact tribute from some of the people of the west coast, but this was rather in the nature of blackmail extorted by war prahus. Natives who made themselves useful to him were often given high-sounding titles. He had absolutely no control over the interior.

Naturally both Sultans were only too glad to transfer their doubtful claims in exchange for what was to them a liberal yearly payment, for they lost little or nothing by surrendering all rights in the territory, and obtained a handsome rent for what was of hardly any use to them. The Directors of the Company, on the other hand, were equally anxious to come to terms in order that they might, before starting operations in Borneo, have some sort of a legal document to flourish in the faces of those who were rude enough to say that they were little better than the pirates and freebooters whose excesses they professed themselves so wishful to stop.

Thus the British North Borneo Company started to possess themselves of the country, without in any way truly consulting the feelings or wishes of the inhabitants, proclamations being merely read which announced that the territories had been leased from the two Sultans. The natives were for the most part too badly organised to offer any resistance, and either, in the case of the more timid peoples, acquiesced without any thought of making an attempt to show that they objected to being summarily disposed of by Sultans whose suzerainty they did not acknowledge, or, in that of the more warlike tribes, pretended, with the somewhat subtle politeness of the Malay, to receive their unwelcome visitors with pleasure, at the same time wishing themselves well rid of them and trusting that something would happen to upset their plans.

When, however, the coastal tribes found that the intruders showed no signs of retiring, that the servants of the Company were attempting to interfere with what they had hitherto regarded as their legitimate amusements, that courts, police stations and other abominations were being established, and efforts made to bring the littoral at any rate under some sort of control, they naturally began to understand the drift of the proclamations, and to what kind of things the Company's rule would lead, should it succeed in establishing itself permanently.

Naturally discontent among the predatory tribes increased proportionately as they saw their freedom of action menaced, and they only required a leader of some parts to set them

A Bamboo Bridge over the Kadamaian (Tempassuk) River at Kaung " Ulu."

The Dusuns turn bamboos to innumerable uses : hats and baskets, posts for small huts, bridges, rafts, walls, fences, water-vessels, emergency cooking pots, boxes, spoons, combs, traps for fish and mammals are all made from this indispensable material.

in a state of open warfare. This leader was found in the person of Mat Saleh, who not only was successful in banding together the Bajaus and Illanuns, but also partly by terrorism, partly by cajolery, at one time managed to get together a considerable following of pagan Dusuns.

The Encyclopædia Britannica, which should certainly be unbiassed, in the course of an article on British North Borneo makes mention of the Mat Saleh "rebellions" as follows:—

"The Company's acquisition of territory was viewed with considerable dissatisfaction by many of the natives, and this found expression in frequent acts of violence. The most noted and most successful of the native leaders was a Bajau named Mat Saleh, who for many years defied the Company, whose policy in his regard was marked by considerable weakness and vacillation. In 1898 a composition was made with him, the terms of which were unfortunately not defined with sufficient clearness, and he retired into the Tambunan country to the east of the range which runs parallel to the west coast, where for a period he lorded it undisturbed over the Dusun tribes of the valley. In 1899 it was found necessary to expel him, since his acts of aggression and defiance were no longer endurable. A short and this time successful campaign followed, resulting on the 31st January 1900 in the death of Mat Saleh and the destruction of his defences. Some of his followers who escaped raided the town of Kudat on Marudu Bay in April of the same year, but caused more panic than damage; and little by little during the next years the last smouldering embers of rebellion were extinguished."

As I have mentioned before, the territory of the Chartered Company is administered by a Governor who is appointed by the Court of Directors. Beneath the Governor are the Residents, of whom there are four, the Resident of the West Coast, the Resident of Kudat, the Resident of the

East Coast and the Resident of the Interior. Under the Residents are the District Officers, the Assistant District Officers and the Cadets; the last-named are usually either attached to some of the Government offices in the towns, or temporarily put in charge of a sub-district—as I was—until they shall have passed their examinations in Malay and Law, soon after which, unless stationed in towns, they are raised to the rank of Assistant District Officers. Outside the Cadet Service are the Railway, Public Works, Medical, Survey, Telegraphs and Police Departments, while officers of the Cadet Service or specialists are attached to the Treasuries, Posts and Telegraphs, Audit and Printing Offices.

One or more European officers are stationed at the following places:—Jesselton, Tuaran, Kotabelud, Papar, Mempakol and Weston on the west coast; Kudat on the north coast; Sandakan, Lahad Datoh, Simporna and Tawao on the east coast; Beaufort, Tenom, Kaningau, Tangkulop, Rundum, Ranau and Tambunan in the Interior Residency, while a Magistrate is also in charge of the Labuk and Sugut rivers. The chief towns in the Company's territory are Jesselton and Sandakan, the latter being the seat of government, but the Governor divides his time about equally between the two, and Jesselton is the headquarters of the Constabulary. The next town in order of importance is Kudat on Marudu Bay, and after this Beaufort on the Padas river. The means of communication I will deal with in another chapter. The territories of the British North Borneo Company extend from the Lawas river on the west coast to the Sibuko river on the east.

A joint Anglo-Dutch Commission has visited the interior for the purpose of adjusting the boundary between the Company's territory and Dutch Borneo, and settling disputed points. All the islands within a distance of nine leagues of the coast of British North Borneo, including those of Balambangan and Banguey, are within the sphere of the Company's jurisdiction.

CHAPTER II

BRITISH NORTH BORNEO—POPULATION & RACES

BRITISH NORTH BORNEO can boast of only a scanty population, a very large part of the country being still under virgin jungle, especially the east coast and the interior. The low-lying regions of the west coast support a fair native population, a great part of which is engaged in the planting of wet padi. In the upland regions, however, where hill padi is the staple crop, the population, owing to the methods of agriculture employed, must of necessity be scanty, even should all available land be in use.

The reason for this is that after a patch of ground has been in cultivation for a couple of years or so it will no longer give a good crop, and, in consequence, clearings are usually abandoned in the second or third year, when the land soon becomes covered by secondary jungle. After a considerable number of years have passed, and, presumably, a certain amount of humus has accumulated, the jungle is again felled and burnt, and the land once more put under cultivation, to be abandoned as before on the exhaustion of the soil.

Possibly a remedy for this state of affairs might be found in terrace cultivation and manuring, but many of the primitive tribes who inhabit the hill country know nothing of such methods of agriculture, and would probably be slow to abandon their immemorial custom, even if skilled agriculturists were to be imported as instructors. To put a stop to the planting of hill padi by enactment would be unthinkable, as it would condemn about half the population of the country to death by starvation.

The people of the littoral and on the more navigable rivers are, generally speaking, lax Mohammedans, those of the interior and the intermediate regions pagans. The tribes of the coastal regions are the most recent arrivals, and are of Malayan or Proto-Malayan stock; those of the interior are Indonesians.

The natives of the up-country regions far excel those of the coasts in good qualities, the latter being usually boastful, lazy, tyrannical over those weaker than themselves, lawless, gamblers, borrowers and spendthrifts, their only merit being their fondness for sport in all its forms. The up-country man, on the other hand, is hard-working, thrifty and usually honest; he has, moreover, a manner which appeals singularly to most Englishmen, since he has no trace of the cringing and fawning style of many of the peoples of India, which, should there be any opportunity, quickly develops into very slightly veiled insolence. He meets the white man with a kind of "man-to-man" manner, which at the same time is perfectly respectful. The best type of native both respects himself and respects you; and, if you are of a friendly disposition, the respect will rapidly develop into liking on both sides.

Nevertheless I do not want the reader to think that the pagan native is faultless; he has his little failings, as most of us have, and among them must be mentioned a weakness for "lifting" human heads from their owners' shoulders—partly as a matter of sport and prowess, partly of religion—and a penchant for stealing buffaloes, which also is considered almost a sport; but I shall have more to say about this subject in another chapter.

I have never been able to settle quite definitely in my own mind whether such difference in character is due to the fundamental difference in race between the coastal tribes and those of the interior, or whether the reason for the essential badness of the natives of the sea-board must be sought for in some obscure influence of the teachings of Islam on the peculiar Malayan temperament. I cannot profess any great admiration for Mohammedanism in general, since it suffers from all the defects of an exclusive religion, but I am inclined to think that we must not by any means ascribe all the shortcomings of Mohammedan natives to the religion, one reason being that, except for a very firm belief that its tenets are true, they pay but little attention to them in matters concerning everyday life.

It is related of a certain local saint—the story is told by the Malays against themselves—that when he arrived in Sumatra he found the people absolutely indifferent to his teachings, since their whole time was devoted to cock-fighting, wagering and the discussion of the merits of the various birds which were to take part in forthcoming matches. The would-be teacher's chances of converting any of the natives to a better way of life seemed poor indeed, until a certain Malay, wishing to obtain a spell or charm to say over his fighting cock to ensure its victory in a contest for which he had entered it, bethought himself of the holy man who had come to live near his village.

Thereupon he took himself off to the wise man's house and besought him for a charm which would help his bird to win. The Arab considered for a while, and, probably seeing little harm and some possible gain in complying with the request, taught the Malay to utter the Mohammedan Confession of Faith. The Malay went away perfectly satisfied with this new charm, and to his great joy his bird, about which he had felt some doubts, beat its opponent, an event which he was not slow in attributing to the saint's spell. Not unnaturally he boasted to his friends of the fine new charm he had obtained from the wise man, the consequence being that the latter was overwhelmed with similar requests from other natives. To each of these he taught the same formula, and thus the Moslem profession of faith was soon heard on all sides throughout the country.

The first Malay, however, soon came again to the saint and protested against the charm, which had been given to him as his own, having become public property. The saint, therefore, to appease him taught him as a fresh charm the Five Daily Prayers, and once more the Malay went away satisfied. From that time to such a pitch did the demand for charms attain that the saint was able to teach the Malays all the doctrines of the Mohammedan religion under the guise of spells to be used in cock-fighting.

The average Mohammedan native in the Malay Peninsula, in Borneo and other islands of the Archipelago is in a perpetual state of *banyak susah* (great trouble) usually with regard to money affairs. Needless to say, his troubles, where they truly exist, as they often do, are generally of his own making; but he seems to regard them as being due to continual bad luck, and he is always quite ready to transfer them to the shoulders of another, especially a European. The method he adopts is to "touch" his unfortunate victim for a loan, of which he seldom repays any part, and still more seldom the whole.

I have heard Malays excusing themselves for their spendthrift nature by saying that their Prophet—I do not know whether such a passage exists in the Koran or not—has said that "*Orang Islam ta'buleh jadi kaya*" (Mohammedans cannot become rich). It is no exaggeration to say that among young Malays, especially in the towns, wages received at the end of the month are spent by the second or third day of that following. When, however, the spendthrift advances in years, he often becomes penurious and grasping; and, though his heart is as flinty as ever, makes some show of conforming to the observances of his religion.

Altogether the Mohammedan native is not usually a very attractive personage. His manners are good, and, until you know him better, he seems to have some real self-respect; but this to my mind consists chiefly in showing resentment to rough methods of address, and avenging slights or insults real or fancied. The Malay word *malu*, meaning ashamed, is continually on the lips of natives, and especially of Mohammedans; but for a man to be ashamed to do, or of having done, some scoundrelly action is rare; he is only ashamed of having been found out.

Probably the best that can be said of the Malays, the Bajaus and the other Mohammedan tribes of Borneo is that they have a saving sense of humour and are keen sportsmen. They will, I think, certainly manage to keep their place in the modern struggle for existence, just beginning to be felt in Borneo; they may not be highly successful, but they will continue to exist, thanks chiefly to their rascality.

To turn again to the pagan natives for a while. These tribes, especially the Dusuns, are the best native agriculturists in the country; they are, generally speaking, frugal and, at any rate at certain seasons of the year, extremely hard workers. They should, with the protection from raiding by the Mohammedans afforded them by the Chartered Company, and the suppression of intertribal head-hunting, be rapidly increasing, but I have considerable doubts as to whether this is the case.

Periodical epidemics of small-pox, cholera and other diseases have undoubtedly done a great deal to keep the population down, but with the gradual opening up of the country these foes may be fought and vanquished. The mortality among children is, I believe, unduly high; and I cannot help having an uneasy suspicion at the back of my mind that the pagan tribes of the interior, being much more unsophisticated than those of the coast, may suffer severely both in numbers and vitality from the encroachments of civilisation. This to many primitive peoples is a deadly poison, and destroys them body and soul, bringing, as it does, in its train new diseases, intoxicating liquors, clothes unsuited to the savage, and which he does not change when they are soaked with rain, new foods, new restrictions, new customs and the destruction of old habits.

Unfortunately the process of disintegration and decay has often been aided and hastened by the efforts of well-meaning but misguided missionaries and others, who, instead of attempting to arrest the progress of many of the innovations (*e.g.* the use of clothing), which have been partly responsible for the decay of savage races, have deliberately aided in their adoption, and have done everything in their power to break down old customs, religious or otherwise. Their fault has, of course, been that they have expected the primitive savage still in, or little advanced from, the Stone Age to turn himself immediately at their behest into a civilised man like unto themselves, quite forgetting how far back in prehistoric times it is necessary to go in Europe to find peoples comparable in their state of development to the uncivilised natives with whom they are dealing. Can we wonder that the results of their well-meant but ill-advised efforts have frequently been disastrous?

Things have fortunately not reached such a pass in Borneo as in the islands of Polynesia and Melanesia, and I hope never will. The inhabitants of those islands have until, comparatively speaking, recent times been absolutely isolated from all contact with the rest of the world, consequently the effect upon them of newly introduced habits and diseases has been overwhelmingly disastrous, all these disintegrating influences being let loose on them at once. The people, before they have had time to recover from the effects of, or accustom themselves to, a single disintegrating influence, have been immediately inundated by a score of others.

In Borneo the situation is, I trust, more hopeful, for the tribes inhabiting the interior of the island have reached a much higher state of civilisation than those of the South Seas, being able to work, and in some cases smelt, metals.

The brewing of intoxicating liquors is understood, one made from rice—though not a true spirit, since it is not distilled—containing a high percentage of alcohol. Thus they will probably be better able to resist the evils of cheap spirits than peoples who have no knowledge of intoxicants; yet the sale of cheap and fiery brandy, whisky, gin and arrack, the vendors of which are the Chinese traders of the gambling and spirit monopolies, should be stringently forbidden. (In some districts near the coast the effects of cheap spirits upon the natives are even now, unfortunately, only too apparent.) The prohibition to be entirely effective would have to be absolute, since, if the sale of spirits were made an offence only to natives of the country, though it might to a certain extent prevent the rising generation from taking to drink, a native would merely go to the first Chinaman he knew and give him a present of five cents to purchase a bottle of gin for him.

The inhabitants of Borneo are also probably fortunate in not having been completely cut off from the outer world; for, though epidemics sometimes commit terrible ravages among them, they have not to fear, to quite the same extent as the Polynesians and Melanesians, the inroads of civilisation. Their powers of resistance to diseases, especially to minor diseases, according to European ideas, such as measles, which have wrought such havoc in the South Seas, are fair, small-pox, cholera and dysentery being their greatest enemies; and I do not think that they will so easily go down before the generally corrosive influence of civilisation as their fellows.

Still, I believe that, even now, the population in some districts is decreasing, while in others it is stationary, or shows a very small increase. Probably for a time this state of things will continue, and decreases even become more numerous and accelerated; but I hope that after a period of decrease the tribesmen will become inured to the new and destructive agencies and will then be able to hold their own and increase fairly rapidly.

The one thing which made me feel somewhat doubtful on this point is the sparsity of the population in the interior, for it has always seemed to me that where a race which has been in part, or wholly, isolated from peoples in a higher state of development is more or less suddenly brought into contact with an advanced civilisation, a quick process of decay sets in, but that whether this decay is to lead to the final extinction of the race depends not only on its recuperative powers, but on the density of the population before it was attacked by the disintegrating influences. That is to say that when the scattered remnants of a population, which was always sparse, have acquired powers of resistance to new conditions and diseases, their fate will probably even then be extinction, or at any rate absorption into the more civilised race of invaders, the remnants being too few, too scattered and too effete ever to be capable of again giving rise to fresh communities.

When, however, the population has been fairly numerous to start with, and where the vitality of the race is moderately good, we may hope that, after a long period of decrease, it may after a time attain a stable condition, and finally begin to increase again.

A case in point is afforded by the Maoris of New Zealand, who, after decreasing continuously for many years — they should now be extinct, according to one writer, who, a good many years ago, calculating on their rate of decrease, estimated that the last Maori should have died some years back—are now actually again on the increase, a state of things which it is to be hoped will be maintained.

Should Borneo ever become largely occupied by Chinese, it is not unlikely that a mixed race between these people and the natives of the interior would quickly arise. The Chinese bring but few women with them from their country, and those members of the race who are settled in out-stations at the present day have very largely married native wives, taking them from one or other of the pagan peoples. Women of the Mohammedan tribes, unless of bad character, they are, of course, unable to obtain, since a father would refuse to let his daughter marry a Chinaman unless the latter would turn Mohammedan, an occurrence which, though by no means unknown, especially in the Malay Peninsula, is nevertheless somewhat rare.

A census of the population of British North Borneo was taken in 1901 and another in 1911; the former is, however, so incomplete that it is to all intents and purposes useless with regard to obtaining any idea of increase or decrease in the native population, many of the districts at the time it was taken being in such a disturbed state that it was impossible to obtain any estimate of their population.

The results of the census of 1911 show how enormously the Dusuns preponderate in numbers over any other division of the natives. The Dusuns are not a single tribe, but an assemblage of tribes, or rather the appellation embraces large numbers of village communities, some of which can be grouped together as closely related owing to identity in dialect and minor details of custom, while the whole of them are roughly classed together as Orang Dusun, owing to their similarity in language, beliefs and general habits. Orang Dusun is not the name used by these natives to describe themselves; the people of each district or each assemblage of village communities employs a different term, but it is a name—meaning people of the orchards (*orang* = people; *dusun* = an orchard)—used by the Malays to denote those inhabitants of the greater part of the interior of British North Borneo who appear to them to be of similar culture, and live in villages surrounded by coco-nut palms and fruit trees.

CHAPTER III

TRADE & INDUSTRIES

THE produce exported from British North Borneo may, with the exception of a few articles, be roughly placed under two headings: firstly, cultivated produce, the chief articles of which are tobacco, rubber, rice, sago, pepper, coco-nuts and copra; secondly, natural products, vegetable or animal, either in a raw or partly manufactured condition. Among the latter may be noticed timber, cutch, gutta-percha, jungle rubber, rattans, beeswax, camphor, damar gum, edible birds'-nests (the nests of a species of swift), mother-of-pearl shells, *trēpang* (dried sea-slugs or holothurians), sharks' fins (dried) and dried fish.

The exploration of the country in search of minerals has, so far, not been a great success, though coal is mined at Sebatik on the east coast, and is used by steamers trading with east coast ports; borings are also being made for oil, especially in the Klias Peninsula, but whether this product is present in paying quantities appears to be a matter for doubt.

Gold is found in several of the rivers, notably the Segama, where dredging has been attempted, but so far gold-working has not proved profitable for Europeans. Copper is known to exist in one or two localities, but has not yet been worked. "Blue ground" was some time ago announced to exist on the Labuk river, and it was said that a second Kimberley was awaiting the attentions of capitalists; but the report proved to be incorrect, the formation not being diamondiferous. A somewhat similar story also became current with regard to manganese in the hinterland of the

Marudu Bay region, but, though manganese exists, the attempt to exploit the deposits was anything but a commercial success.

Of the cultivated products, estate tobacco is grown chiefly in the Darvel Bay district on the east coast and around Marudu Bay in the north, this industry being largely in the hands of Dutchmen. Bornean tobacco leaf is used for the wrapping of cigars, a purpose for which it is particularly well suited. Rubber, since the "boom," has been a good deal planted, and many estates have been opened up, chiefly on the west coast. The British North Borneo Government, in order to foster this industry, has guaranteed planters that no duty shall be levied on exported estate rubber for a period of fifty years; while in the case of some companies it has pledged itself to pay five per cent. interest on the capital to the shareholders, until such time as the trees shall come into bearing.

Land for rubber-planting is let by the Government on 999 year leases. The labour chiefly used on the rubber estates is Chinese, Javanese and native. The supply of the last is somewhat irregular, and daily labourers are liable to desert the estates in a body at the rice-planting and harvest seasons. Chinese labour is, or was, almost entirely contract labour, the coolies signing an agreement to work for a certain number of years.

With regard to the two districts of Borneo which I know, there were three estates in being—one of these had just been opened at the time that I left the country. The labour was Chinese and native, the native labourers being Dusuns and Bajaus, the former excellent workers and the latter in most cases the exact reverse. I remember once going round an estate in the Tuaran district with my manager, fairly late in the afternoon. He drew my attention to a gang of labourers who were all Bajaus. "Do you see that gang?" he said. "Well, I put a gang of Dusuns and a gang of Bajaus on to weed round these trees this morning.

I gave each man a task of a fixed number of trees, and when a man had done his task he was at liberty to knock off work for the day. The Dusuns finished—some at eleven, some at twelve, and some at one o'clock, but you see that most of the Bajaus won't have finished their jobs by five."

The majority of the Bajau labourers are under contracts, these being generally made for a term of six months or a year, but a large proportion of the Dusuns are free labourers. The labour laws of British North Borneo require drastic revision in order that Bajau labourers may be protected against themselves; the actual contracts are fair enough, but owing to the Bajau's reckless habits he often becomes little better than a slave on the estate for which he is working, with the exception that he receives pay for his work. Matters are now (1915) somewhat improved, and most estates seem to be using Chinese and Javanese labour more than native.

The usual method of recruiting coolies, as far as my experience goes, is something of this kind. The manager of an estate takes out a licence to recruit coolies in a certain district and dispatches a recruiter, whom he has entrusted with anything between two hundred and five hundred dollars, to obtain labourers. The recruiter goes and hangs about outside the gambling-shop—unless he is inside gambling with his employer's money—and on seeing that a native has lost goes up to him and says: "Hullo, So-and-so! do you want a loan to try your luck again with?" The native, especially if he is a Bajau or Illanun, will almost certainly reply that he does. "Very well," says the recruiter. "How much do you want?" The Bajau replies that he wants ten, fifteen, twenty, or even thirty dollars, as the case may be. The recruiter advances the money with the stipulation that the native shall come and work on Blank Estate for a period of six months, an agreement to that effect to be signed in the presence of the District Officer.

When the recruiter has obtained sufficient labourers

he, after a great deal of trouble, and probably some heart-searchings on his own part as to how he is going to account for the money he has himself lost in gambling, gets together his gang of coolies and takes them to be signed on.

In the Tempassuk, where I was stationed for some time, the coolies did not have their contracts signed at the Government post, Kotabelud, but were taken down on foot to Tuaran, since they were to work in the district of that name. The District Officer, North Keppel, who resides at Tuaran, is in charge of the Tuaran and Tempassuk districts forming the northern portion of Province Keppel. An Assistant District Officer or a Cadet is stationed in the Tempassuk, and is, of course, under the former officer. Before leaving the Tempassuk, any coolies who had not yet paid their poll-tax for the year were obliged to do so; and I found that almost invariably this necessitated a further application for money to the recruiter, the usual demand being for two dollars, one to pay the tax, the other for expenses by the way. The money borrowed previously had, in nearly all cases, found its way into the hands of the gambling-shop keeper.

Arrived on the estate, the coolies were without money and without food, and moreover had a considerable debt to work off, though, provided they did not borrow still more, one which could easily be settled during the period of their contract, instalments not exceeding a fixed percentage of the wages being deducted monthly. Borrow again almost immediately is, however, just what they usually did; and, so long as their debt did not assume huge proportions, the estate managers were not particularly averse from giving loans, since this only meant that the coolies would have to work the longer for them.

Facilities for gambling, if the coolies were unable to visit the gambling farm, were to be found on the estates, some Chinaman being sure to start an illicit establishment.

Coolies who are heavily in debt often desert, but are

almost invariably caught, their captors, generally either police or native headmen, being given a capture fee. The deserter is brought up in court, and only two courses are open to the magistrate: he may either fine the man and send him back to the estate, the fine being paid by the estate manager, and the amount of capture fees, fine and costs added to the wretched coolie's debt; or he may, if the coolie has run away before, order him a whipping with a rattan cane, the coolie's debt in this case—he is sent back to the estate just the same—only being augmented by the costs of the case and the capture fee.

It usually comes about that unthrifty coolies, especially Bajaus, are still heavily in debt when the period of their agreement is over. They thus remain on the estate, often for several years, and by constant borrowings keep themselves in a miserable condition. Should they run away, they will be brought back, fined, and the amount of the fine and any costs incurred added to what they already owe.

Now, though I do not approve of the whipping of runaway contract coolies, it cannot be said that there is anything unfair in the contracts or the treatment of the coolies. The most objectionable feature with regard to Bajau contract labour seems to me to be that advantage is taken of the weakness of the Bajaus in the matter of borrowing money. That this should be so is no credit to the Chartered Company. A short enactment providing that coolies should be free to leave any estate on the expiration of their agreements, however much their indebtedness, would place on the estate manager's shoulders the onus of seeing that coolies should not obtain such large or such constant advances that they should go home still owing the estate money.

I well remember a poor old couple coming to me to ask for assistance, shortly before I left Borneo. They told me—they were both almost in tears—that their son had signed on for six months as a coolie to work on an estate near Beaufort, some four years before, "and now," said they, "we hear from a man who has just come from Beaufort that he is still there, almost without clothes and heavily in debt. If you can find him for us we will pay his debts so that he can come home." I wrote to try and find their son for them—they did not know the name of the estate and their informant had left the district—but I had not received an answer when I left Borneo. I often wonder if they saw their prodigal again.

About the tobacco estates I know very little, since I have never been in a tobacco district, but from hearsay I believe that the Chinese coolies are often very badly swindled by their headmen or *tandils*. These men become very well-to-do, and on account of their exactions are much disliked by their compatriots the coolies. In consequence, it is not uncommon for a *tandil* mysteriously to disappear.

Of objects of cultivation other than rubber, coco-nut palms do very well near the coasts, but hitherto their cultivation has been principally carried on by natives and Chinese. Pepper was some years ago fairly extensively cultivated by Chinese settlers, but for various reasons many of the estates were abandoned. There is now, however, I understand, some revival of pepper-planting, especially in the neighbourhood of Sandakan. Sago mills for treating the pith of the sago palm exist at Mempakol, but lately, at any rate, I believe they have not been a financial success. Timber, which is chiefly exported to China, is of excellent quality, two hard woods called by the natives *bilian* and *selangan batu* being especially worthy of remark.

The natural products of the jungle are sought after by native collectors, the Dyaks, small parties of whom frequently come to British North Borneo from Sarawak to hunt for rubber, being especially expert jungle men. The Dusuns, the Muruts and other tribes are also skilled collectors, and bring down to the markets, or to the Chinese shops of the out-stations, loads of beeswax, rattans and damar gum, the last being collected either at the bases of the trees from which it exudes, mostly species of *Shorea*, or dug for in the earth around the trunk.

Mother-of-pearl shells are obtained by Bajau or other native divers.

Edible birds'-nests, made by the Chinese into soup, which is supposed to be a great luxury and also to have strengthening properties, are obtained chiefly from caves near the coast or on islands, especially the Mantanani Group, though there are also caves up-country which yield them. In a good many cases these caves are the property of families of natives, who collect the nests for market. From those in the Mantanani Islands as many as four collections are made yearly, the Government selling the nests and taking a proportion of the proceeds, while the balance is handed over to the native proprietors and the collectors. White nests of good or even fair quality may realise as much as sixteen or seventeen dollars per kattie (1⅓ lb.) locally, but the Singapore price for first-class nests is much higher. Black nests—that is, nests in which feathers are mixed with the gelatine-like secretion of which they are formed—fetch only about four to six dollars per kattie locally, though when they have been carefully cleaned they probably command almost as high a price as white nests of fair quality.

The British North Borneo Company does not itself engage in trade, its revenue—some of which, when there is a surplus, goes to pay interest to the shareholders—being derived from a poll-tax of one dollar imposed on every adult male native, the letting of the gambling, opium and spirit monopolies, duties under a somewhat comprehensive import tariff, which ranges from five per cent. *ad valorem* on imported food-stuffs to ten or fifteen per cent. on most manufactured articles, export duties, the letting of public markets, royalties on certain products, tobacco licences, the sale and rent of forest-lands, suburban lots and town sites, and land revenue.

That the Company shall not engage in trade, which is forbidden under its charter, is, of course, an excellent rule, but for all this the existence of a Chartered Company at the present day is not easily justified. The fates and destinies of a large native population rest entirely in its hands, and it must be remembered that such a concern is not a philanthropic association, nor has it the disinterestedness of the Government of a British colony: it is, if possible, "out to get dividends."

Now I have not the slightest wish to make any charges against the Chartered Company's administration, much less against its servants in the East, whom I believe to be extremely conscientious, but I consider it a mistake to allow any body of men, who have monetary interests, to have absolute control over a large territory; for as long as human nature is what it is there must always be a temptation for the directors and shareholders in such a company to sanction —all honour to them if they do not—revenue-producing schemes which may be exceedingly damaging to the native peoples entrusted to their care. In fact there must be a possibility of those who are largely interested in a company caring little from what sources and in what manner dividends are procured, so long as they obtain them.

Unfortunately it is not necessarily the case, though some officials would seem to think so, that the larger the revenue extracted from a country the greater the happiness of its inhabitants.

The articles chiefly imported into British North Borneo are European manufactured goods, those designed for the native trade being in the majority of cases cheap, flashy, and made in Germany. (This was written before the war.) Among them are gaudily printed cloths of various kinds, beads, knives, toilet soaps, scent, tobacco-boxes, enamelled ware and mirrors. These are to be found in every Chinese store in the out-stations, together with various kinds of cloth of better quality, kerosene, soap, spices, sulphur, copper sulphate, cooking pots, yellow soap, matches, thread, needles, etc., etc.

Means of communication in Borneo are but little developed; but a narrow-gauge railway, of which the construction is extremely bad, runs from Jesselton to Beaufort on the Padas river, fifty-seven miles distant. Beaufort is a junction from which two branch lines start, one running to Weston, twenty miles away on the coast, nearly opposite to Labuan; the other to Tenon, the present terminus of the railway to the interior.

The British North Borneo Company has recently raised a considerable sum of money by means of issuing Mortgage Debentures, and a portion of this is to be devoted to the reconstruction of the railway. An extension from Jesselton to Tuaran was projected, but this, owing to the war, has been postponed indefinitely.

A telegraphic system links Jesselton with Kudat via Kotabelud, and also Jesselton indirectly with Sandakan via Mempakol on the west coast, through which place runs the cross-country line connecting Sandakan with the latter station. Thence the line is continued as a submarine cable to Labuan. Separate lines also connect Kaningau in the Murut country with Tambunan, and Batu Puteh on the east coast with Lahad Datu, the headquarters of the East Coast Residency.

Bridle-paths link up many of the out-stations, especially on the west coast, one system extending from Jesselton through Tuaran and Kotabelud to Kudat, another from Kotabelud to Bundutuhan and the Interior. Wireless stations have also been recently opened.

CHAPTER IV

THE TUARAN & TEMPASSUK DISTRICTS

THESE two districts, with which this book chiefly deals, form the northern half of Province Keppel, on the west coast of British North Borneo. Formerly a District Officer was in charge of each of them, but of recent years a senior officer, with the title of District Officer, North Keppel, has been stationed at Tuaran, the Government post in the district of that name, and an Assistant District Officer, or a Cadet, at Kotabelud, the Government post in the Tempassuk district. During my residence in Borneo, except for a couple of months at Tuaran with the District Officer, I was in charge of the latter district, receiving a visit of inspection from my superior officer about once a month.

The easiest way to reach Tuaran is by boat from Jesselton. Embarking in a Bajau prahu, adapted either for sailing or rowing, and pushing off from the iron pier at Jesselton, we have the prospect of some hours' journey before reaching the little Bajau fishing village below Gantisan Head, where a disembarkation is made. On the way we pass the mouths of the Inanam and Mengatal rivers, in days of "not so very long ago" the haunt of bands of Bajau "rebels."

On reaching the headland the boat is left behind; the boatmen shoulder our baggage; we climb the steep sides of the long promontory, reach its summit, and descend again to the Mengkabong river—rather an inlet of the sea than a true river, which runs out beyond Gantisan Head. Here we find another boat with a crew of Bajau paddlers waiting for us. By cutting across the promontory we have avoided the long journey round it and possibly a rough time on the bar at the river mouth.

Paddling up the mangrove-fringed Mengkabong, we at length arrive at a large Bajau village which has the same name as the "river." This village is built entirely on, or rather over, the water: the pile-dwellings of the inhabitants are sometimes connected by crazy gangways, but the only method of getting about for more than a few dozen yards is by embarking in a little cockle-shell of a dug-out canoe.

Arrived at Mengkabong, we disembark for the second time, and a three-mile walk lies before us ere we reach Tuaran. Once well away from the Mengkabong, we leave the Bajau villages behind us and pass into swampy plain-lands, the padi-fields of the Dusun villagers. As we near Tuaran we see the belt of trees which marks the Tuaran river, with Dusun villages straggling along its bank; and at length we arrive at Tuaran with its District Officer's bungalow on a hill, its police barracks, office and lock-up on the level ground below.

The easiest way of reaching Kotabelud, the Government post in the Tempassuk district, is to take a passage in the small local steamer, which makes a trip round the coast once a fortnight. This boat puts in at the wooden pier in Usakan Bay, about seven or eight miles away from Kotabelud.

Leaving Usakan wharf, the path passes over the hills, which lie in a ring around the bay, and dips again to the inlet of the sea called the Abai. This has to be crossed in a Bajau prahu, and during the crossing we have leisure to observe the columns of smoke which arise from near some of the Bajau houses, which are scattered here and there along the mangrove-fringed shores of the inlet. These indicate that the inhabitants are at work making salt by a peculiar process, which I describe in another chapter.

Arrived on the other side, there remains a walk or ride partly over hills covered with *lalang* grass, partly below their bases along the edge of a plain converted into padi-fields, on the other side of which lie the Illanun villages around Fort Alfred, formerly the Government post. Past

Fort Alfred we again meet with a little up-and-down travelling and finally arrive at Kotabelud.

This settlement consists of rather under a score of Chinese shops, while the European officer's house stands at one end of a long hill covered with scrub and *lalang*. The upper part of the fort—also on the hill—is used as barracks for unmarried police, while the lower parts are protected by a wall of river stones built up within two fences of corrugated-iron sheets. Quarters for married police lie below the fort, on the side of the hill facing the Tempassuk river. The Government office is on the hill-side above the shops; and below the ridge, at the fort end, comes the Bajau village of Kotabelud, in charge of which is Keruak, one of the best Bajaus I have ever known.

From the top of the hill, on which stand the European officer's house and the barracks, magnificent views can be obtained. Seawards there is the mouth of the Tempassuk river; the sandy sea-shore fringed here and there with *Casuarina* trees, and the low, swampy plains which lie behind it, while away in the distance can be seen the Mantanani Islands, from the caves in which are brought large quantities of edible birds'-nests.

Inland, towering up to the skies, is Mount Kinabalu, its seaward face rising sheer up, apparently almost from the plains, its black and forbidding rocks relieved only by two white streaks, made by waterfalls which plunge sheer down its face for many hundreds of feet. To the left of Kinabalu is the range of hills of which the great mountain is itself a member. This range, none of the other peaks of which approach Kinabalu in height or grandeur, is covered with big jungle and runs almost parallel with the sea in the direction of Kudat. The *lalang*-covered foot-hills below the range, among which nestle a few Dusun villages, gradually die away into mere undulations, and these in turn give place to dry plains, and finally to the marshlands of the coast.

From the hill at Kotabelud too can be seen the Tempassuk or Kadamaian river, which flows beneath it, while its course can be followed with the eye for several miles towards the interior, walled in on the right by the hill ranges that separate its valley from that of the Tuaran river, which also takes its rise in Mount Kinabalu. To the right of Kinabalu lies a conical hill named Nunkok, also on the farther side of the Tempassuk river.

Dusun villages, Piasau, the two Tamboulians and others, are dotted about the plains on the other side of the Tempassuk opposite to our post of observation, while Perasan, the most inland Bajau village, which has the reputation of sheltering some of the worst characters and biggest cattle-thieves in the district, lies up-stream, on the same side of the river, and almost at our feet. The whole length of the Tempassuk valley inland is inhabited by the Dusuns, whose villages are mostly perched on hill-tops on either side of the river.

Away over the swampy plains in the direction of Kudat runs a narrow bridle-path. Beyond the swamps the ground rises slightly and the traveller comes to the Bajau and Illanun villages around Pindasan, once the haunt of pirates. At this place the big jungle from the main range runs down towards the coast and the country is more or less jungly as far as Metanau, a Dusun village near which there is a halting-hut. Never having been farther than this point, I cannot speak of the country which lies beyond, but the path continues right on to Kudat.

With the exception of the plains that lie between the sea and the range running parallel with it—of which Kinabalu is the highest point—the Tempassuk district consists of little but the valley of the Kadamaian river and the hills on either side of it. The farthest point in the district, at the divide over which it is necessary to pass to the Interior, can be comfortably reached on foot in five days from the coast, and with a little harder walking in four. From Kotabelud

AN UP-COUNTRY VIEW IN THE TEMPASSUK DISTRICT.

This view, taken on the bridle-path to the Interior, shows the Kadamaian River far below, Mount Nabalu in the clouds on the left of the picture, and Mount Nunkok on the right.

the ground rises almost continuously as far as the divide, which is said to be about 8000 feet above sea-level. The bridle-path to the Interior, which is, in the up-country regions, cut into the steeply sloping side of the valley, follows the left bank of the river, winding in and out according to the contours of the hills.

Leaving Usakan, a traveller would probably sleep for the first night at Kotabelud, the European officer in charge, judging from my own experience, usually being only too glad to put up any chance European wanderer. Coolies being procured, a start would be made next day for either Tamu Darat (seven miles or so away), or more probably for Ghinambur, a little farther on, at both of which places there are halting-huts. If, however, there is need for haste, Kabaiau halting-hut, nineteen (?) miles from Kotabelud, and on the river-bank facing the village of the same name, can be reached in a day's journey. The villagers were ordered to move down to the river as a punishment for misbehaviour. They have now (1915) gone back again to their old village on a hill above the river. This, however, is rather hard going for a traveller who wishes to observe and note everything he passes.

The fourth day's journey will take him on to Kaung, and here again the resting-hut faces the village across the river. On the fifth day, if he does not take the branch track to Kiau village, which is situated on the other side of the river on the slopes of Kinabalu at a height of 3000 odd feet, he should reach the last halting-hut in the district at a place called Singarun.

This is built on a spur of the hills at a height of about 5000 feet, and opposite to Kiau village, on which it looks down. From the spur a magnificent view of Kinabalu is obtained and, looking seaward, of the valley of the Tempassuk. In fine weather the air is most exhilarating, but if rain comes on, the traveller, unless provided with warm clothes, will find it distinctly chilly. The only drawback to the place is that there is no spring near at hand, and water has to be brought from a distance by means of a cleverly constructed aqueduct, built of bamboos split lengthwise, which are supported here and there on slight trestles of saplings.

From Singarun, sometimes called Dallos, after a walk of a few miles along the bridle-path, the top of the divide which separates the Tempassuk district from the Interior province is reached. Here in my time the bridle-path came to an end, not having been linked up with that from the Interior, which stopped short at Bundutuhan, or a little beyond it. These two sections have now, however, probably been joined.

The Tuaran district, of which I have much less knowledge than of the Tempassuk, consists of the valley of the Tuaran river and a strip of land near the coast, extending nearly as far as Jesselton. It contains—but can scarcely be said to be watered by—the Mengkabong, Menggatal and Inanam rivers. Farther back from the sea the country becomes rugged, while the hills which divide off the district from the Interior are really a continuation of the range of which Mount Kinabalu is the highest point.

Along the coast, to the northward of the mouth of the (Kuala) Tuaran, is an inlet of the sea called the Sulaman, into which there flow various small streams. On this inlet, and near its mangrove-fringed shores, are scattered Bajau villages, built on piles like those at Mengkabong. A bridle-path runs from Tuaran to Kotabelud, but the journey is made easier by walking or riding the first six miles to Kindu on the Sulaman, and thence, taking a Bajau prahu across the inlet, ascending a side-channel, or stream, and disembarking about a mile from the Dusun village of Tenghilan, near which the North Borneo Trading Company has fairly recently (1911) opened a rubber estate. The distances given in this chapter are not, I believe, very correct. In some cases they may be "out" to the extent of a couple of miles.

Spending the night at Tenghilan halting-bungalow, the next day's journey will see the traveller reach Kotabelud, distant thirteen miles, after traversing a very up-and-down bridle-path along the top of a range of small hills. The boundary of the two districts is some little distance from Tenghilan on the Kotabelud side of it.

The British North Borneo Company has recently been negotiating for fresh capital; this, if obtained, is to be used among other things for repairs to the railway, of which it stands in great need, and the construction of a branch line from Jesselton to Tuaran. At present a bridle-path, known as the Likas path, covers this ground.

The Tempassuk, *laus Deo*, has not yet been "developed," and both this beautiful country and its natives are free from the blighting influence of the European capitalist. Its main exports are cattle, fowls, hides, ground-nuts, edible birds'-nests from the Mantanani Islands, native-grown tobacco, damar gum, mother-of-pearl shells and a little wild rubber and beeswax. The wide plains of the district, although the grass is somewhat coarse, afford pasturage for large herds of buffaloes and cattle, while a herd of mixed breed, a cross between Indian humped sires and native cows, is kept by Government. Little sure-footed native ponies are also reared in fair numbers, though natives pay little or no attention to the mating of desirable animals, both ponies and cattle being allowed to run wild until required for use. The buffaloes and cattle go about in big herds, and are only interfered with when the calves are marked by their owners, which is generally done by nicking or cutting the ear with a knife, each man having his own mark or marks, or when an animal is required for a feast, for training as a beast of burden, or for riding.

The articles imported into the district are such as are calculated to be of use to the natives, or to attract them by their flashy appearance: blue-black cloth for making coats and trousers, cheap singlets and shirts, ready-made coats and trousers, hats, belts, thread, buttons, beads, needles, German cutlery, cooking-pots, looking-glasses, parang blades, tin lamps, kerosene, soap, tinware, flashy jewellery, cheap brands of canned salmon and sardines, beer, Chinese-made aerated waters, tobacco, dried fish, shrimp-paste, rice, spices, gambier, betel-nut, scissors, brass tobacco and betel boxes, all of which, with many other things, are to be found in the Chinese general shops at Kotabelud.

During the time that I was stationed at this place there was also a shop run by the Gambling Opium and Spirits and Pawnshop Farmer's representative. This retailed vile spirits and opium, and had a separate room set apart for gambling. Spirits are no longer sold at Kotabelud—a very good thing. The gambling part of the establishment was always crowded with lazy Bajaus, mostly intent on losing everything they possessed; but several of the local shopkeepers and their assistants were also bitten by the gambling mania. I am, as a rule, very much opposed to any interference with the liberty of the subject, but I have special reasons for thinking that natives should not be allowed to gamble with the Chinese, or to buy drink from them; these I have set forth in another chapter. Drink is not as yet much purchased by natives, with the exception of some lowland Dusuns, but matters are worse in this respect at Tuaran. A few of the Bajaus and Illanuns, and especially some of the chiefs, are opium smokers, but luckily the Dusuns have so far not taken to this vice.

The coasts and river estuaries of both districts are inhabited by the Bajaus, a Proto-Malayan people, who are essentially maritime. They appear to be fairly recent invaders, who have driven back the Indonesian Dusuns from those parts of the country in which they are now settled. On the east coast of Borneo the Bajaus are still wanderers, sea-gipsies, who are born, live and die in their boats. On the west coast they are settled, either building pile-villages in the estuaries or constructing dwellings on the land close to a river.

They eke out a living by fishing, salt-making and cattle-rearing, and in addition they are padi-planters on a small scale; but their crop is rarely large enough to support them till the next harvest. In the old days they were renowned as pirates, their name in this respect being only a little less dreaded than that of the Illanuns, another tribe which is found in the Tempassuk, but not in the Tuaran district.

The latter are, like the Bajaus, nominal Mohammedans. They also are invaders, having come in their piratical craft from Mindanao, the southernmost of the Philippine Islands, but are much more recent arrivals than the Bajaus. They formerly had a settlement in the Tuaran district, but the Dusuns made things so uncomfortable for them, by hanging about and cutting off stragglers, that they eventually abandoned it. At present their villages in the Tempassuk are to be found near Fort Alfred, and around and beyond Pindasan.

The Dusuns, an Indonesian people, with a slight penchant for head-hunting, inhabit the plain-lands, foot-hills and upland regions of both districts. They are excellent agriculturists and generally hard workers, hospitable, though somewhat given to drunkenness, peaceful, and even rather cowardly, in spite of their head-hunting exploits.

I have so far spoken of Dusuns and Bajaus as if these were the names of two tribes or peoples, and they certainly are the names by which they are generally known to the Malays and other strangers in the country, but they are not the designations which they apply to themselves. The Bajaus call themselves Orang Sama or Sama men. The tribe which we speak of as Dusun or Dusuns is known to the Malays by that name, which means the "people of the orchards," to the Bajaus of the Tempassuk as Idaan, and to the Sulus (or Suluks) as Sun Dyaks. In the

Tempassuk the Dusuns call themselves *Tindal*, but the people of Tuaran, or at least the inhabitants of the villages near the Government post, seem to dub themselves Suang Latud (men of the country?). The up-country people of the Tuaran district I have not visited, but I believe that they also acknowledge *Tindal* as a designation.

According to the census of 1911, the native population of the two districts by race was—

Tuaran District

Bajaus	5,683
Dusuns	16,785
Illanuns	7

Tempassuk District

Bajaus	3,448
Illanuns	1,299
Dusuns	10,256

In addition there were in the Tuaran district: Europeans 3, Chinese 495 (many employed as coolies on rubber estates), Japanese 1, Philippines 6, natives of India 4, natives of Netherlands East Indies 2, natives of the Sulu Archipelago 9, Bruneis 54, Dyaks 14, Muruts 3, Tidongs 1.

In the Tempassuk district: Europeans 1, Chinese 62, Philippines 3, Malays 1, natives of India 2, natives of Netherlands East Indies 15, natives of Sulu Archipelago 21, Bruneis 8, Dyaks 26, Muruts 6, Orang Sungei 4.

The total population of the Tuaran district was 23,067; that of the Tempassuk 15,152.

Since the rubber boom three estates have been opened in the Tuaran district, worked partly with Chinese contract labour, partly with locally recruited natives. Of these three the North Borneo Trading Company owns two, one on the Damit river near Tuaran, the other at Tenghilan. The third estate, belonging to the Beaufort Borneo Rubber Company, is at Menggatal. Probably the labour question and high prices will be the greatest difficulties with which Bornean rubber planters will have to contend. Native labour is insufficient in quantity and unreliable. Among the Chinese Borneo has rather a bad name, and the Indian Government will not allow its subjects to be recruited for labour in the country.

The Tempassuk district is policed by a force of about twenty native constables, who are armed with carbines. The native police are recruited from any of the tribes of Borneo, and at the time I was stationed in the district the following were represented:—Sea Dyaks, Dusuns, Muruts, Bajaus, Illanuns and Orang Sungei, the Dyaks being in the majority over the members of any other tribe. At Tuaran also there were formerly only native police, but, owing to the threatening attitude of newly imported Chinese coolies on the Sungei Damit Estate, a small number of Indian police were stationed there shortly before I left the country, but they have now been withdrawn.

I will here set down clearly that when in the succeeding chapters of this book I speak of Tuaran or the natives of Tuaran, I mean, unless otherwise stated, the part of the district around the Government post and the inhabitants of the neighbouring villages. I have never visited the Ulu (head-waters of the) Tuaran, though I have met many natives of that region, as they frequently come into the Tempassuk district to trade. I believe that their manners and customs are very similar to those of the up-country Dusuns of the Tempassuk.

CHAPTER V

THE JUNGLE

WHAT is the average stay-at-home reader's idea of an Eastern jungle? Judging by what I can remember of my own early impressions, gathered from reading various books of travel, I believe that I pictured a dark and gloomy forest where the light of day hardly penetrated, and where walking was almost an impossibility. This sombre scene was relieved by the presence of gorgeously coloured and strongly perfumed flowers depending from trailing creepers which hung from tree to tree. In addition to the flowers there were brilliantly plumaged birds, which flitted from bough to bough before the traveller, while troops of monkeys chattered and screamed among the branches overhead. Enormous butterflies with jewelled wings sailed across the open spaces in the forest, and gigantic horned beetles watched the intruder from every log of rotting wood. Pythons curled themselves round branches overhanging the only track, herds of tapirs, pig or deer, frightened at the approach of human beings, stampeded through the undergrowth of graceful palms and tree ferns which reared their heads on all sides, and the atmosphere was that of a hot-house in Kew Gardens.

The reality is apt to be somewhat disappointing, as, though there are plenty of interesting objects, the beautiful birds and flowers refuse to display themselves, nor are herds of game or enormous snakes commonly met with in the jungle. As a matter of fact, though there are some lovely flowers, especially orchids, they are rarely seen, and an Eastern jungle can show us nothing which can compare with the spectacle of an English wood carpeted with primroses, hyacinths or anemones. Graceful palms, rattans, creepers and enormous buttressed tree-trunks constitute its chief charm, but the foliage in general is of a rather sombre hue and never shows the glories of late spring or autumn in England.

Birds, as has been remarked above, are little seen, but if we listen for a while they will probably be heard calling gently in the thick undergrowth or in the mass of foliage overhead. Sometimes as we are poling up a narrow river shut in by the jungle on either bank a gorgeous kingfisher will dart away ahead of us, or we may hear a sound like that of an axe ringing on wood, followed by several deep-voiced chuckles and the creak of wings, as a hornbill of the kind which the Malays call *Burong tebang mentua* flies off at our approach.

The name means "the bird who felled his mother-in-law," and a legend tells how a man once went to his mother-in-law to borrow some salt, and that on being refused he flew into a rage and chopped through the posts of her house, bringing it to the ground. When the house fell he went into fits of laughter, and for these impious actions he was transformed into a bird, whose note, as a warning to mankind, resembles the sound of a man working with an axe and laughing. The crooning note of green pigeons, the kind which are caught with call-bamboos, is also often heard.

Butterflies there are in plenty in the open spaces, particularly, I think, in clearings near secondary jungle—*i.e.* jungle which has been felled once and has grown up again. In the Tempassuk district the bridle-path leading to the Interior is a favourite haunt of theirs. Wherever a trickle of water crosses the path butterflies swarm; in some places dozens of yellows and whites, all busy drinking up the moisture; in others species with the outer sides of the wings like dead leaves, but with reddish brown colouring within; handsome fellows with black wings marked with patches of blue; swallow-tails yellow and black or green and black; enormous insects chiefly black, but with patches of brilliant yellow—all these are to be seen. Many of the most beautiful butterflies, like the English Purple Emperor, have a taste for very unsavoury food, and the filth under native houses, dead animals or buffalo dung are all fruitful hunting grounds for the entomologist.

Big game is seldom met with in the jungle. Deer and pigs have a liking for the neighbourhood of native gardens or padi-fields, much to the detriment of the crops and the annoyance of the owners. Timbadau, a kind of wild cattle (*Bos sondaiacus*), are found in the Tempassuk in the big jungle around Metanau, which lies beyond Pindasan, and there may be an occasional rhinoceros on the range which runs from Kinabalu in the direction of Kudat. Elephants are not found on the west coast. The muntjac or barking deer and the mouse deer are common.

Snakes are to be met with but rarely, though occasionally one may be seen swimming a stream or gliding away through the undergrowth.

Two kinds of animals in the jungle force themselves on every traveller's attention; these are leeches and ants. The former are the most insistent, but they can be warded off to a certain extent by wearing putties. Leeches are found in damp places, chiefly on decaying leaves; here they often form little colonies and when somebody has passed near them may be watched standing on end and reaching out in all directions in search of an unwilling host. Their pertinacity is marvellous: they will mount a boot and either climb straight away till they reach the leg, or will march with their loping gait to the eyelets of the boots, squeeze through one of these, and then climb up inside till they get to the top, and so over the sock until they reach their feeding ground; or if there should happen to be a hole in the sock—not an unknown thing among Bornean bachelors—they will find it at once, and begin blood-sucking.

I can well remember my feeling of disgust the first time that I turned down one of my socks and saw a full-fed leech, which looked more like a small black grape than anything else I can think of. Sometimes a leech-bite is felt quite sharply, but if one attacks any part of the body which is not well supplied with nerves, the first intimation that the creature has been at work is a gradually spreading crimson stain on the clothes, the leech having fed to the full and dropped off. It is advisable never to pull a leech away, as, if this is done, a bite often refuses to heal—I believe through the animal leaving its jaws in the wound. I generally get rid of them by lighting a cigarette and putting the burning end on their backs, but I have seen Dyaks carrying some salt for the purpose, which they had tied up in a little screw of rag. This when moistened and applied to a leech makes it let go very quickly.

Ants do not as a rule give much trouble unless provisions are carelessly left exposed or are not packed in ant-proof receptacles; but jam, open tins of sugar, or condensed milk, if not placed in a saucer of water, will in about half-an-hour become alive with them. Two kinds of ant commonly met with have very painful bites: one is the fire ant or *semut api* (Malay), which goes in processions, the other a species of large red ant called *kĕrengga* by the Malays, which builds nests among the foliage of the smaller trees.

Small jungle-crabs are sometimes seen scuttling over the leaves near the banks of a stream, while centipedes and scorpions are also to be found, but I have seen the former more commonly in houses than elsewhere, and with the latter I have only had one little adventure, though I have occasionally come across them. Millipedes are common and attain a large size; in the Malay States I have seen a mass of, I should think, several hundreds of them collected together in one place. A Sakai who was with me at the time said that it was a mother with young, and certainly one was considerably larger than the rest and of a rather red colour, while all the others were greyish. Sometimes curious frogs are met with; these have two projecting horns over the eyes and markings and a coloration which makes them look like dead leaves.

Borneo produces some very fine hard-wood timbers, and among the best of them are two kinds called *salangan batu* and *bilian*. *Rita* is a soft wood, which, undressed, makes excellent timber for rafters under thatch and for other parts of buildings where it is not exposed to damp. Its only drawback is that it sometimes becomes riddled with, and weakened by, the burrows of a species of large boring bee, which is very fond of using it as a nesting-place. The stems of the *nibong* and *bayas* palms, as they are called in Malay, split into lengths, are used for the flooring of houses and small bridges. Large bamboos hacked longitudinally here and there with a *parang* (chopping knife), cut along one side, and spread out in sheets, form the walls or floors of native houses. The leaves of the sago palm and of the *nipa* are made into "attaps" for thatching. The bark of one tree, which I believe is a species of *Artocarpus*, is used for making rope, and that of another for the sides of padi bins.

Bamboo has, of course, hundreds of uses other than for walling and flooring houses; rafts are formed from large stems, and sections are used for water vessels; the posts of temporary houses, bridges, fish-traps, boxes, combs, hats are all made from this most useful plant. The various kinds of rattan canes found in the jungle are perhaps only second to bamboo in their usefulness. The rattan palm has graceful feathery leaves, the petioles of which are covered with hook-like recurved thorns. Long runners hang down from the stem and these when split form the rattan cane of commerce. The natives use rattans for basket-work, for cord, for binding together the posts and beams of houses, and in many other ways.

In big jungle the atmosphere is apt to be distinctly chilly at nights, and also in the early mornings before the mists have risen. Sunlight does not find its way between the leaves of the trees sufficiently during the daytime to make the wearing of a hat necessary, but it is quite hot enough for half-an-hour's hard walking to cause free perspiration.

The Malays recognise three kinds of jungle: big or virgin jungle, which they call *rimba*; secondary growth or *bĕlukar*, which has grown up on the site of old clearings; and bush jungle (*sĕmăk*). The *sĕmăk* stage precedes the growth of *bĕlukar* on a clearing which has been abandoned. If the soil is good, small secondary jungle should arise in five years and reach its maturity in about thirty. After this the soft-wood trees which abound in *bĕlukar* begin to die out, giving place to that hard-wood species which is predominant in big jungle. Probably true big jungle would not be produced for at least a hundred years, possibly much more.

The trees in an Eastern forest are of so many species that even a botanist who had resided for years in the country would be hard put to it to identify at sight all that might be pointed out to him. Beautiful tree ferns are common in the higher regions of the Tempassuk district, while epiphytes and trailing creepers are everywhere. In some places bamboo forest is met with, and the stems of these giant grasses are then cut, made into rafts and floated down to the plains, where they can be sold profitably.

CHAPTER VI

TRAVELLING UP-COUNTRY & ELSEWHERE

BORNEO is no land for the globe-trotter; facilities for travel are *nil*, and roads, outside the towns, do not exist; it is true there are bridle-paths, but these are often very rough, and are of course impassable for vehicles of all kinds. It is necessary, therefore, to travel either on foot or horseback, preferably the latter, as the little Sulu ponies, bred in the country, are as sure-footed as cats.

Natives, most of whom ride buffaloes, follow tracks which have been used from time immemorial, as these heavy animals are not allowed on the bridle-paths for reasons sufficiently obvious to anyone who has ever seen a buffalo track in wet weather. Owing to their peculiar blundering, jumping gait when going over heavy ground, buffaloes will soon reduce a decent path to a series of deep rectangular holes, each separated from the next by a narrow razor-back ridge of mud. It is usually best when following a path much used by these animals not to stride from ridge to ridge, but to push along on one or other side of the track, as an unlucky step on an apparently firm-looking ridge will land you up to your knees in mud and water, with a separate hole for each leg—I know this from personal experience.

Walking along a track or bridle-path in jungle country is not all unpleasant, as there is sufficient shade to be a protection from the heat of the sun; but a march from, say, Kotabelud to Pindasan over sun-scorched plains and marsh-lands is by no means so pleasant, especially if the sun is full on the back. Hence on a journey of this kind it is advisable to start as early as possible, preferably at daybreak or before, as the sun will be high enough to be unpleasant by about nine o'clock.

To those who, like myself, are not expert equestrians, a well-trained water-buffalo is by no means a steed to be despised, as being quite a difficult beast to fall off. An animal with a nice even gait is quite comfortable, and not nearly so slow as might be supposed, a trained riding buffalo keeping up a good steady trot for a considerable number of miles without showing signs of fatigue, even if taken into the plains, where it is exposed to the full force of the sun. The beast is fitted with a ring through the nose, to which is attached a long cord. The rider holds the loose end of this and steers the animal by pulling it in the direction in which he wants to go.

The native saddle is a curious article with a wooden peak sticking up in front and a body padded with the inner bark of some kind of tree, I believe the *Tĕrap* (*Artocarpus kunstleri*). The peak-board leans backwards at an angle from the perpendicular, and from the saddle hang down rope stirrups.

Natives often ride with one stirrup so short that their foot is on the animal's back, or, if they do not shorten the stirrup, simply put up their foot. People with long legs should be careful when riding a buffalo in the plains. Here the small streams have often cut down the banks many feet below ground-level, and consequently the track which crosses them leads down to the water between two high banks of earth, the passage between being only just large enough to allow a full-grown buffalo to pass. When approaching one of these streams it is advisable to kick the feet clear of the stirrups and put them up on the animal's back until you are safely on the other side, or ten to one you will get both your legs most unpleasantly squeezed between the buffalo and the sides of the passage.

Buffaloes can be also highly recommended for crossing rivers; they are not afraid to enter water, as they are amphibious, and are far more sure-footed on the slippery stones of a shallow river than a pony. Needless to say, they are excellent swimmers. Turned loose after his day's work, the buffalo strolls off in search of good pasture, and when he has fed to the full, retires to a wallow, a pool filled with filthy mud which may be capable of holding anything from one to forty animals. Here he will lie for hours, protected from the bites of insects, with little more than his eyes, ears and nose above the surrounding sea of mud. Wallows are made by buffaloes lying down in any small depression, which may hold a little water after a rain-storm, and rolling about until the earth and water are churned up into the evil-looking mud in which they delight. Besides buffaloes and ponies, bulls and cows are pressed into service for purposes of riding or carrying burdens.

Coolies for Government work in Borneo are easy to obtain, as any native failing to obey when his headman orders him to work as a coolie is summarily fined. The rate of pay is twenty-five cents a day, about sixpence in English money, but it is customary for private individuals to give another five cents. This rate, however, has now been raised slightly. Occasionally natives show reluctance to come as coolies when called, and a fine has to be inflicted, but this is rare. It is a good rule never to take Bajau coolies with you if Dusuns—preferably up-country men—are obtainable. Bajaus give constant trouble owing to their laziness, and besides this, as is to a lesser extent the case with lowland Dusuns, they are quite unfitted for the work through their being unaccustomed to walking far or carrying loads, a Bajau never stirring out on foot while he has a beast of any kind to carry him.

Once started and the loads arranged, up-country coolies give little or no trouble, and you have not the worry of providing food for them unless you are going into the jungle away from all habitations, as rice and fish are procurable in any village you pass through. In fact from mouth to source of the Tempassuk river you are hardly ever out of sight of cultivation.

All Bornean coolies expect to be allowed to stop for a short rest when they come to a stream. Here they drink, bathe, and take a chew of *sireh* or smoke a *nipa*-leaf cigarette. Where a stony and shallow mountain stream crosses the path you will generally see one or two of your men draw their *parangs* (working-knives) and squat down in the middle of it to sharpen them. The most conveniently situated stone is chosen for the purpose, and, as nearly every man goes to the same stone, wherever a stream crosses a regular track there will be found a small boulder which has been worn away by constant knife-sharpenings.

In the Tempassuk it is seldom necessary for a Government officer to go into big jungle, since nearly all the villages are accessible without passing through it, being surrounded by secondary growth, which has grown up on the sites of old clearings. The virgin jungle in the district is now confined to the hills, except beyond Pindasan, where in one place it runs down almost to sea-level. I have had but little experience of big jungle in Borneo, though I have seen a good deal of it elsewhere; what I have had, chiefly beyond Pindasan and in the head-waters of the Tempassuk river above Kiau, was not particularly unpleasant, as little or no clearing had to be done to make a path. In extremely heavy jungle it is sometimes necessary to *rentis* (hack a path) for every yard of the journey, but I have never yet met with such heavy going.

With regard to provisions, rice, fowls and eggs can generally be procured in Dusun villages, and possibly vegetables, cucumbers, a kind of French bean, or green Indian corn. Another vegetable not to be despised is a kind of white fungus which grows freely on old tree-trunks. Fish can sometimes be obtained from up-country villagers, who build complicated fish-traps in the rivers. Honey too

—the produce of the little domesticated species of bee which the Dusuns hive in old tree trunks, fixed against the walls of their houses—can often be bought. Fresh coco-nuts form a refreshing drink after a long tramp, and are usually brought as a present when a European visits a village. Still, there are few white men who would care to depend on local supplies alone, and tinned provisions should always be taken.

There are, unfortunately, certain firms whose goods should never be purchased, but for obvious reasons I am unable to mention their names. A good choice of tinned fish, salmon, haddock, sardines, kippers, lobsters, is obtainable, but the question of tinned meat is much more difficult. I usually take several tins of "army rations" with me, as they are excellent and contain both meat and vegetables. These can be supplemented by tinned mutton cutlets, tongue and local fowls. All tinned meat seems to have a tendency to become stringy, and is, I think, bad for the health if eaten continually.

Instead of bread, it is usual to take cabin biscuits or cream crackers, to my mind preferably the former. Many people buy oatmeal to make porridge, but this necessitates either carrying a large number of tins of fresh milk—and weight is a thing which has to be considered—or, if condensed milk is used, mixing it with water, which, if your boy is lazy, may not be boiled. Tinned vegetables are put up by various firms, both English and foreign, and nearly all the brands of these are good.

In wet weather, or before an early morning start, a good cup of hot cocoa is both "grateful and comforting," but cocoa is too heating to be drunk during the day. My usual drink when travelling in Borneo was either tea or the juice of a green coco-nut, but most people prefer whisky and water or whisky and coco-nut juice. Water, unless obtained from mountain streams—and even these are not too safe—should always be boiled. A Primus cooking-lamp is exceedingly useful when on a journey, as it saves the trouble of hunting for dry wood—which is almost impossible to find in wet weather—to make a fire, and burns but little oil, one tin of kerosene lasting almost a month.

When visiting villages away from the bridle-paths, in most of which there is no halting-hut, it is necessary to put up for the night in a Dusun house. I used generally to sleep in the public verandah, as this is the airiest place, and family rooms in a "long house" are generally all occupied. The Dusuns manifest a considerable interest in your belongings and yourself, which is at times apt to be a little embarrassing, but are always willing to do whatever lies in their means to make you comfortable; and as compensation for a little discomfort you obtain an insight into native life which you would not do if stopping in a halting-bungalow. Native houses are usually fairly clean, but nearly always harbour bugs, which their methods of construction particularly favour; however, a Dusun is not worried by such small matters as these.

When setting up your camp-bed it is advisable to see that it is not close to one of the posts of the house, or you may wake up in the middle of the night with the impression that a small earthquake is taking place. The fact is that one of your host's buffaloes is sheltering underneath the house—all Dusun houses are raised from the ground—and is rubbing his back against the post close to your bed. Other disturbing agencies at night are the pigs and the dogs, the former especially. After experiencing a night in a Dusun house and listening to the stealthy crunchings and noisy munchings which go on under it, it is easy to realise how the Dyaks are led to believe in a kind of spirit which comes at night and eats up the remains of cooked rice which are thrown down through a hole in the floor.

The Dusuns are a most hospitable people and always produce a joint of bamboo full of "toddy" to regale the traveller. Seated in a circle, hosts and guests pass the coco-nut-shell cup merrily round, at the same time helping themselves to boiled or broiled fish, which is placed in the centre of the group on a banana leaf or an earthenware plate. The fish is not necessarily eaten because the drinkers are hungry. When the Dusun sits down to a good toddy drink, he fully intends to become intoxicated, but this desirable state should be obtained very gradually. It is the getting drunk the Dusun enjoys, not the being drunk. As old Lengok of Bengkahak once remarked to me: "We like to get drunk slowly, and so we always eat something when we are drinking, otherwise we get drunk quickly, have had no pleasure, and have put away very little liquor." Dusun hospitality to travellers is well illustrated by a certain custom which has almost the force of law. Any wayfarer passing a Dusun garden is entitled, if he be hungry, to gather whatever he wants to eat on the spot, but nothing must be taken away with him, as an act of this kind is regarded as a theft.

Government halting-huts in Borneo are built of the same materials as native houses. They are frequently divided into two portions, one being a coolie room, the other, which is for the use of Europeans, consisting of an unfurnished bedroom with a small verandah. The local headman keeps the hut in repair, but it is necessary to bring your own camp furniture, food and cooking-pots, and at least one personal servant. A "boy" who knows a little cooking is worth his weight in silver, since he is almost impossible to find, at any rate in country districts.

On navigable rivers and on inlets of the sea such as the Sulaman and Mengkabong it is necessary to hire a native boat, the small dug-outs locally called *gobang* often being the only craft obtainable; but when a larger kind can be got, the centre should be covered with a palm-leaf roof supported on a simple framework of trimmed branches, the lower ends of which pass into eyelets cut from the solid wood of the hull. The steersman sits at the stern with a steering-paddle in his hand and the paddlers in front. Boats larger than the *gobang* are usually floored with slats of *nibong* or bamboo.

The crew of the boat will be Bajaus or, if in an Illanun neighbourhood, men of that nationality. Both these races are in their element on the water, in fact, properly speaking, the Bajaus are not land-dwellers; but, though many of their villages are found on dry land, they are never far from a river. The villages on the Sulaman inlet and the Mengkabong are typical, being pile-dwellers over the water, but I shall have more to say about Bajau villages in another chapter.

All the truly native boats I have ever seen in Borneo are essentially dug-outs, though their freeboard may be heightened by the addition of planks which are attached to the dug-out body by means of wooden pegs, the edges of the planks meeting those of the body and the pegs being inserted as "secret nailing."

Travelling in a boat at night on one of the salt inlets is very pleasant, provided that there are not many mosquitoes, which there frequently are on these mangrove-fringed waters. Each stroke of the paddle leaves behind it a swirl of phosphorescent light, and its blade sheds showers of jewelled drops, emeralds and diamonds. The Bajau boatmen set up a weird and haunting chant to the stroke and grind of the paddles, and as the canoe shoots forward into the darkness a native squatting in the bows, with his right hand shading his eyes to enable him to pierce the gloom ahead, calls out to the steersman, "*Gebang, gebang!*" "*Kuanon, kuanon!*" as he makes out the winding of the stream to left or right. I used always to encourage my boatmen to sing, as the paddling chants are to my mind singularly attractive, and chanting keeps the men all paddling in time, and seems to make them quite enjoy their work.

There is yet another method of travelling by water which is chiefly used where boating would be impossible, this being rafting. Though the Dusuns of the Tuaran and Tempassuk —except where there are villages near the coast and the streams are navigable for prahus—know practically nothing of boat work, they are often extremely expert raftsmen. Rafts are chiefly used for going down-stream when rivers are in flood. The fabric consists of a number of enormous bamboos lashed together and secured with shorter bamboo cross-pieces at front and back, while sometimes a hand-rail and seat of the same material are added. The steersman stands either in front or at the back, as occasion demands, keeping the raft on its right course with the aid of a long pole. In the deeper reaches the raft is carried along swiftly by the current and requires but little attention beyond an occasional guiding stroke with the pole; but every here and there a rapid formed by a bed of big round stones is met with, and the raft bumps and bangs noisily over these, the occupants of the small seat getting wet with spray up to the waist. It is below these rapids that the raftsman needs to show his skill, for there is often a deep pool with the current sweeping directly towards a large rock jutting out from the bank. The raft requires very careful guiding here, and exact judgment and hard work are necessary if it is not to be smashed to pieces.

Natives generally have a cheerful way of telling you of approaching difficulties: for instance, your raftsman will say: "We are coming to a very bad place in a little while, Tuan. I have never fallen off a raft yet, but who knows what my luck will be this time!" In the same sort of way when crossing an estuary in a tiny and very unstable little cockle-shell of a dug-out, which has its gunwale level with the water, and in which, unless used to this sort of boat, it is necessary to sit in a kind of cataleptic condition, your solitary paddler will remark: "Lots of crocodiles here, Tuan!"

The chief drawbacks to travelling in Borneo are bad paths, flooded rivers, torrential rains and a hot sun, but in spite of these I look back on my experiences with nothing but pleasure.

CHAPTER VII

THE LIFE OF AN OUT-STATION OFFICER

EVEN in Borneo there are out-stations and out-stations; some of them, if there be estates in the neighbourhood, can produce quite a little colony of European men, while there may even be one or two ladies. In the outposts of civilisation which have advanced to this extent, tennis courts and other luxuries are to be found; and, since the presence of Europeans in a place signifies that there "is something doing" either in the way of planting or mining, the Asiatic population will be much more heterogeneous than that in the smaller stations, which can boast of only a single European, generally a Government officer. As I am chiefly acquainted with the second type of post, I will confine myself to trying to give some idea of the life there.

The vast majority or the whole of the people who inhabit the surrounding country will be Bornean natives; if near the coast, partly Mohammedans, partly pagans—the Mohammedans occupying the littoral and lower river reaches; if in the interior, wholly pagans.

The European officer's house, especially if the post is an old one, will stand on a commanding eminence, such a position having been chosen owing to the likelihood of attacks by the natives, as well as for reasons of health. Possibly on the same level as the European's house, but at some little distance from it, will be the police barracks, while at the foot of the hill are the office, the houses of the clerk and the telegraph operator, and the lock-up. Not far away are sure to be found a row of palm-leaf thatched and walled Chinese shops.

The European official has of necessity to learn to be

something of a jack-of-all-trades; he is his own Police Officer, Chief of Public Works Department, Land Revenue Officer, Magistrate, Accountant, Treasurer, Doctor, Coroner and possibly Customs Officer. He must, if Government allows him to reside in the district for any length of time, get to know all the chiefs and village headmen; while, if he has lived in the country for several years, in addition to Malay—the *lingua franca*—he will probably have a fairly good working knowledge of one or more of the native languages. His duties comprise the collection of revenue from the poll-tax, land-rent on native holdings (if the district has been demarcated), boat and fishing licences, and from other less productive forms of taxation; supervision of the repair and construction of bridle-paths; court work, which includes the hearing of both civil and criminal cases; the monthly making up of the accounts both of revenue and expenditure, besides the sending in of various quarterly and monthly returns. In addition he is expected to visit the villages in his district as frequently as may be, in order to hear complaints, to become acquainted with his people, and to see that all the men are paying poll-tax.

Each district has a certain number of native chiefs, who receive anything from fifty dollars or more down to five dollars for placing their services at the Government's disposal. Among the Mohammedans these chiefs are sometimes men of rank who have been given an official position owing to their birth and influence, sometimes men who have risen owing to their own ability. The Government chiefs among the pagans are usually those headmen of villages who show themselves most capable. The Government chiefs are supposed to attend the court on Thursdays with regularity, to assist the European officer to administer justice and to aid him with their knowledge of native affairs and customs. Minor cases, especially those which concern native custom only, are often dealt with by the chiefs alone.

Every native village, whether Mohammedan or pagan, has

GUMPUS, THE HEADMAN OF TAMBATUAN, WITH SPEAR AND PIDA.

He is wearing his headman's badge, received from Government, of which he is very proud. The *pida*, a broad-bladed knife, or short sword, is in its origin a Sulu weapon.

its headman, who, although he receives no direct pay, is recognised by Government. It is his duty to see that good order is kept in his village, that any crimes committed are reported to the police, to settle small disputes, and to collect the annual poll-tax from his people. In consideration of the latter service he receives ten per cent. commission on the total of his collection. A headman who misbehaves himself is removed by the District Officer, some more trustworthy native being appointed to fill the position.

Out-station life in a district with few other European residents, or none, is, however keen be the Government officer's interest in the people over whom he has charge, naturally rather depressing owing to the isolation, and this depression may sometimes become almost intolerable should fever or other illness attack him. A man accustomed to mix much in society, a lover of card-parties, dancing and other such forms of amusement, will probably suffer from his loneliness much more than one who is sufficiently self-centred to be able to dispense with the companionship of his fellows. The evenings spent alone after the early tropical night has fallen are the times when he is likely to feel his isolation most; his native friends—if he cultivates any—have gone home to their villages; he has read each volume of the last batch of books from cover to cover; and, provided he cannot apply himself to work of some kind, he has nothing to do but sit and think—not a particularly healthy occupation in Borneo—or betake himself to bed, by far the best thing he can do.

On Saturday afternoons or Sundays he may have a chance of enjoying a little sport; a deer-drive can often be organised without much trouble, or taking his gun he may stroll out in quest of green pigeon, and, if it be the season, snipe. Pigs, and the male of the Bornean wild porker has very fine tusks, can sometimes be shot, either by beating them out of places which they are known to frequent, or by waiting for them in the evening near their usual track till they come out of a patch of jungle on their way to raid native gardens; while, if the district harbour them, there may be an occasional opportunity of getting a shot at wild cattle (Timbardau) or rhinoceros.

Near the coasts crocodiles abound in the river estuaries and their lower reaches; but, though crocodile shooting is useful, it is not such good sport as shooting deer or pigs, and besides this not a very large proportion of the animals accounted for are actually secured, since, unless the brutes are lying well away from the river on some mud-flat, they usually manage to fall back into the water when hit, the carcasses being probably found farther down-stream some days afterwards.

To my mind the most enjoyable part of district work is the travelling, though this may be attended with considerable discomfort, heavy rain-storms, flooded rivers and shockingly bad tracks, or none at all, being among their number; but there is freedom from all official routine—though this is not very strict in Borneo—change of scene, intercourse with the natives, for whom I cherish a great affection, and a feeling of having almost cast off the shackles of a paid servant, tied to a country in which it is not good for a white man to spend his whole life. Many times have I thought, when some glorious panorama of upland country unrolled itself before me: "How I should enjoy all this were I only a free man—free to go when and where I like, free to stop as long as pleases me!" Some people do not seem to be galled by the yoke of officialdom; unfortunately for myself I am not one of these.

However, in spite of discomforts—and they are many—to anyone who likes the peoples and customs of the Malay Archipelago and the neighbouring countries the call is irresistible. To me it would be unbearable to think that I should be obliged to live for the rest of my life in England without chance or hope of ever returning to those regions which attract me so greatly, and to the peoples for whom I have so great a regard.

Wherein, with the exception of certain favoured districts, lies the charm of this part of the East it would, I think, be difficult to say; but it is there, and when the old hand returning from Europe encounters again those indefinable Eastern smells at Colombo, he feels that he is nearing home. It is much more easy to give reasons for liking the uncivilised tribes and peoples of the Malayan region, since they possess those good qualities so often found among primitive people who have not yet been corrupted by the all-blighting influence of the white man. True, they have their faults, but perhaps they are not less likeable on that account.

One of the worst troubles of an officer is the probability of being shifted from station to station, these moves being, when I was in Borneo, very frequent, especially in the case of junior members of the British North Borneo Service. I do not know what policy dictated these constant changes, possibly it may have been due to shortage in the staff, or to a desire that newly joined recruits should gain experience of different kinds of work; but, whatever was the cause, appointments often made for a comparatively short time can scarcely have fulfilled the latter purpose. One man I knew had, if I remember rightly, been in six different places in eighteen months.

Moreover, this constant shifting of officers is much disliked by the natives, and tends to a certain extent to unsettle them. Native headmen have said to me on several occasions: "When we are just beginning to know an officer, and he to know us, he is shifted." I gathered, furthermore, that they would sooner have a European whom they disliked set over them for a considerable time than the constant procession which at that time seemed to be customary, since they would at least have known the man with whom they had to deal.

Another thing which probably makes the more unsophisticated natives dislike changes of officers in charge of districts is the fact that, according to their ideas, the advent of a new influence gives rise to some disturbance of the normal conditions of the country, the disturbance being often supposed to be inimical to its inhabitants. Thus any event out of the ordinary occurring soon after the arrival of a new officer is put down to the influences which he brings with him. The results of a new officer's arrival may of course be beneficial, such as plenty of rain when it is required before ploughing the wet-padi fields, a dry spell at the time when the felled jungle is being burnt on the hill-clearings, or a bumper padi crop; but since most human beings, and especially agriculturists, are more prone to grumble than rejoice, I suspect that if any fault can be found with the condition of affairs at the time, the things which are unsatisfactory are put down as being due to the fresh arrival rather than those which are entirely satisfactory.

The unpleasant happenings which may be ascribed to the arrival of a new European are a drought just before ploughing time, floods of rain at the season for burning the jungle in hill-padi cultivation, plagues of rats, and also, I believe, epidemics among buffaloes or human beings.

These favourable or unfavourable events are, I think, in no way connected with the natives' estimation of an officer's character, unpleasant events frequently following the arrival of an officer whom the natives get to like very much. Whether these consequences are considered to be the result of the European's personal influence on the tide of affairs, or whether they are due to outside influences, evil or good, which he may bring with him, I am not certain; but I rather incline to the former opinion, for, since the European is the head of the whole district, his personal spiritual influence would probably be considered strong enough to affect the normal course of affairs.

At the same time it must be remembered that, according

to the ideas of the up-country people, a native returning to his village after a residence elsewhere may bring home a whole crowd of evil spirits or influences with him; hence the custom of performing a religious ceremony over the returned wanderer with a view to their dissipation. Natives think, I suppose, that all diseases are of supernatural origin, certainly small-pox is; therefore a man coming back to his village from a district infected with the disease, developing it himself and so starting an epidemic, would afford to the villagers' minds an extremely forceful proof of the truth of this theory.

The question of the arrival of good and benevolent men having an evil influence on the affairs of others is extremely interesting, cases somewhat analogous being not unheard of in Europe. For example, Pope Leo XIII. was credited with the possession of the Evil Eye; the effects of his glance were therefore dreaded by the superstitious peasants of Italy, and were warded off by surreptitiously making the well-known sign for averting the maleficent influence of the "jettatore."

One trouble which frequently besets Europeans living in places far from the beaten track is the difficulty of obtaining efficient servants. In British Malayasia it is customary for a European to employ at least three, if not four: these are a cook, sometimes a Tamil, but more frequently a Hylam Chinese (native of Hainan); a "boy," either Chinese, Tamil or native; a *tukang ayer*, who draws water and does all the rougher work of the house, again a Chinese, Tamil, or native, but very rarely a Mohammedan; and a *kebun* or gardener. In out-stations in Borneo the European officer's garden is often kept in order by prisoners working in charge of a guard, while the *tukang ayer* may be also a prisoner who has conducted himself well.

Well-trained "boys" and cooks are difficult to get outside the towns, Chinese servants especially being unwilling to go to out-stations, even if tempted by big wages. In the Federated Malay States the only Chinese servants are Hylams, a people not recognised as being true Chinese by the inhabitants of the mainland. The Hylams have, I suppose, gained their position through natural aptitude for this sort of work, but they have a very strong secret trade union or "kongsi." In these states, at any rate, it would be almost impossible to make use of Chinese servants from any of the mainland provinces, as they would be driven out by threats and boycotting or, if these failed, by even more active measures. Many Europeans have found it absolutely impossible to obtain any Chinese servants at all, if a man on leaving, or being discharged, has harboured a grievance and lodged a complaint with his "kongsi."

In Borneo, not being stationed in a town, I had to do the best I could with regard to retainers. I picked up a Chinaman, who turned out to be a most excellent little fellow, as cook; there being no Hylam "kongsi" in such out-of-the-way places, he did not belong to that division of the Chinese, but was a Keh. My first "boy," a very raw and exceedingly objectionable Tuaran Dusun, I got almost immediately on coming to the country. As I think I have remarked elsewhere, a boy who is already trained and has a knowledge of camp cookery is a treasure without price; so, having suffered internally, and otherwise, from the culinary efforts of my Dusun servitor, I decided after some months' trial always in future to take my cook with me when travelling.

Some bachelors of economical tendencies, where such servants can be obtained, dispense with a cook proper and keep a cook-boy instead, but the experiment—I have tried it myself—is not, I believe, generally very successful.

Though a good Chinese servant has some excellent qualities not often found among the natives of the Malayan region—notably gratitude—I cannot say that I like the Chinese as a whole, and for some reason, difficult to state, they fill me with feelings of repulsion.

THE DUSUNS

CHAPTER VIII

RACES OF THE TUARAN & TEMPASSUK DISTRICTS—THE DUSUNS

AS I have previously remarked, Orang Dusun means "people of the orchards," and is a term used by the Brunei Malays to describe a large section of the Indonesian inhabitants of British North Borneo.

The Dusun social unit is the village community, governed by a headman assisted, perhaps, by some of the older men. Roughly speaking, the Dusun groups are more or less similar in habits, customs, beliefs and language, though there are minor differences—and others somewhat more important—from district to district, or even from village to village.

The Dusuns apply different names to themselves in different parts of the country; for instance, I have it on the authority of Father Duxneuney that the Putatan people call themselves Kadasan, while I found that the natives of the Tempassuk dub themselves Tindal.

With regard to the distribution of the Dusuns in British North Borneo, as I have not travelled extensively, and the evidence available is scanty, I cannot speak dogmatically, but I believe that I shall hardly be incorrect if I say that the communities known under this style inhabit the whole of the northern part of the interior of British North Borneo, as far south as the Murut country. On the northern and western coasts (on the west coast they reach the Klias Peninsula) they are to be found living fairly close to the sea, though generally with an intervening fringe of Mohammedans—in most cases Bajaus. On the east coast they inhabit the upper river reaches, while in the interior they extend at any rate to Tambunan, Kaningau being in Murut territory.

Judging from the few measurements that I have taken, they appear to be long-headed Indonesians. The dialects spoken by the Dusuns belong to the Malayo-Polynesian family of languages, and their grammar is far more complicated than that of the Malay language itself.

The Dusun man is generally a rather lithe and muscular individual of low stature. He cannot as a rule be called in the least good-looking, his face being too broad, and the angles of the lower jaw frequently showing extraordinarily heavy development. His nose is concave towards the root and has widely spread nostrils, while the forehead is low, and often bulging. The eyes are generally straight and without the Mongolian fold over their inner corners (a fold of skin over the corner of the eye next the nose, such as is found in the Chinese and other Mongolian races), though in some cases both slanting eyes and the epicanthus can be found. The body is well proportioned, but many growing youths have a very weedy appearance, probably due to their hard life and poor diet.

On the other hand, it is not uncommon to meet Dusuns who are handsome, even when judged by European standards; such a man was my friend Sirinan, one of the headmen of Kampong Piasau, who was the narrator of many of the folk-tales that I collected in the Tempassuk.

On my leaving Borneo he followed me down to Jesselton to say farewell, and several Europeans drew my attention to him as he stood on the steamer among a crowd of other natives, remarking: "What a fine fellow that is." And so he was, not only in appearance, but in character. He was a skilled craftsman, a quick learner, and a hard worker, who could always be trusted. He had, I think, the most perfectly respectful and gentleman-like manner I have ever observed; yet in his respectfulness there was no touch of servility or cringing, and if one word was said to him in an insulting or slighting manner his eyes would flash, his whole body stiffen, while it was evident that very little more provocation would be required to make him draw his *parang*. This is a large chopping-knife, which is used either for work or as a weapon, chiefly for the former purpose.

In all our dealings he was "as honest as the day," but, I think, just possibly, he may have known a little of the sport of buffalo-thieving, which according to Tempassuk district ethics is scarcely a crime, but a kind of game of "I catch your buffalo and you catch me—if you can."

To return, however, to the Dusun in general. His skin colour, especially in the hill districts, is often exceedingly fair for a native of the tropics, being a light yellowish with just a touch of brown in it. This colour was sometimes quite startling, when, on rounding a bend in an up-country bridle-path, I came upon a gang of nearly naked coolies repairing the track, as their light skins were thrown into strong relief by the dark green tints of the surrounding jungle.

The Dusun of the plains is usually a good many shades darker, since he is continually exposed to the direct rays of the sun, which do not affect the up-country man to the same extent, partly owing to the shade of the jungle, and partly to the much smaller amount of sunshine in the rainy upland regions. Probably the low-country man has a greater mixture of blood in his veins than the hill-man, and this may also to some extent account for his darker colour. In the coastal district I think it would not be easy to pick out a man and say, "This is a typical Dusun," but the difficulty would not exist up-country. This fact again, apart from the probabilities of the case, gives some countenance to the idea that the Dusuns of the plains are a mixed people.

On the whole, the percentage of handsome natives is probably higher in the lowlands than in the highlands.

Dusun women, when young, are often quite pretty, what

they lack in regularity of features being balanced by a cheerful and intelligent expression. Their hands and feet are nearly always small and neat, and their bodies well developed. Field labour, however, the carrying of heavy burdens and child-bearing unfortunately soon age them, and a woman is middle-aged at twenty-five and old at thirty. In some of the up-country girls the skin colour is so light that they have quite rosy cheeks.

The Dusun does not seem to attain to a great age; I certainly sometimes saw old men with grizzled hair and crippled limbs left behind in the houses to look after the children when the other members of the family had gone to work in the padi-fields, but I imagine that Englishmen of the same age would be still enjoying a day's shooting or hunting, or a round of golf.

Let us pass, however, from the Dusun's appearance to his character. He is, I think, a good family man. Sons are, of course, more valued than daughters, but the latter are always a good investment, as will be seen in the chapter dealing with courtship and marriage. Extravagance is certainly not a failing of the Dusun, as it is of the Bajau or Illanun; he is as a rule very frugal, and at intervals, if not always, a hard worker—in up-country districts of necessity, since hard labour must be performed to clear the jungle and prepare the ground for padi-planting.

His worst vice is drinking; but this is chiefly indulged in at those times of the year when work is slack—that is, after harvest, and when the jungle has been felled and burnt ready for planting, so that the business of sowing can be safely entrusted to the women. Native-brewed drink seems, however, to have but little, if any, after effects, though one kind made from rice contains a high percentage of alcohol.

In villages situated at some distance from a river, as many of them are—probably owing to hill sites being chosen in old times in order to guard against surprise attacks—the population often leaves something to be desired in the matter of personal cleanliness; and on a few occasions I have seen natives from very out-of-the-way villages who were not merely grimed but caked with dirt.

The Dusun is at first a little apt to be suspicious of a European, especially if he knows that he is a Government "Tuan," the reason for this being that his conscience, which is usually in a healthy dormant condition, is disturbed by the visit and the uncertainty as to whether one or more of his little peccadilloes may not have come to light. When once his confidence is gained, however, he rapidly expands, and in a short time will probably be quite friendly. He will, if you let him, kill fowls for you and bring you presents of vegetables, probably both belonging to somebody else, if he be the headman of the village. In associating with him you can treat him almost as an equal, and be assured that he will not take advantage of it, an impossibility with any of the races of India, with perhaps the exception of the Gurkhas.

But though, if you show yourself sympathetic, you can easily gain some insight into his ways of thought, religious beliefs and superstitions, it is more difficult to get him to tell you truthfully all the affairs of his village. For instance, the true details in a buffalo case, how so-and-so's buffalo, which was attached by a rope to a post of his master's house, managed to run away during the night and tie itself carefully to a tree a couple of miles away in the jungle. Such things will remain mysteries for ever as far as voluntary information from him is concerned, probably for the following reasons:—firstly, he may be in the "job" himself; secondly, if he is not, he has no special reason for giving away his friends, unless he has some grudge against them; thirdly, there comes into play that peculiar dislike to meddling in another's affairs which is so common all over the East.

Again, a man will see a murder taking place and say or do nothing, for why should he interfere in the ways of Providence? If the victim is fated to be murdered, he will be murdered. As to reporting the crime at the nearest police station—well, it is the business of the police to find out these things for themselves; and, if he did, who knows into what trouble he might get through his being mixed up in the affair? Should a serious crime, such as a murder, have been committed, it is often a matter of the greatest difficulty to obtain evidence, even if the police are almost sure that certain individuals have knowledge of the affair; and, if the headman or any other influential person has any reason for screening the offenders, he will have the whole affair hushed up with the greatest care, while it is no uncommon thing for all the people who may be called upon by the police to bear witness to be specially drilled in their evidence beforehand.

Buffalo-stealing expeditions are frequently planned a long time in advance, and in case the thieves should be caught it is arranged what stories are to be told. Luckily for the prosecution, however, when a gang of thieves has been caught, one or other of the prisoners, finding himself in a tight place, usually gives away all the others, meanwhile taking care to try and exculpate himself. Immediately this is known the other participants follow suit, and it is thus fairly easy to piece together the whole story.

This habit of "giving away" companions in crime in order to save his own skin is perhaps one of the worst traits in the Dusun's character. On the other hand, one of the pleasantest things to observe in Dusun society is the method of treating those who have committed some offence and have subsequently returned from a long spell of imprisonment in Jesselton or Sandakan; for, unless the ex-prisoner is a notoriously bad character, no stigma seems to attach to him—he has paid for what he did, and there is an end of the matter. In out-of-the-way villages, indeed, where not many of the inhabitants can speak Malay, the man who has been a "guest of the Government" is, in fact, rather inclined to give himself airs as a man of the world who has received a liberal education, and it is generally he who welcomes the "Tuan" on his arrival in the village, his attentions often being rather overwhelming.

Here I would like to add a word with regard to the confinement of long-sentence prisoners in town gaols. Though I believe the prisons of Jesselton and Sandakan are everything that can be desired, yet from what I have heard the death-rate among up-country natives under sentence is far in excess of what it should be. This, be it understood is in no way the fault of the officers in charge of these institutions, but is due to the peculiar psychological characteristics of the prisoners. It has been described to me by a Government officer how strongly-built natives pine and die under these conditions, apparently becoming home-sick and heart-broken. On the other hand, it is a rare thing to have a death in an out-station lock-up, unless through epidemic disease.

I cannot help thinking that if local lock-ups could be enlarged so as to hold long-sentence prisoners as well as those confined for minor offences, this high death-rate might be materially reduced, for the prisoners would then be working in a country they knew, and would probably not become affected by home-sickness to the same extent; while the station grounds and buildings would be better kept, owing to the larger number of prisoners working on them.

But to return again to the Dusun. With the capacity for forming deep and complicated plots, there is often a large vein of childishness in his character, and his excuses for faults that he has committed are often exceedingly ingenuous.

A case in point was as follows. The prisoners at Kotabelud used to be taken down to the river on Sunday to wash their clothes and bathe, as no work was done on that day, a policeman armed with a loaded carbine being in charge of the gang.

One Sunday a Dusun prisoner, noticing that the police-guard was asleep, dropped quietly off the raft on which the other prisoners were washing and let the current carry him to a small brushwood-covered island some hundred yards down-stream, where he landed and hid himself. Having finished his snooze, the policeman collected his prisoners and marched them back to gaol without noticing that he was a man short. When the relief guard turned up, according to orders, he counted the prisoners, and, not finding the correct number, asked for an explanation, which, of course, policeman No. 1 was unable to give. Meanwhile the missing man lay safely concealed on the island until he saw the other prisoners return to the lock-up, and then, as his disappearance seemed to be still unnoticed, slipped quietly into the river again, swam to the opposite bank and made his escape.

When the matter was reported to the European officer in charge of the post the sleepy policeman was, of course, suitably dealt with. The next thing was to find the prisoner, so police were sent up to his village to make inquiries, as an escaped prisoner nearly always makes straight for home. Sure enough he was found there, and was arrested and brought back. On being charged with running away, he replied that he had not tried to make his escape, but while bathing in the river he had suddenly remembered that he had not paid poll-tax to the Government for that year, and so had returned to his village in order to get the money.

Another story will well illustrate the Dusun's wiliness, which was, however, unsuccessful in this case. In the old days, when the Dusuns' crops were getting damaged by pig or deer, it was the custom to set spring spear-traps for these animals, the traps being operated by means of a bent sapling and a trigger-cord, the latter being stretched across the track used by the marauders. Certain marks were placed on neighbouring trees to warn passers-by of the presence of these traps, but, in spite of this, cases of injury or death occurred so frequently that the setting of spear-traps was forbidden.

Nevertheless the traps are still used "on the sly," and the following events happened as the result of the setting of one. A's padi was being damaged by pigs so he set a spring-trap for them. B, passing along near A's clearing, did not notice the trap-sign and ran into the trigger-cord, firing off the trap and receiving the spear right through the calf of one leg. B was consequently laid up in his house for some time.

A, hearing that B had been wounded and was going to report the matter as soon as he could move, thought out a plan for saving himself and incidentally "getting one back" on B for threatening him with trouble. He therefore made two superficial wounds, one on each side of the calf of his leg, limped down to Kotabelud and reported that he was walking along near B's clearing when he was struck in the leg by the spear of a spring-trap. Inquiries being set on foot and B's presence requested to explain the matter, it was found that he was lying ill, quite unable to walk, and suffering from a serious wound. Result: A retires to gaol to repent of his sins.

A considerable amount of insight into the Dusun's character can be gained from listening to his folk-tales, which are often not without a certain touch of dry humour in them: they show him in his daily round of labour, and they make the auditor understand the things which largely occupy his mind: the felling and burning of the jungle for padi-planting, the prospects of the crop, the Spirits which have to be propitiated in order that they may not molest him, the warnings which he believes come to him in dreams, and the omen-animals to whom he pays heed. The subject of Dusun legendry is, however, dealt with at some length in Chapter XVIII.

CHAPTER IX

DRESS AND ADORNMENT

THE costume of a Dusun man is usually designed with two objects in view, utility and comfort. In hot climates clothes, if worn, should be loose to the body, a fact which all Easterns have long ago realised; but this is a lesson which the stiff-necked and superior Briton, with his tightly fitting suits of khaki or drill, has been slow to learn.

The dress of the up-country Dusun male is beautiful in its simplicity, consisting as it does of a simple T bandage loin-cloth, generally of European material, so disposed as to leave a loose end hanging down at both front and back, in addition to a hat or head-cloth to protect his head against the rays of the sun. This "costume" is both comfortable and cheap.

Slung over his left hip, by means of a string round the waist, he carries the inevitable *parang* (working-knife), which is fastened by a loop and toggle, the latter being often made from a Chinese "cash" or a Sarawak one-cent piece, stamped with a hole in the centre.

The more civilised Dusuns of the coast have adopted coats and trousers, those of Tuaran wearing a rather loose coat of the dark blue cloth sold in the Chinese shops, and very long baggy trousers of the same material, gathered in tightly around the ankle. In addition, head-cloths of turkey-red are much in favour. In the Tempassuk, among the Dusuns of the plains and the more advanced up-country natives, the costume is rather different, a fairly tightly fitting coat of dark blue or black cloth, and loose trousers of the same material, the jacket being often ornamented with two rows of buttons on each side and with embroidered facings.

The head-cloths which are most commonly used in the Tempassuk are the products of Bajau and Illanun women's looms; they are bartered with the Dusuns, as the Dusuns supply these two peoples with sun-hats (*seroung*) which are not made by them. Sun-hats may be either conical or rounded, and the materials of which they are made are strips of bamboo or rattan cane. Frequently they are decorated with quite elaborate patterns, which are worked in with dyed strips of the same materials as the framework. Most varieties are bounded at the edge by either a circular strip of wood or a length of whole rattan cane; but I deal with hats at greater length in Chapter XVI., as the making of them is quite an important Dusun industry.

Dusun men wear a large handkerchief round the waist, and in this is generally carried the brass *sireh*-box, without which no native leaves his house. Occasionally I have seen *sireh*-boxes in the shape of a crescent; these rest on the left hip and are tied to the waist by means of two strings which are attached to brass loops at the points of the horns. *Sireh*-baskets of plaited rattan, which have a strap to go across the chest, and are slung under the left arm, are also common.

Dusun men do not usually decorate themselves with ornaments to any extent, but pretty bracelets and armlets of dyed and plaited rattan, coloured either red and black or yellow and black, are not uncommon in up-country villages, while strings of beads, or beads woven into a plaited band of fern-fibre, are worn diagonally across the chest. Young dandies at Tuaran sometimes carry a small cone-shaped object of buffalo-horn or wood, with a ring at the top, tied to one end of the waist-scarf, or hung on a Chinese or European key-chain. It is hollow below and contains wax for dressing the moustache.

In hill villages such as Kiau, where the weather is apt to be both chilly and rainy, the natives make sleeveless coats of brown bark-cloth, the material being, I believe, obtained from the *Tĕrap*-tree (*Artocarpus kunstleri*). The Dusun name for this bark-cloth is *dampon*, and no doubt, before European cloth became so easy to obtain, it was used for making loin-cloths as well. *Dampon* coats are often skilfully decorated with lacings of native cord.

In the Tempassuk it is now the general fashion to cut the hair short, but formerly long hair was very generally worn by the young bloods—even now men with long hair are still to be met with, and in one or two villages it is almost customary. At Tuaran many Dusun youths wear the hair long, as in love-making it is usual for the swain to rest his head in the lap of his loved one, while she searches vigorously for what a German once called "the little things which go about." Sometimes up-country Tempassuk men shave the head entirely or leave a fringe three or four inches broad from the front reaching down to the ears. Little girls at Tambatuan wear a thick tail of hair from the centre or back, and have the rest of the head shaved: boys may either have the hair cut short or wear a small tail.

Tooth-filing is general, and Tuaran Dusuns have told me that they would be ashamed to have long teeth, probably because they think it like an animal. One youth I knew had the six front teeth in the upper jaw filed down to the level of the gums, while the teeth in the lower jaw had also been rubbed down to a much less extent; but this was an extreme case. Many natives blacken their teeth with a compound which is, I believe, made from young *pinang* fruits and copper sulphate; but the custom is rather dying out. The stems of some kind of plant are also chewed to blacken the teeth. In the Federated Malay States wood-tar made from burnt coco-nut shells was formerly used for this purpose, and very likely the Dusuns may use it too. I have never seen teeth inlaid with brass or other substances, though this method of decorating the person is common among the pagan tribes of Sarawak.

To turn now to the subject of women's dress. The chief garment of the up-country women is a short skirt reaching to a little below the knees. This is of native-woven cloth dyed dark blue with a kind of native indigo. Cloth does not seem to have been manufactured at Tuaran, at any rate within recent years. All Dusun women wear girdles of split and coiled rattan; at Tuaran these are the natural colour of the cane, while in the Tempassuk they are dyed red or black. Numbers of small brass rings are often threaded on the girdle, which consists of a single length of cane, coiled many times round the waist. Several girdles may be worn at the same time.

In the up-country villages of the Tempassuk young women wrap a length of European or Chinese blue cloth about eight inches broad around the breasts, but this is discarded on the birth of the first child. The women-folk of the low-country Dusuns have a short jacket of black or blue cloth, the material for which is bought at the Chinese shops, and a dark blue skirt of the same kind of cloth as their up-country sisters. Jackets are also sometimes worn by up-country Dusun women. When a covering for the head is used, it is either a hat similar to those worn by the men—there are special women's hats made at Saiap and Koung, and one or two other villages, but their use is local—or a cowl-like hood of native-woven cloth similar to that which is used for the skirt. Occasionally the hoods, especially those used for ceremonial purposes, are ornamented with a broad band of beadwork along the edge at the back, the old shell (?) beads called *bongkas* being very much in favour for this purpose.

Apart from the cane girdles and other decorative objects already mentioned, the Dusun woman does not adorn herself to any great extent; young unmarried women wear large flat-topped brass ear-studs which considerably distend the lobe of the ear, and the same kind of articles are sometimes made of silver. Bracelets and armlets of coiled brass wire are fairly common, and occasionally a woman will wear a finger-ring made of silver, or from a piece of a sea-shell.

The hair is dressed into a compact "bun" at the back of the head, but a "fringe" is often left in front and cut straight across the forehead. Up-country the "bun" is ornamented with a bone pin, which is usually slightly engraved. From the head of the pin there depends a string of small European beads about six inches long. Combs are of wood, but are not worn in the hair as ornaments. Among the young women of Tambatuan and some other Tempassuk villages the eyebrows are shaved to thin almost straight lines.

Large discoidal brass collars and others of thick brass wire can sometimes be found stored away in the more remote villages, but these are now to all intents obsolete. Heavy brass anklets are in favour among the belles of Tuaran and Tenghilan and must considerably impede their movements. Embroidery in coloured threads is employed to a small extent to decorate the seams of Dusun women's skirts, and sometimes also their breast-cloths.

CHAPTER X

HOUSES—DOMESTIC AFFAIRS—GOVERNMENT

A DUSUN village invariably stands in a grove of coco-nut palms, the houses being scattered about, apparently without any attempt at arrangement. As is the case with all Bornean dwellings, they are raised from the ground, though sometimes only slightly so; and the space between the house and the earth is the favourite hunting-ground of the wild-looking, gaunt and razor-backed Dusun pigs, which come to feed on the slops, refuse from cooking, and stale rice thrown down through a hole in the floor.

In wet weather Dusun villages, especially if they are situated on a hill, are most unpleasant to approach, since, before reaching the houses, it is necessary to wade through an expanse of evil-smelling mud, which consists partly of refuse washed away from below the houses, and partly of the ordure of domestic animals. Lying about in this sea of filth are pigs of all sizes, evidently thoroughly enjoying the opportunity of a good wallow. Coco-nut shells, husks and leaves are littered over the quagmire and add to the general air of untidiness.

When once the worst of the mud zone is passed, the next thing is to climb up into the house to which you are making your way. This is not quite so easy as might be thought, since the Dusun's idea of a ladder is often merely a tree-trunk with a few notches cut in it, though some houses have quite good steps. In many houses, especially in the lowlands, there is an open platform in front of the door. Here the children play, clothes are dried and various kinds of domestic business performed. These platforms are fairly common in the lowland villages of the Tempassuk, but not up-country.

Dusun houses are of many types. First there is the communal dwelling, which is inhabited by several families; this consists of a wide public verandah, the bachelors' sleeping-place, in which there is sometimes a raised platform at one end or along one side. Doors open off the verandah into the room, or rooms, of each family. Very often the first room leads into a second, which, besides being used as a sleeping-place, contains the family valuables. Occasionally the sleeping-chambers do not lead straight off the common verandah, there being a walled-in passage between them. The cooking-places consist essentially of a square of hardened mud, planked in around the edges. These are placed in the living-rooms, but sometimes also in the verandah; and, chimneys being unknown, when the fire is smoking badly, a native house is almost unbearable to a European. In Tambatuan I have seen fireplaces made of a thin slab of stone slightly concave in the centre. These were placed at intervals in the public verandah.

Though there are many varieties of dwellings, the general plan, whether of a communal house, or of a house for a single family, is much the same. Above the fireplaces used for cooking is a framework supporting shelves for holding firewood and cooking-pots. Both the inner and outer walls of the house, especially in communal dwellings, are frequently made of wooden planks or panels fitted to the roughly squared main timbers, these being generally set vertically with a skirting board at top and bottom.

Considering the tools at the Dusuns' disposal, the work is remarkably well executed. The planks and panels are smoothed with a light native-made adze, and the work done with this tool is often so fine that at a little distance it might well be thought to have been produced by a plane.

In smaller houses the walls may be made of beaten-out sheet-bamboo, and, if the occupants are very poor, the whole dwelling may consist simply of one room. The common verandah is sometimes open along the outside, especially at Tuaran, sometimes closed in; but in the latter case there are small windows, longer than high, each fitted with a board shutter, which is hinged above with a rattan binding or with wooden bars. Large windows of a peculiar kind are found in the roofs of some houses. In these a square piece of the thatch is left loose except along the edge towards the roof-beam, where it is hinged. When more air or light is required somebody climbs up and props this piece of thatch open with a stick. The doors of the living-rooms are frequently pivoted in wooden sockets.

Nails, unless the natives have become very much accustomed to European methods, are never used in house construction, though, if I remember rightly, wooden pegs are occasionally employed instead. Native houses are bound together with rattan cane, large beams and posts usually being joined by removing a section from each, fitting them together, and lashing them firmly with a rattan binding; but rough methods of mortising are understood. Floors are made of sheets of bamboo, more rarely of slats of palm-wood. The house thatch, which slopes away from the roof-beam on either side, is a series of "attaps," made of the doubled and plaited leaves of some kind of palm-tree, generally either *nipa* or sago palm, the former in the low-lands, the latter up-country, though sago attaps last the longest. In up-country districts huts are sometimes roofed with bamboo shingles; when this is done the building is generally of the lean-to type, with an almost flat roof.

The life of a house is about seven years, or until the main posts become rotten, the first parts of them to become decayed being just above ground-level. Re-thatching may have to be performed as often as once in three years, but the frequency of this depends partly on the kind of attaps used and partly on the closeness with which they have been applied to the roof.

Above the roof-beam, at both ends of the house, stick up a pair of wooden decorations called house-horns. These are found upon both Bajau and Dusun dwellings, and are cut out of flat pieces of wood—they may be simply prolongations of the beams upwards, but are often separate—which are frequently roughly carved to represent weapons or mythical animals. I am inclined to think that they may have been originally intended to protect the house against evil spirits, though I could obtain no evidence that the idea persists at the present day.

On some cross-beams of the house, generally over the sleeping rooms, are placed the large tree-bark store-bins for padi which are called *tangkob*. Sometimes, however, padi-stores, little huts, are built separate from the house, or a small store is built on the platform outside the front door. In other cases a separate room in the house is set aside for holding padi. Over the door, or on the walls of a padi-store, there are occasionally to be seen rows of short perpendicular marks made with lime. These indicate the numbers of measures taken out of the store by each inmate of the house, who, on taking some rice, dips a finger into his, or her, lime-box and adds a fresh smear to the series.

The communal houses of the Dusuns are nothing like so long as those of the Dyaks, and one consisting of more than five or six family compartments is rarely seen. The largest I ever saw in the Tempassuk held eight families. I have heard that among some of the Dusuns of the Murudu district one long house constitutes the village, as among the Dyaks. The Dusuns always talk not of a house of so many rooms, but of so many doors. Many villages have but few, or no, communal houses; others consist chiefly of small dwellings of this type.

In addition to the large numbers of pigs already mentioned, a Dusun village has numerous other inhabitants, besides human beings—fowls, cats, dogs, buffaloes and probably also cattle and goats. The lean and mangy pariah-like

THE WIFE OF THE HEADMAN OF TAMBATUAN AND HER FAVOURITE PIG.

Every householder has its pig, razor-backed, unpleasant-looking animals, which though scavengers, are regularly fed by their owners.

dogs are allowed free access to the houses, as the Dusuns do not consider the dog an abomination, as do their Mohammedan neighbours. Though they value good hunting-dogs, they seldom, or never, give the animals sufficient to eat, and consequently they are continually on the prowl to steal any food which may have been carelessly left exposed. I seldom remember having seen a Dusun fondle or make much of his dog.

Cruelty to animals, either intentional or by neglect, is one of the worst faults of the Dusuns. They will torture to death monkeys, which they have caught robbing their crops, in the most horrible manner; and it probably never occurs to a Dusun that a dog should be anything else but a sneaking, shrinking, hungry, mangy cur. Monkeys, chiefly *kra*-monkeys (*Macacus nemestrina*), are sometimes kept as pets, and these wretched beasts generally have their long tails chopped off. I have asked Dusuns why they did this, but never could obtain a satisfactory answer, the reply usually being that long tails were dirty, or did not look nice.

I kept several pets while at Kotabelud, among them a bear cub, a tame deer and a monkey; but I found that it was quite useless to rely upon my Dusun "boy" to feed them. One day I noticed that the monkey, which was tethered to a pole outside the kitchen door, had a bad cut on its tail; so, calling up my Chinese cook, whom I knew was invariably kind to animals, I asked him how it had got wounded. He said he was not certain, but he thought that the "boy" must have done it, as he had seen him near the cook-house and had heard the monkey shriek.

The boy, called and questioned, denied that he had hurt the animal, but admitted that he had thrown a piece of wood at it "in fun." Taking him by the arm, I led him up to the monkey, which immediately started screaming with fright and rushed away to the full length of its chain.

Thinking this sufficient proof, I took the boy into the

house and gave him a good thrashing with a rattan cane. He was only a youth of about fifteen, and I had given him a beating on several occasions before for various sins of omission and commission without his making the slightest demur, since he knew quite well that he deserved everything that he got and a bit more. On this occasion, however, he protested violently, saying that he did not assent to his getting a beating. Nevertheless he got it, and, after writhing at every blow, he rushed out of the room yelling: "The Tuan has half killed me, and all for a monkey that I could buy by the hundred at fifty cents apiece!" It was quite useless explaining to him that he had been punished for his cruelty and not for damaging my property.

Cats in Dusun houses are generally as thin as the dogs. They are of the curious Malayan variety, which has a short, stumpy tail with a bend in it. The vertebræ towards the tip of the tail curve so sharply that the end is almost at right angles to the rest.

The Dusuns are careful enough about animals which it pays to keep in good condition, especially their pigs. These, besides managing to find a good deal of food by routing about on their own account, and often eating the most unpleasant garbage, are fed regularly twice every day, once in the early morning, and again a little while before sundown. At these times in up-country villages the valleys resound with cries of "Kay! Kay! Kay!" with which the Dusun women call home their pigs to be fed with boiled *kaladi* stems and other vegetables. Every pig knows its owner's voice and trots up quickly when called. I still well remember the young and pretty wife of Gumpus, the headman of Kampong Tambatuan, standing on a rounded boulder in front of the house and distributing delicacies among the waiting herd of porkers below; it was quite a picture of Beauty and the Beasts.

Bees are kept in many up-country villages, more, I think, on account of the wax they produce than for their honey.

The hives are made by getting a section of hollow tree-trunk, stopping it up at top and bottom and boring a hole in one side as an entry. The species of bee in these hives is a little, dark-coloured, rather thin-bodied insect, and the inmates of a hive frequently collect in large clusters near the entry. When anyone passes a hive with a cluster of bees hanging to it, the whole assembly is set in violent motion with a curious vibrating movement; but its members never seem to make any attempt to attack the intruder, and in this their behaviour differs very much from that of one wild species which makes its nests in hollow trees. These frequently make themselves a great nuisance by flying out and attacking travellers and often following them for a considerable distance. The domesticated species cannot give much trouble, as the hives are fixed to the walls of the houses, often quite close to a window or sometimes actually within the house itself. The Dusuns do not, I believe, understand anything about hiving swarms. They simply hang up a hive and it is taken possession of by the bees, which are a wild species.

The honey is not considered particularly valuable, and at Tambatuan I once bought three large combs for ten cents (about 2½d.). These I took with me to the Government halting-bungalow which stands just above the village, where I was spending the night with Dr Piltz of the British North Borneo Exploration Company. We indulged in some of the honey on the spot, but unfortunately wild bees found out that we had it, and came into the hut in such numbers that we were forced to make a hasty exit, while the remainder of the honey had to be thrown away and the hut smoked out before we could return.

Dusun women's main household occupations, other than looking after their children, are the husking and winnowing of rice, cooking, fetching water from the river, and weaving cloth. The unhusked rice or padi is pounded in a large wooden mortar. The pestle, also of wood, is quite a heavy affair, and strenuous work is necessary to beat the grain out of the husk. One of the prettiest sights to be seen in Borneo is a bevy of native girls all pounding rice together. The pestles keep perfect time, and it is a sheer delight to watch the graceful movements of the lissom, brown-skinned young beauties.

When the rice in the mortar has been sufficiently pounded, it is taken out and put into a large circular winnowing-tray of basket-work, which has a slightly raised rim. In winnowing the grain from the chaff, the operator grasps the tray firmly at the edges with the hands wide apart, the index fingers being from time to time extended along the tray-edge so as to be better able to control the utensil. The tray is held horizontally in front of the operator, while, by a series of rotatory movements, accompanied by little taps of the index fingers, the husks are shaken towards the far edge of the tray and the padi towards the operator. When a large amount of chaff has collected, the tray is given a little toss which sends the husks over the edge. The process is repeated again and again until no husks are left.

Rice before being cooked is always thoroughly washed. The grain is placed in the cooking-pot and water poured over it; it is then well stirred round and handfuls of it taken and pressed repeatedly in the water. The water in the pot becomes milky, and in village-grown rice is coloured by the starch, dirt and other substances in suspension. The dirty water is poured away and the process repeated until washing no longer discolours the water. When the rice is thoroughly clean, sufficient water is added to just cover it, and then the pot put on a slow fire to heat until the water has all been driven off and the rice next the inside of the vessel has begun to cake and brown.

Dusun cooking is generally exceedingly rough, quite large animals being roasted whole in their skins, sometimes without even removing the intestines. Fish are either boiled or grilled.

A great part of the Dusun's time is spent away from home in attending to his padi-fields. In fact at harvest and just before it the villages are almost deserted, whole families migrating to their clearings, which are often as much as a couple of miles or more away. Here they live in a temporary hut or *sulap*, the crop requiring constant watching by night and day to protect it from the attentions of birds, pigs, deer and rats.

At other times of the year, when there is rather less work, the men, and often many of the women-folk, leave the village shortly after daylight, the former all carrying spears and some of the latter baskets on their backs, in which they are going to bring back tubers for the evening meal. They work in the fields during the morning and lie off during the heat of the day, returning home towards sundown. Frequently if a village is visited at any hour between eight in the morning and four or five in the afternoon nobody will be found at home except the very oldest men and women, whom age and infirmities have rendered incapable of field work, or the young children left in their charge.

When harvest is over, more people are to be found at home in the villages, for then work is at a minimum and the Dusuns give themselves up to feasting, drinking and other forms of enjoyment. Parties are made to renew the fish-traps in the river below the village, while a good deal of time is spent in repairing the long stone walls of the shoot-traps, and in fishing with rod and line.

The Dusuns never seem to have evolved any higher form of organisation than the village community, and in the old days neighbouring settlements were often at feud. Over each village is a headman, who at the present day is responsible to the Government for the good behaviour of the people under his charge, settles small disputes concerning native customs, and collects poll-tax of a dollar a head from all adult males, receiving ten per cent. commission for his trouble. In some villages—Tambatuan, for instance—I do not know if in all, the headmanship nominally descends from father to son, though I expect that formerly anyone who was capable of getting together a following would have been able to seize the leadership.

CHAPTER XI

AGRICULTURE, FISHING, HUNTING & TRAPPING

THE Dusun is primarily an agriculturist, but that is not by any means to say that he neglects other employments which may provide him with food. Everything is "fish which comes to his net," from a maggot to a buffalo.

In the lowland regions the staple crop is wet rice. This is at first planted out in nurseries; then when the seedlings have attained a certain height they are dug up, their tops are cut off, they are tied into bundles and carried by the women to the swampy padi-fields where they are set out in rows with the help of a short wooden dibble. The fields require a good deal of preparation each year before the seedlings can be planted out, and for this rain is a necessity. As soon as sufficient has fallen operations are begun.

Each field is bounded on its four sides by a bank of hardened mud, and the water, if an insufficient amount collects, naturally is conducted from the nearest brook, which is obstructed by a dam. The water finds its way from field to field, the embankments being temporarily breached for this purpose. When enough has been admitted the breaches are again closed and, after the water has stood for some time and the weeds have died down, the land is ready for ploughing.

The Dusun plough is an extremely simple contrivance of wood with an iron-shod share. It is drawn by a buffalo, which is attached to it by very primitive harness and is driven by means of a nose-cord and a switch of rattans. After ploughing, the soil, now in a semi-liquid state, is harrowed by harnessing a buffalo to a large bamboo frame under which are fitted projecting spikes of the same material as the frame, or of *nibong* palm-wood. This contrivance is dragged about the field, often with the driver standing on it. Two other contrivances drawn by buffaloes are also used for smoothing and levelling the soil: one is a kind of large rake with a rail-like handle which enables the driver to raise or depress the implement as required; the other a heavy and almost semicircular beam of hard wood which is dragged about to level inequalities of the ground, the driver mounting the implement to increase its weight. Harrowing having been completed, the land is ready for the reception of the young seedlings. Between planting out and harvest the crop requires to be kept free of weeds, this work being apportioned to the women and children.

When the grain is ripening it attracts large flocks of weaver-birds, and is, besides, liable to be destroyed by inroads of rats, pigs and deer. To protect the padi against these visitors the Dusuns build small huts in the fields and station watchers in them, or sometimes a whole family will live there until the harvest is completed. One method of scaring birds is to plant a number of bamboo poles loosely in the ground at various points in the fields. These are connected by strings to which are attached rags, bunches of grass and other suitable objects. The different strings lead up from the posts into the watcher's hut and are usually tied altogether to a beam. The watcher is thus enabled to take his ease in the shade, and at the same time to keep birds away from the whole field by jerking at the bunch of strings which sets all the scarers in motion.

Reaping, which is done with a special type of knife, is left to the women and children, as is all but the very heaviest field work. There are two special kinds: one type consists of a thin blade of iron set at right angles across, and in about the centre of, a wooden handle; this is grasped in the right hand, so that the blade is between the second and third fingers. In reaping, the padi stalks are drawn with these

DUSUN WOMEN AT WORK IN THE FIELDS BELOW TAMBATUAN.

The women are cutting down the grass, this, where the plough is not used, being one of the first steps in the cultivation of wet-growing rice. Water is subsequently let in to convert the land into a swamp suitable for receiving the seedlings, which are transplanted from the nursery.

two fingers against the blade and thus cut through. The other kind of reaping-knife has a blade which is broad at the end and narrow near the handle, the back curving upwards towards the end farthest from the handle.

The Dusuns of the hill villages plant dry rice as their chief crop. The cultivation of this necessitates the making of a fresh clearing in the jungle every season. When the forest has been felled with adzes and chopping-knives it is left to dry for a while and is then fired. The burning does not entirely destroy the tree-trunks, but the ground is sufficiently cleared to allow sowing to take place. This work is done by the women, who drill lines of holes with sharpened stakes of hard wood and drop several grains into each. The holes are not filled in, and a watcher is generally set for a few days to keep away birds until the earth has tumbled down so as to cover the seed or has been washed over it by rain.

The hill padi needs just as much looking after as wet rice, or rather more, since the clearing is surrounded by jungle, the haunts of deer and pig: in fact, during the padi season the up-country Dusun lives more on his clearing than in his village, the tiny little hut (*sulap*) which he builds being crowded with himself and his family. After harvest, if it has been plentiful, the Dusun gives himself up to eating and drinking.

Occasionally, if the weather has been very wet at the burning season, the Dusuns are unable to clear their ground properly and the crop is a failure; in this case they have to support themselves as best they may on jungle tubers and whatever small animals and fish they are able to catch in their traps.

The planting of hill padi is destructive to large stretches of jungle, but it is difficult to see what method could be substituted for it, unless the Dusuns could be taught to terrace the sides of the valleys and plant wet padi. The shallow soil of the hill-side will support crops of padi for a few years at the outside, and actually the Dusuns only use it once, planting, when the padi has sprung up, *kaladi* (*Caladium*) among the young crop. For the next season's padi crop a new piece of jungle has to be felled and burned, and when the *kaladi* tubers have reached maturity and been dug up the old clearing is abandoned.

After some years, perhaps about twenty, when tall secondary jungle has grown up on it, it may be used again, the soil having had a rest and a certain amount of new humus having accumulated. In the coastal regions dry or hill padi is a good deal planted on flat land which it is difficult to irrigate. The plough and harrow are used in preparing the ground, and the land will support a crop for two or three years running. A few of the up-country villages of the Tempassuk, for instance Tambatuan, have a little wet rice land in the valley. Probably old ground might be used more frequently, but as it is very troublesome to clear the grass, weeds and brushwood which spring up in a year or two, the people prefer to wait until comparatively large trees have grown up and killed the undergrowth.

As mentioned elsewhere, a considerable amount of tobacco is grown at Kiau, and in various villages of the Interior province. Other crops occasionally planted are tapioca and Indian corn, the last to a very small extent among the Dusuns. Sometimes also quite large patches of native cucumbers are met with, which, though they have not so much taste as those grown in Europe, are nevertheless a very welcome vegetable. Small onions, like spring onions or little leeks, a French bean, as well as pumpkins and a kind of vegetable marrow, are other vegetables occasionally obtainable. The fruit grown in the Tempassuk and other parts of Borneo I have dealt with in a former chapter.

The Dusuns are particularly clever at obtaining both small and large animals by means of traps. For catching deer spring spear-traps and nooses are prepared, while for pig spear-traps, trigger fall traps and pit-traps—the bottom of the last-mentioned studded with pointed bamboo stakes—are most generally used.

The *blantek*, *blatek* or *tuil*, names under which the spring spear-trap is known, has the spear set at different heights according to the kind of game it is required to kill; thus for pig it is set at about the height of the calf of a man's leg from the ground and for deer at the height of a man's chest. Owing to numbers of people having been killed or wounded by traps of this kind, they are now illegal, and are only set by stealth; consequently I have never seen one, but I understand that the spring power is supplied by a bent sapling and the trap exploded by means of a trigger-cord stretched across the game-track. The long bamboo spears with which *blantek* are armed were several times during my residence in Borneo brought into court when Dusuns were charged with setting them. This type of trap is, I believe, essentially similar to that called *peti lanchar* in Sarawak, an example of which is figured in Ling Roth's *Natives of Sarawak and British North Borneo* (vol. i., p. 440).

The pit-traps for pig are covered over with sticks and leaves, so as to resemble the surrounding earth: they are, of course, dug in the middle of a game-track, generally close to the spot where the pigs have broken through a garden fence.

Deer, when not hunted with a pack of dogs and spears, are frequently driven against a row of rattan nooses suspended from a long cord of the same material. A large number of beaters is necessary to accomplish successfully one of these drives, and a section of jungle known to be haunted by deer must be found, which is of suitable shape for the purpose—*i.e.* one which is rather triangular, so that the line of nooses may be set not far from its apex, the deer being driven down from the broader portions. The Dusuns are also exceedingly clever at making fall- and noose-traps for small animals, chiefly rats and squirrels, and a very common type of squirrel-trap worked by a trigger and a bow is illustrated by Burbidge in *Gardens of the Sun.*

When the harvest is over the hill people are at a loss for regular employment, and so betake themselves to the river to set their fish-traps in order. The most common type of large trap consists of two converging stone walls with a basket fixed at the end. The trap is built in the form of a **V** with the broad end facing up-stream, and its walls are composed of large rounded boulders collected from the river bed. These walls are of considerable length, and are built so as more or less to dam a considerable portion of the river. Thus the water within the stone walls, especially near their apex, is at rather a higher level than that of the stream outside them. The long conical basket affixed to the narrow end of the trap retains the fish and at the same time allows the pent-up water to escape. As the walls of the trap and the water between them are above the level of the stream, the basket is also elevated considerably above the surface, and the water from the trap plunges down through it to join the main body of the river again. A slight bridge of two bamboos, one for a hand-rail and one for the feet, is often built from the bank to the end of the trap in order to facilitate the collection of the catch.

Few fish are caught in these traps unless the river is swollen by heavy rain, but then large hauls are the rule; for at such times the fish make their way down-stream in search of suitable holes and eddies in which they may shelter themselves from the force of the stream, and thus pass in large numbers between the stone walls and into the basket. When the river is badly in flood—frequent occurrence—the bamboo bridge becomes almost a necessity, for it is an extremely dangerous experiment to try and wade the Tempassuk after heavy rains, many Dusuns, swept away by the rush of water, having paid for their temerity with their lives.

Another method of trapping fish occasionally employed is to select a shallow stretch of river where the bed is wider than usual and the current not very swift, and there to build a series of large stone-walled chambers, each connected with the next by a small opening, the main entrance to the trap, as before, facing up-stream. Fish make their way into the chambers and are then easily captured and dispatched.

One very ingenious form of trap is a bottomless conical basket of natural or wait-a-bit rattan twigs. The reflexed thorns of the plant are left adhering on the inside, the strands of rattan being so arranged that the thorns point backwards—that is, towards the apex of the trap. Walls of stones with small holes in them at intervals are built at right angles across the river to receive the traps. These are inserted with their opening facing up-stream, so that fish descending the river put their heads into what appears to them to be breaches in the wall, but are unable to withdraw again owing to the thorns of the traps catching them under their scales. Often this type of trap is used without thorns. The fish get their heads wedged in and cannot escape. A similar kind of trap is made in the Malay States, where it is called *tengkalak onak*.

Several varieties of basket fish-traps are made by the Dusuns, the principle of all being that of easy entry and difficult escape. The usual method is to make a conical entrance to the trap out of strips of rattan or other material, the point of the cone being directed inwards. The fish can thus easily make their way into the trap, but when they try to make their way out again, even if they can find the place at which they entered, they are unable to push apart the converging strips of cane which form the point of the cone.

Several methods of rod-and-line fishing are employed, one of which resembles fly fishing with a grasshopper or other insect for bait. For fishing the pools in the river the line is weighted with a small piece of lead and baited with a worm, or anything else which will attract the fish. A light float is often used on the line in ditches and other still waters.

A rather remarkable method of fishing is by "splashing"; to perform this a man walks along the bank of a deep and rather sluggish stream with a rod and a short line, to the end of which is attached a small piece of sheet-brass armed with either one or two hooks. He drops the bait into the water and then splashes the water about with the top of the rod, the movements of the rod top causing the bait to jump about as if alive. Fish lurking under the banks or on the bottom come and seize the bait, and sometimes quite large catches are made.

Among the lowland Dusuns small streams are often dammed, in order to catch the fish which lurk in the deeper holes, while scoop-like baskets or hand-nets are used for bailing out the catch. The flat, marshy country between Kotabelud and Pindasan is a favourite place for this method of fish-catching, and also for hunting for tortoises and fresh-water turtles. The juice obtained from the roots of the tuba plant (*Deris eliptica*) is sometimes used for stupefying fish in rivers and pools, the roots being pounded up and the juice poured into the water. Catching fish by torchlight is a favourite pursuit of both Dusuns and Bajaus, and, when the water in the Tempassuk is low, parties are out along the river bank night after night. The fish are dazed, or even attracted, by the glare of the torches and allow themselves to be killed with a chopping-knife or a fish-spear without making the slightest effort to escape.

Any European can make himself popular with a whole Dusun village by dynamiting a couple of pools in the river. Everyone in the place turns out to take a share in the fun, grandfathers, fathers, mothers, grandchildren and bevies of Dusun girls, whose partly assumed modesty and shy giggles greatly add to the amusement of the occasion. The women and children, armed with hand-nets or scoop-shaped baskets, stretch themselves in a line across the river in the shallows below the pool. The cartridge is thrown in, a dull boom is heard, and a small column of water leaps from the surface of the river. Then all is excitement, hasty grabs at escaping fish are made by the watchers in the shallows; the younger men of the village dive again and again into the pool, bringing up each time half-stunned fish which are lurking near the bottom; sweeps are made at floating fish with hand-net or basket, and finally, when nothing more remains to be caught, a move is made to the bank and the catch counted and divided.

CHAPTER XII

FOOD, NARCOTICS & INTOXICANTS

THE Dusun is nearly omnivorous. Rice, fish, meat, vegetables, fruit, jungle roots, squirrels, monkeys, rats, snakes, tortoises, lizards and frogs are eagerly devoured, even such foul and musky smelling reptiles as the monitor-lizard not being despised. I remember shooting one of these animals on a small creek near Tenghilan, where I used occasionally to stop for the night on the way from Tuaran to Kotabelud. Wishing to preserve its skin, but not being willing to skin the animal myself, I turned it over to a coolie, on condition that he should have the body to eat if he would take off the skin for me. The offer was accepted with alacrity and I was afterwards informed that the meat was splendid!

Around many of the villages monkeys and small game, such as rats, have been almost exterminated, a fact which has struck several zoologists who have visited Mount Kinabalu in search of specimens. Of course, as with most Eastern people, the staple food of the Dusuns is rice, but in addition large quantities of *kaladi* (*Caladium* sp.) and tapioca root are consumed. Fresh-water fish, as has been shown, are easy to obtain, for the rivers teem with many different kinds, and dry or fresh sea-fish can be purchased in the markets.

Occasionally, when the padi crop is a failure, and the produce of supplementary cultivation is insufficient to maintain him, the Dusun has to fall back on jungle roots to supply the deficiency. Certain poisonous tubers called *kadut* are dug, cut into thin slices, and placed for some hours in a basket, which is set down in a shallow stream

A Dusun Family Party on the March.

The old man has a spear in his right hand, which he uses as a walking stick, or against a pig, or other animal he may encounter. The point of the spear is protected by a two-piece wooden sheath bound with strips of rattan cane. Note the inevitable chopping knife on the left thigh.

A Dusun Fish-Trap in the Kadamaian River.

A trap of this kind is constructed at the narrow end of two long V-shaped, converging walls of stones, built in the river bed, and having their larger opening up-stream. It consists of a long shoot of bamboos leading to a removable, conical basket, into which the fish fall.

so that a constant current of water shall flow over its contents. When all the poisonous elements have been thus removed, the tubers are ready for cooking. I once saw this vegetable being washed at a Dusun village not far from Pindasan. The padi crop had been a failure, and the people were half starving. Measures were taken for their relief.

With regard to food in general, the Dusun appreciates quantity more than quality. An Illanun chief once remarked to me: "These Dusun coolies eat like buffaloes; a whole saucepan of rice per man is not enough for them." Some epicures like their game high. Burbidge, in *Gardens of the Sun*, tells us how a Dusun "had two rats —rather high they were too—which he roasted entire and ate with great gusto."

The Dusun methods of cooking are boiling, stewing and roasting. Small fish or bits of meat are often roasted by putting them into the cleft of a stick, which is sharpened at the other end for sticking into the ground. Three stones or three short stakes of wood or bamboo are used to support the cooking-pots.

But to return to the subject of high food, the Dusuns have one delicacy — a kind of potted meat — which to European ideas is a most disgusting compound. The basis of it is raw salted meat of some kind or other, usually buffalo, treated with powdered seeds of the tree which the Malays call *kapayang*, the Dusuns *pangi*. This is put away in jars, where it is left till far advanced in decomposition, when it is considered ready for use. A jar of potted meat is often opened at a drinking-party, and its vile stench corrupts the air of the whole village.

The Dusuns obtain their salt from the Bajaus and Illanuns of the coast, but the subject of salt-making is one with which I will deal later. Cooking is largely done in native pots of greyish-coloured clay or brass vessels, purchased, in the latter case, from Brunei traders or Chinese store-keepers, but

H

European saucepans are coming more and more into use. Fish, caught in traps in the river, when not eaten fresh, are split open and sun-dried. A disgusting smell arises from these during the drying process, clouds of flies settling on and buzzing around them. According to Whitehead, in *Exploration of Mount Kinabalu*, p. 183, "rats are often split and fixed on bamboo frames, then smoked and stuck over the fireplaces in the houses until required"; but, though no doubt his observations are correct, I never remember having seen this done myself.

The water-vessel in all Bornean houses is a length of bamboo, the body of the vessel being a long single inter-node, and the bottom an adjacent node. In the morning women carry down a number of these to the river on their shoulders, fill them and bring them back to the houses, the supply of water being generally sufficient to last for the day. Occasionally, when a village is far from a supply of drinking water, an aqueduct of bamboos split into halves and supported on slight poles is built to the nearest spring.

Dusuns have a rather curious habit of preserving the skulls and bones of animals they have eaten, a piece of the under side of the thatch often being decorated with numbers of these trophies. Among them are generally remains of squirrels, pigs, rats, and sometimes of the muntjac or of deer.

Rice, as has been remarked before, is the staple diet. Various condiments, red peppers, etc., are sometimes mixed with the rice and fish to give spice to the meal. The mixture is pressed into boluses with the fingers of the right hand, and transferred from the plate to the mouth, the head being tilted backwards. Spoons cut from joints of bamboo are used in Dusun cookery, as are also wooden stirrers or spatulæ. For figures of these Ling Roth's *Natives of Sarawak and British North Borneo*, vol. i., p. 380, should be consulted.

At Tuaran the women have the abnormal habit of eating

earth, which is also found in other parts of Borneo, in Java and the Federated Malay States. Not far from the Chinese shops at this station there is a gully, which at the time of heavy rains has a small stream running at the bottom of it. The sides of the gully are made of a bluish grey clay with one or two bands of a hard dark purplish red clay running through it. At about six o'clock in the evening it is usual to see anything up to about a dozen women digging out this red clay with pointed sticks or small knives, and putting it into baskets. I have been told that the clay is roasted before being eaten, and that some women consume very large quantities. It is said to be a good medicine for women who are *enceinte*. I have several times dug out a sample and eaten it myself; it has rather the consistency of chocolate, but is almost tasteless.

To the native mind a *sireh* chew and tobacco to smoke are only a little less necessary than food. The ingredients of the quid, as made up in Borneo, are a *sireh* leaf—*sireh* is a climbing pepper—a piece of nut from the betel palm, a piece of gambier, which is bought from the Chinese in small cubes, a little native-grown tobacco, and a smear of lime obtained by burning sea- or fresh-water shells or coral. The coarsest veins are stripped out of the *sireh* leaf, and a smear or two of lime put on its upper surface. Sufficient quantities of betel, gambier and tobacco are then put into the half-folded leaf, and the whole made into a bundle and pushed into the mouth. Occasionally, when too little lime has been added to the chew, a native will produce his lime-box and taking out some of the lime-paste on his little finger smear it on a back tooth.

Chewing causes a copious flow of saliva and colours it red, so that a new-comer to the country, following a path much used by natives, might think that a wounded man had preceded him along it. The habit is certainly not particularly pleasing, and the appearance of a quite pretty young woman is often spoiled by her having a ragged-looking wad of half-chewed sireh and tobacco protruding from one corner of her mouth. Old people, who have lost their teeth, find it impossible to manage a quid made up in the manner described above; but for all this they are not to be deprived of one of their chief pleasures, so they put the ingredients of the chew into a tabular mortar of iron, brass, or bamboo, and pound it up with a pestle with a sharpened end.

A *sireh* quid has an aromatic, pungent and astringent taste, and, speaking from my own experience, is distinctly stimulating. When a guest visits a Dusun house the host immediately produces *sireh* and tobacco, the former being contained either in a tray or in one of those beautiful old brass caskets so treasured by the Dusuns. These are always much worn at the bottom from being perpetually pushed along the floor of the house from guest to guest. The caskets contain small boxes for the lime, tobacco and gambier, with a pair of special scissors for cutting up the betel-nut. Not to offer a guest *sireh* would be a breach of the laws of Dusun hospitality.

Tobacco is used not only for chewing, but also for smoking, though pipes are not known among the Tempassuk and Tuaran Dusuns; they are used, however, by other tribes, notably the Muruts. The Dusun medium of smoking is the cigarette, which is covered with a wrapper made from the flower-spathe of the *nipa* palm. These wrappers, which are called *kirai*, can be bought ready cut and made up into bundles at all the markets. Native cigarettes are not a bad substitute for the European variety, if anyone runs out of stock, but the wrapper tastes rather more than the tobacco, and they are drying to the throat, and tend to produce a cough.

The Dusuns have, rather unfairly, I think, got a certain reputation as drunkards. It is true that they often drink to excess, but this is a rule only at nights after the day's work is done, or when work is slack, as, for instance, after harvest, which is the general season of rejoicing. Then you may sometimes find whole villages drunk, men, women and even children; but it is rarely that a Dusun takes to drink, as many Europeans do, to such an extent that he becomes incapable of doing his daily work. This is not for want of opportunity, as every man makes his own liquor, and the supply is limited only by the number of coco-nut trees.

One good point about native intoxicants is that they seem to have comparatively little ill effect; a man will be dead drunk at night and get up the next morning without even a headache. Natives have often told me this, adding that gin, arrack or whisky bought at the Chinese shops made them feel very ill the next morning: not that native drink is not strong, especially the kind known as *tapai*, which contains a large percentage of alcohol, but it is made from good materials and is free from adulteration. Luckily so far the Dusuns do not seem to have taken very much to the vile products sold as brandy and whisky by the Chinese, this probably being chiefly owing to their high price compared with native-brewed drink. Around Tuaran some of the men drink arrack and gin, and illicit stills run by Chinese sometimes give trouble to the authorities.

The Dusun is a great man at convivial gatherings and a regular connoisseur with regard to the liquor he drinks. It is the height of hospitality to make a visitor drunk, and the guest will probably regard his host as mean if he does not give him enough drink to make him go home staggering. In deference to native custom, whenever Dusuns came to see me, I used to provide a stock of liquor, native-brewed, and on one occasion when I was doling it out rather sparingly, partly because I did not want to have a noisy party in the house, and partly because I did not wish to encourage drunken habits, one of the Dusuns asked for some more, saying: "Look here, Tuan, you would not like us to go home to our villages and say you had not made us properly drunk, would you?" After this nothing remained but to send out for some fresh drink and be truly hospitable.

The liquor chiefly drunk is toddy, locally known as *bahr*. It is made from the sap of the coco-nut palm, obtained by cutting the end of a young flowering shoot, which, of course, has a great sap pressure in it. A large bamboo receptacle is hung underneath the cut end of the shoot, and into this the liquor trickles. A piece of a certain kind of tree-bark called *russak* is placed in the bamboo tube, and this is said to hasten the fermentation of the drink, and to give it the peculiar bitter taste which the Dusuns like. The end of the shoot has a fresh slice, a very thin one, taken off it at least once a day in order to keep the sap perpetually flowing, and at about half-past six, when the people return to the village from work in the padi-fields, each tree which is being tapped has a brown-skinned human monkey concealed somewhere among its leaves, who is collecting the drink which has accumulated, reslicing the end of the shoot with the peculiarly shaped knife used for the purpose, and hanging on a fresh receptacle.

Sometimes the trees are notched to help the climbers, but the majority of natives will "walk" straight up a coco-nut palm trunk without any other assistance than that of their hands and feet. This they do by planting their feet firmly against the trunk of the tree so that their legs are almost at right angles to it, at the same time embracing it with both hands; their bodies, which are bent at the hips, being thus almost parallel to the tree-trunk. Next they jerk both hands forward a little and, when they have got a good grip, bring up their feet to the same extent. In this way they are enabled to climb the trees in a few seconds.

Newly collected toddy ferments very fast, and it is impossible to keep it in a corked bottle. In colour and density it looks something like ginger-beer, but occasionally has a pinkish tinge. When fresh it is sweet and faintly reminiscent of very bad cider, but it leaves a nasty sour taste in the mouth. After standing for some few hours it becomes bitter, and is then, according to Dusun ideas, at its best, though a European would probably prefer it freshly drawn. A large bamboo of toddy can be obtained for from ten to twenty cents, a couple of bamboos being sufficient to have "the desired effect" for two or three men.

Toddy drinking in markets is supposed to be prohibited owing to the quarrels which occur among the Dusuns when under the influence of liquor; however, if the "Tuan" would like a drink, one can usually be procured at short notice, as I know from personal experience; and in the lesser markets, which are infrequently visited by the police, the coco-nut-shell cup passes round merrily without any fear of a thirsty private annexing the brew under the pretext that Government regulations are being infringed.

Tapai, which is the intoxicant most in favour about harvest time, though not a spirit—since it undergoes no process of distillation—is, nevertheless, extremely potent. It is made by pouring water on rice with which has been mixed some fermented rice-flour. The yeast for setting up the fermentation is, in Tambatuan in the Tempassuk district, made as follows. Rice-flour is mixed with sugar and water and made into a small ball, which is tied up in *lalang*-grass leaves and hung up under the thatch till it has become quite hardened and mouldy. It is then pounded up and mixed with more rice-flour and water. This compound is made up into small balls, which are hung up outside the house for three or four days and are taken in at night. After they are sufficiently matured, a quantity of rice is boiled and allowed to cool, and then the balls of yeast are pounded up and mixed into it. The *tapai* rice is put into a jar, and, after a day or so, when it begins to taste sweet, water is poured in and the top of the jar tied up. After three or four days the liquor is ready to drink. If the *tapai* is kept for about ten days or so it becomes sour, and is no longer good. The *tapai* rice will keep for a long time, but if water is added the *tapai* resulting must be drunk within a few days. This account of *tapai*-making was given me by Gumpus, headman of Tambatuan.

Tapai, even when not drunk straight from the jar, is served up with the rice still in it, and for straining off this, while drinking, I have seen one very ingenious type of filter. A short piece of bamboo with a node at one end is taken, and long and narrow slots cut in it longitudinally, these being sufficiently small to prevent grains of rice passing through. This strainer is placed in the *tapai* with a rather long reed or small but fairly long joint of bamboo loose inside it. By applying his lips to the bamboo tube, which is much longer than the filter portion of the apparatus, the drinker is thus able to suck up the *tapai* without getting any rice into his mouth.

Not only is the *tapai* drunk, but even the rice which forms a thick layer at the bottom of the jar is not rejected, this having a strong taste of the liquor. I have both drunk *tapai* and eaten rice from the *tapai* jar, but I am at a loss to know to what European drink I can compare it, unless it be to bad brandy. *Tapai* rice has a burning taste and *tapai* itself is quite fiery to the throat. The Malays of the Malay Peninsula make a kind of *tapai* cake, which is exactly similar in taste to the *tapai* rice of Borneo.

Besides the harvest season, every event of any importance, birth, death or marriage, is an excuse for a good deal of drinking, and toddy is, of course, drunk daily in the houses, and in the huts (*sulap*) which are built for watching the padi-fields. The Dusuns nearly always drink and eat at the same time, otherwise, they say, they get intoxicated too quickly, small fish, boiled or broiled in the embers of a fire, being much in favour for consumption at drinking-parties.

As remarked above, native-brewed drinks apparently do but little harm, but the British North Borneo Company should follow the excellent example of the Federated Malay States Government and make the selling of foreign spirituous liquors to natives a punishable offence. Unfortunately a Chartered Company which has to do its best to pay interest to its shareholders, and which depends for a large amount of revenue on the leases of the spirit, opium and gambling farms, can hardly be expected to act in so disinterested a manner, having indeed every temptation to obtain money in any way it can.

CHAPTER XIII

COURTSHIP, MARRIAGE & DIVORCE, BURIAL & PUBERTY CUSTOMS

THE Tuaran villagers are comparatively well off, and their *bĕrians*—*i.e.* the purchase prices paid for wives—are much larger than those of the natives of the Tempassuk or the up-country parts of the Tuaran district. I was, unfortunately, never present at a Dusun marriage; but information obtained from natives was to the effect that there was little or no ceremony beyond a feast, at which a buffalo was killed and eaten and a good deal of toddy drunk. These statements are further borne out by Mr Whitehead's account of a Dusun marriage at Melangkap in *The Exploration of Kinabalu*, p. 110.

As far as I know, the wife goes to live with the husband, and not the husband with the wife's parents, as is done in some tribes. Whitehead says that in Melangkap the husband lives for a while with the wife's parents. Monogamy is the general rule, but I occasionally heard of a man with two wives. Shortly before I left the Tempassuk, Yompo, a young headman of Kiau, was meditating taking a second wife, as his first had proved barren; but probably he woul divorce his old wife before taking a new one, since divorce is easy, and depends only on the husband's wish.

If a man divorces his wife on account of some serious fault on her part, he can obtain the return of at least a part of her *bĕrian* from her relations, but if he sends away his wife merely at his own wish, the *bĕrian* cannot be recovered. The *bĕrian* paid for a widow or a divorced woman is about half that for a virgin. Formerly the punishment for incest was death.

Among the pagan races of Borneo much greater facilities for courtship are allowed than among the Mohammedans, though the women of the Mohammedan tribes are free as compared with their sisters in other countries. The Sea Dyak lover visits his inamorata stealthily by night, when the family are supposed to be asleep, though, as a matter of fact, these visits are usually known to the girl's relations and connived at. It is said that this method of courting seldom results in immorality. (Various authorities quoted by Ling Roth, *Natives of Sarawak and British North Borneo*, vol. i., pp. 109 and 110.) Sarebas Dyaks have now, however, given me a different account. One man informed me that if the parents of a girl did not connive at her responding to her lover's advances there would be little chance of the girl marrying. As far as I have been able to discover, Dusun methods of courting are somewhat similar to those of the Dyaks, though I am inclined to think that their nocturnal visits are not always so blameless.

As mentioned in another chapter, at Tuaran, where many of the youths and young men wear long hair, it is customary for the maidens to search for insects among her lover's locks, and it is said that these are often eaten! In some villages of the Tempassuk it is usual for a man, when he wishes to notify the parents of a girl that he intends to court their daughter, to take off his coat and hang it up near the door of the house.

At Tuaran, marriages, especially those of the children of people of importance, are often arranged at an early age. The chief negotiations which must be gone through before marriage can take place are concerned with the fixing of the amount of *bĕrian* (*lit.* a giving), which must be paid by the suitor to the girl's brother, as the *bĕrian* becomes his property. The aged women-kind of both parties usually take a considerable share in the discussions relating to this subject. When the price is fixed the marriage can take place. Sometimes a *bĕrian* is paid in kind, sometimes in money; and an example of a Tuaran *bĕrian* is given in another chapter.

When a Dusun dies, the first thought of his relatives after burying him is to rid themselves of the presence of his ghost, in case it should be still lingering about the house, or should be able to find its way back from the graveyard. At Piasau in the Tempassuk the women who lament at the burial cry aloud to the spirit of the deceased: "Do not stop here, for your way lies to the left" (*i.e.* to Mount Kinabalu, the home of dead Dusuns). At the same village the bamboo bier on which the body is carried to the grave-side is hacked to pieces, and I have heard that in some localities the people, on returning from a funeral, slash at the steps and door of the house in which the death has occurred, in order to drive away the spirit of the deceased.

After returning from a funeral, all the mourners betake themselves to the river to bathe, I imagine in order to cleanse themselves from the pollution of having taken part in a burial. In the village of Tambatuan, and probably elsewhere, the inhabitants of a house in which a death has occurred are tabu, and remain secluded for a week. According to Dusun ideas it would be very unlucky to wear the clothes of a dead person, so these are hung up over the grave, and at Tambatuan those of virgins are embroidered before disposing of them in this way. I believe that this only applies to the clothes actually in use at the time of death. Valuable cloths, etc., stored away are, I think, kept and used.

After a funeral, the grave is left to fall into decay untended, the Dusuns being generally unwilling to enter graveyards unless it is necessary to bury a corpse. The grave is surrounded with a fence, which at Kampong Piasau and many other villages is decorated with wooden models of the possessions of the deceased—fowls, buffaloes, spears, guns and *parangs*, or of other objects, such as snakes, tortoises, wild cattle and deer. Probably in bygone times, when the Dusuns were not so well off as they are now, all the personal belongings were deposited on the graves, as are clothes at the present day. An offering of this kind to the dead would not involve such sacrifices then as now, since most of the articles in use before the Dusuns were able to obtain brass-ware and other luxuries, and had few if any cattle, would be easy to make at home.

With the growth of wealth and the increased desire of acquiring it, it is likely that excuses would be made that models were quite as acceptable to a spirit as the real articles; since spirits, fortunately for those troubled by them, are known to be notoriously stupid and easy to deceive. It thus became customary to place on the grave models of all the objects the deceased had used in life, and of such animals as he was accustomed to eat.

The only case in which the actual objects themselves are offered to the spirit, as mentioned above, is that of clothes, which are usually inexpensive; and, having been worn on the body of the deceased, are probably supposed still to be animated by a portion of his spirit, somewhat as pieces of cloth from the shroud or garments of a saint are in Roman Catholic countries supposed to retain part of his virtues and to be capable of performing miraculous cures. The Dusuns, moreover, owing to their belief that the spirits of the dead only work mischief when they linger near the dwellings of mortals, would hastily get rid of anything which they suspected of having an intimate connection with a dead man's ghost.

Before describing Dusun graves and methods of burial, it may be as well to say a little about Mount Kinabalu, the home of departed spirits. The Dusuns relate how the ghosts of the dead on their way to their last home cross a small river at the foot of Mount Kinabalu, and also leave certain traces of their passage at a large rock on the way up. This rock, which is said to be situated between Kinabalu and Mount Nunkok, is called Pomintalan. Here the ghosts place, the men a cigarette wrapper, the women some thread, and the children some bits of dirty rags. The following little legend tells of the passing of the ghosts over the Koraput (or Uraput):—

The Path of the Ghosts

Told by Sirinan of Kampong Piasau, Tempassuk District

There is a small river to the *laut* (seawards) of Kampong Kaung named Koraput. There are large stones in the middle of it, and the people say the ghosts stop there on their way to Kinabalu. If the ghost of an old man is passing the sound of his walking-stick is heard tapping on the stones, if of a young bachelor the sound of his *sendatang* (a kind of native banjo), if of a young unmarried woman the sound of the *toreding* (a kind of wooden or bone jews' harp), and if of a child the sound of weeping.

In consequence of the Dusuns' beliefs with regard to Kinabalu, an ascent of the mountain is not to be undertaken lightly. The spirits of the dead must be propitiated with offerings and a gun fired to warn them of the approach of human beings. Sompat, one of the headmen of Kiau, usually performs the ceremony when a European wishes to climb the mountain, and from him I obtained the following details. The sacrifice to the spirits consists of seven eggs and a couple of fowls, and there is a *menghaji* (religious ceremony). It is said that when the ceremony is being performed a spirit is often heard to cry out in answer.

On the way up the names of streams passed or of places in the jungle may not be mentioned, nor may the mountain be called by its usual name, but if it is necessary to refer to it the Dusuns instead of *Nabalu* say *Agayoh ngaran* (big name). If no ceremony were performed, it is thought the party making the ascent would be unable to find their way home. One European who undertook the climb refused to fire a gun before starting, and the continual wet weather which was met with was put down to this cause. Unfortunately I never had an opportunity of getting farther than Kiau village, on the lower slopes of the mountain, where I met old Sompat. Mr J. C. Moulton, curator of Sarawak Museum, who has recently climbed the mountain, says that two shots are also fired at the top, the gun being pointed upwards, facing north (*Sarawak Gazette*, November 1913).

The word Kinabalu, as Mr Moulton, I think rightly, observes, is probably derived from *Nabalu* (the Dusun word for the home of the dead), and does not mean "Chinese Widow" (mountain), "China Balu or Kinabalu," as stated in so many works on Borneo. There is a village in the Tempassuk valley which seems to be called indifferently Kinabalu or Penelabu, and probably this also has nothing to do with China or the Chinese.

To turn now to methods of sepulture. All good Dusuns wish to be buried in a jar; but a jar is expensive, and so the bodies of poor people are buried in a rough wooden coffin or wrapped up in mats. If the deceased is sufficiently well off to afford a jar, the body is slipped into it legs first and pushed, or even stamped, down till it does not protrude.

Some few years ago there was a bad epidemic of smallpox in the Tuaran district, and the father of my Dusun servant, Omboi, caught the disease and "died." Whereupon his relatives, having obtained a jar of sufficient size, slipped the body into it, intending to bury it immediately. The neck of the jar was, however, rather narrow, and when the mourners began to stamp the body home with the flat of their feet, the "corpse" got up and objected to the process in forcible language. The patient had merely been in a state of coma, and he eventually recovered.

If the mouth of a jar is too narrow to admit the body, the vessel is cut in two horizontally at its greatest circumference, the body packed into the lower portion and the top replaced and fastened down with some kind of resin. The jars are not buried at any great depth and it is common, in walking about near villages, to come upon an old graveyard with many of the jar tops showing above the ground.

At Tuaran, after a period of years, old jars are dug up and used again; but at Tenghilan, not far from the boundary of the Tuaran and Tempassuk districts, I was told that such an act would be looked on with the greatest horror, and that the desecrator of a grave would have been put to death in the old days. As far as my experience goes, I believe that in the Tempassuk the feeling about opening a grave would be similar to that of the Tenghilan people.

Here we have a good example of the differences which can often be found in small areas, and this may well serve as a warning against making hasty generalisations, a thing which is unfortunately only too common. It is obviously unsafe to say that the Dusuns do such-and-such a thing on evidence obtained from one or two villages, for it is always quite possible that exactly the reverse may be the custom two or three miles away.

But to return to the subject under review. Occasionally, when the only jar obtainable is not quite big enough to receive the corpse, the body is buried in a rough wooden coffin and the jar set upright at the head of the grave. I observed an instance of this at Kampong Ghinambur. In the graveyard of Piasau village I have also seen very small jars set in the same position. Presumably these were the graves of poor persons whose relations could not afford to buy big jars, as the vessels did not seem to have been used for holding food or water. I was, in fact, told that it was not customary to make food-offerings at the grave in this village, but at Tuaran I have been informed by natives that it is the general usage. At Piasau the graves were surrounded by a rectangular bamboo fence decorated with wooden models, put there as offerings.

The graves themselves, which were marked by raised mounds, were covered with a *chevaux de frise* of sharp bamboo points to prevent wild pigs from routing up the body. Over the mounds were erected small wall-less huts roofed with palm leaves, the eaves of which were sometimes roughly carved, or in place of this a couple of umbrella-like structures covered with European-made calico were set up. Occasionally a wooden figure was placed under the hut, but whether this represented the deceased, or was an offering, I was unable to find out.

It is possible that if placed there with the latter intention it may have represented a slave slaughtered in order that the dead man might have company on his journey to the land of shadows. This is only a suggestion, and I have never heard of that special kind of sacrifice having been made among the Dusuns in former times, though, according to Mr W. B. Pryer, some of the inland tribes used to kill slaves (*surmungup*) in order to send messages to dead relatives by their aid (W. B. Pryer, *J.A.I.*, vol. xvi., p. 234), while various writers bear testimony to the fact that among other tribes slaves were frequently sacrificed on the death of a chief or any important man (Ling Roth, vol. i., p. 157. Various writers quoted).

Among the Dusuns, I believe, as among so many primitive people, death is scarcely looked upon as a natural event, at any rate in the case of the young.

CHAPTER XIV

MUSICAL INSTRUMENTS, MUSIC & DANCING

GONGS, those instruments so beloved by the Dusuns and by all the native races of Borneo, have been mentioned several times elsewhere; they are regarded as valuables, and have become a sort of currency. A Dusun is almost as great a connoisseur in the matter of gongs as a European collector is with regard to old china or silver. Should he be of industrious and saving habits, his money will be expended, if not in wife-buying, in the purchase of either a gong or a buffalo; but either wives or buffaloes can be paid for in gongs, or in the case of the latter *vice versa*.

When an expensive instrument is for sale, great is the gathering of the *cognoscenti*; it is tapped for flaws, its workmanship examined and criticised, its age estimated, and its tone tried by frequent beatings. An intending buyer having been found, there comes a long haggle as to the price to be paid, and when at last this has been agreed upon, the purchaser carries off his bargain in triumph to show to his friends at home. Everybody being interested in gongs, the native virtuoso has the advantage over his European brother, for a Dusun returning home after having "picked up a bargain" is not met with the same blank faces and inane remarks that so often greet the collector at home when he displays his latest acquisition to the circle of his friends and acquaintances.

New gongs are considered of comparatively little value; but old specimens of the *tawag tawag*—a gong with a deep tone, a large and prominent boss, and a deep edge—or of the *chenang*—a shallow gong with a boss almost on a level with the face—are most sought after. The price of one of these may run to as much as two hundred or three hundred dollars, a variety of the *chenang* called the *chenang kimanis* being especially prized. Besides the *tawag tawag* and the *chenang* there are two other kinds of gongs which are comparatively cheap: one of these, the *agong*, is a large shallow gong with a fairly big boss; the other, the *tenukol*, has, in some cases, no boss at all.

Gongs are struck with a wooden mallet, which is padded with raw rubber or cloth. The note of a gong struck with an unpadded mallet is too hard, while treatment of this kind tends to ruin the instrument by cracking it where the boss joins the face, the metal here, which is usually rather thin, having to take the full force of the blows.

Though Dusuns are capable of casting a few small articles in brass, I do not think that they have ever attempted to manufacture gongs. Those which are valued by them at the present day seem to have been made in Brunei, Java and perhaps China. The Dusuns, however, are not without musical instruments of their own. The young bachelors strum on the *sendatang*, a kind of two-stringed banjo or mandolin, which, with the exception of its face, is roughly carved, belly, stem and all, out of a single block of soft wood. The strings, made of some vegetable fibre, are inserted under a small piece of wood attached to the face or sounding-board, and are tied at their other extremities to a couple of keys, which pass through the stem. A slight bridge keeps the strings from contact with the face of the instrument.

Bamboo flutes of two kinds are in common use: one of these is played in the orthodox manner with the mouth, the other with the nose, the end of it being placed against one nostril, while the other nostril is stoppered with leaves, rags or tobacco. Small jews' harps (*toriding*) are very cleverly cut out of a single piece of palm wood or bamboo, the tongue being usually weighted by two little pieces of wax or wild rubber. The instrument is held before the mouth and played by jerking a string attached to one end. Another wind instrument which I have not yet mentioned is the so-called Dusun organ (*sempatan*), which is made by the natives of the interior.

Most of those seen in the hands of Tempassuk people have been brought from up-country by natives when carrying down tobacco to market, but, if I remember rightly, they are sometimes made by the people of Kiau and a few other Tempassuk villages.

The instrument consists of a long, straight-necked gourd or calabash into which are fixed eight reeds, four shorter in one row, and four longer, but of different heights, in another, which together form a bundle of two rows with a rectangular section. These are bound round with lashings of thread and are fixed into the gourd with some black waxy substance, I believe dirty beeswax. The neck of the calabash forms the mouthpiece, and the notes are produced by blowing into this, while opening and closing the free ends of the short reeds with the fingers of the right hand, and working on two stops, one at the base of each terminal long bamboo, with the left. Every reed has a hole at the base above the level of the gourd, and a small tongue of bamboo skin (?), which is partly responsible for the production of the sounds, fixed into its lower end.

A peculiar instrument which is sometimes called a "harp" is played by the women. It is made from a length of bamboo, and the strings are formed by carefully cutting thin, narrow, longitudinal strips from the outside of the section all round, leaving them attached to the body of the instrument at the ends. They are then keyed up by pushing little pieces of wood under them at the ends till each one will give the right note. Sometimes a round hole is made in the body at one side, presumably with a view to increasing the sound.

Another favourite instrument is a wooden dulcimer or

xylophone. By travellers in the hill districts the sound of one of these instruments is frequently to be heard, coming, as a rule, from some *sulap* (small hut) in which a family is living in order to guard their padi crop from marauding beasts and birds. Sets of small gongs (*kulin-tangan*), specially made for the purpose, are played like a dulcimer, being placed on two strings stretched across a long wooden frame.

I have only once seen a whistle in Borneo, and do not know whether it is a truly native instrument or not. This particular specimen, which is double, is cleverly made from two small pieces of bamboo. I remember that I got it from a native headman, who produced it when I visited his village, and wanted to summon the owner, a small Dusun youth, for blowing it under his (the headman's) house. I gave the youngster a lecture on good behaviour and appropriated the whistle.

Drums with bodies made out of sections of hollow tree-trunks are common. The skin facings of these—they are single-ended—are tightened by wedges driven in below the rattan bindings which hold the facings fast to the wood. At Tuaran I have seen a large cylindrical piece of wood, about four feet long, hollowed out on the inside, and opening to the outside by a comparatively narrow slit running almost the whole length of the wood. The instrument when struck with a sort of club gave out a fairly clear note. The particular specimen that I saw was used for striking the hours on an estate, but was, I suppose, of native manufacture. An exactly similar instrument is made by the Malays of the Peninsula, who call it *kerantong*.

As I have mentioned in another chapter, the general season for rejoicing, feasting, the telling of folk-stories and musical parties is after the harvest has been gathered in. Judging by the number of instruments they make, and their fondness for playing them, I should say that the Dusuns are distinctly a musical people. Of course native music can scarcely be judged by European standards, but some of the tunes they play on the xylophones and on the so-called "organs" are not at all unpleasant.

I do not remember that I was ever particularly struck by their singing, and I never had time to take down any of their songs, but Witti says that the inland Dusuns have "pretty songs of their own." The chief thing that I can remember about Dusun singing is that my boy used to give vent to dismal-sounding love-songs in the servants' quarters about a girl of whom he was enamoured, but who did not return his affection. So thoroughly miserable did he succeed in making himself that the tears used to course down his cheeks and fall to the ground. Having suffered from the youth for some months, I did not wonder that the lady disliked him, and heartily sympathised with her.

Gongs and drums are used at all native dances, but except for the religious kind performed by the women of Tuaran, which are largely of a posturing nature, I can only remember having seen a Dusun dance on one occasion. This was a war-dance performed by a Tuaran youth, and in it, after a good deal of preliminary posturing, he went in pantomime through all the actions of a native engaged in warfare—the spying of a foe from a distance, the stealthy creep through bushes or tall grass, the gliding behind tree-trunks, the sudden rush of a surprise attack, the rout of the enemy and the swaggering bravado of the victors.

CHAPTER XV

WEALTH, CURRENCY, TRADING, MARKETS

THE Dusun's wealth, at any rate until fairly recent times, consisted almost entirely of property, money being only obtainable with the greatest difficulty; and, even at the present day, so deeply is this love of property ingrained in him that probably not a very great deal of hard cash would be found hoarded up in the villages, the Dusun man's or woman's one idea being to turn his or her savings into goods. This is perhaps scarcely a subject for wonder, as an up-country native has remarkably little use for money, unless it be to buy luxuries at the Chinese shops—a method of dissipation to which, fortunately, he has not so far taken very kindly.

The forms of property which chiefly find favour are old brass gongs—concerning the age and tone of which the Dusuns are great connoisseurs—other articles of old brass-ware, such as the large betel boxes called *chelapa*, buffaloes, cattle, rolls of dark blue cloth to be purchased at the Chinese shops, and in Tuaran and Papar the old Chinese jars which are regarded as sacred and to which an annual sacrifice is made.

In the old days brass cannon, krises and spears were also regarded as desirable property, but, with the passing away of the use for such things, they are not now so much sought after, though the first still command a good price as old brass. All these articles being particularly in request, and trade being formerly entirely conducted by means of barter, there arose gradually a sort of standard in values by which the dearer articles were appraised as being worth so many of those which were less expensive; a gong worth so many buffaloes; a jar worth so many pikuls[1] of brass (cannon); a kris worth so many *kayu* (the usual term for a standard roll) of cloth. In this way a sort of rough system of currency was established, since all the articles mentioned above were readily taken and received—*i.e.* became a sort of legal tender.

To obtain a wife a Dusun man has to hand over a certain sum, termed a *bĕrian* (a giving), to the girl's parents. At the present time this is occasionally paid in money, but the annexed example of a typical Tuaran *bĕrian* demonstrates clearly some of the articles which were formerly considered valuable and passed as currency, this particular selection of articles being the price of a wife. The inertia and conservatism of ancient custom have preserved for us this record of the value which used to be attached to articles which are rapidly becoming obsolete.

A Tuaran "Bĕrian"

2 *chenang*	A kind of gong which may be worth anything up to $200 or more.
1 *tawag tawag*	A kind of gong which may be worth anything up to $200 or so.
1 *rantuka*	A small brass cannon.
2 *kamuggi* with two silver cones on each	The *kamuggi* is a ceremonial necklace.
1 spear	
1 kris	

At the present day silver and paper dollars have become fairly easy to obtain, but a great part of the trade of the district is still carried on by barter, and though a native may tell you that such-and-such an article on which he has set his heart is worth so many dollars, he is probably himself calculating its value in buffaloes and turning the result into

[1] The pikul = 100 katties. The kattie is 1⅓ lb. English. I believe the Sarawak Government still fines recalcitrant tribes so many pikuls of brass.

Photo by] BUNSUD, A LOWLAND DUSUN, [*L. H. N. Evans*

Headman of Tamboulian, Tempassuk District. The ornaments on the coat are silver buttons.

THE DUSUN "ORGAN" AND BANJO.

These sweet-toned native organs (sempatan) consist of a gourd body and mouthpiece, and a number of bamboo pipes. The fingers are moved on the tops of the pipes to produce the various notes.

dollars for your benefit—for it is in buffaloes that he intends to pay the purchase price—or, if he be well accustomed to talking about dollars, he may think of the purchase price in dollars and then reckon how many buffaloes will be equal to them, always with the idea of paying in cattle and not in cash. The price of buffaloes does not vary much from year to year: a fully grown and trained buffalo bull is generally reckoned as being worth about $25, a fully grown and trained buffalo cow about $20, while half-grown animals are priced more or less by the length of the horns measured in spans. A weaned buffalo calf will fetch anything from $5 upwards.

This method of bartering buffaloes often gives great trouble in civil cases. For instance, a man A sues B for a buffalo calf or the price thereof, for which B is said to be indebted to him. When the case comes into court it looks as if it were going to be a fairly easy matter to decide, until, after a little inquiry, it is found that it is necessary to go back into buffalo dealings which have taken place between the plaintiff and defendant during the last couple of years or more. Probably something like this has occurred: A buys a buffalo bull from B, which is priced at $25; for this he pays on account a cow buffalo worth $15, thus being still in debt to B for the sum of $10. After a long time and much dunning on the part of B, A, not having a buffalo of the exact value of $10, pays up with an animal whose price is agreed at $15, thus putting B into A's debt to the extent of $5. B promises to settle this debt with a small calf as soon as one of his animals shall have calved. Eventually B repudiates the debt and A takes out a summons for the buffalo calf.

This is very likely by no means the end of the matter, cases of this kind often have several side-issues. The ball having once been started rolling, B's father-in-law turns up and wants a summons, stating that the original buffalo which was sold for $25 to A is his property, and that his son-in-law borrowed it when he saw an opportunity of doing good business with A. He has repeatedly requested the payment of buffaloes equivalent in value to the animal lent, but his son-in-law has been undutiful enough to tell him that he owes him nothing. He therefore asks for a summons.

To do the Dusuns justice, this kind of case is commoner among the Bajaus, but still the same sort of thing does sometimes occur among the Dusuns of the lowland villages. Occasionally a buffalo-dealing transaction is settled straight away, the difference in price between two animals being made up with any small articles which the vendor may be willing to accept. Thus X may buy an animal worth $25 from Y and pay for it with a buffalo worth $18, a brass betel-nut box worth $4 and a spear the price of which is fixed at $3.

In connection with the Dusun love of property, mentioned above, my old friend Lengok of Bengkahak—according to native ideas a man of some wealth—in whom the bump of acquisition was strongly developed, used to enrich himself very considerably at the expense of his Bajau neighbours by taking advantage of their improvidence.

This was his description of how he obtained the goods with which his house was well stocked. "You see, Tuan," he said to me, "the Bajaus are a very lazy people, who scarcely ever plant enough padi to last them through the year: a few months after reaping, when they have eaten up all their rice, some of them are sure to come to me and ask me to lend them some padi till next harvest. I say: 'Very well, I will lend you some padi, if you will bring me a nice piece of brass-work of some kind, and deposit it here as security until you pay me back.' So they bring me some brass which is worth a good deal more than the padi that I give them. Of course they never pay me back, for the next year they don't plant any more padi than they did in the year they came to me to borrow, but Bajaus never reckon on what will happen afterwards, so long as they can get what they want at the time, and, when their stomachs are empty, they don't trouble themselves as to how they are going to pay for the rice they borrow, nor do they remember when they are planting padi how hungry they were in the year before, their only thought being what a trouble it is to plant at all. So they go on from year to year."

Lengok had a contempt for the Bajaus which it was quite refreshing to meet with in a Dusun, as the latter people are generally peaceably inclined, while the Bajaus are, by training and instinct, plunderers and robbers, and in former times oppressed the Dusuns very badly. Being lax Mohammedans, they of course pretend to look down on the Dusuns, saying that they are infidels, that their villages are unclean owing to the pigs they keep, and that they are always drunk. All this is said in the most irritatingly superior manner, and must be extremely galling to the Dusuns. Many Europeans, myself among them, get angry at hearing this sort of talk, since the Dusun man is generally a very decent, hard-working fellow, while the Bajau is almost invariably one of the biggest "wasters" to be found anywhere.

Lengok's opinion of the Bajaus, as remarked previously, was the reverse of complimentary. "Why," he said, "they are always hungry, and they have got nothing worth having, no pigs and no toddy; they must lead a wretched life. A Bajau dare not tap his coco-nut-trees to make toddy and get drunk for fear of what the other people in his village would say, for it is against the Mohammedan religion to drink intoxicating liquors, so those who want toddy come and hang round our villages and ask for drink, making out that they are not feeling well, and that they want it as medicine."

But to return to the subject of trade. The Dusuns are the chief collectors of jungle produce, which now consists almost entirely of damar gum (*salong*), though small quantities of rubber, beeswax and rattans are still brought in. Some years ago wild rubber used to be obtained in fairly large quantities; this has, however, been worked out to such an extent in the Tempassuk that very few natives go into the jungle with the express purpose of collecting it. The Chinese are the chief buyers of jungle produce, and a great deal of trading in these commodities is carried on at the local markets, about which I shall have something to say presently.

Formerly, when affairs in the Tempassuk were in a very disturbed condition, the Bajaus acted as middlemen between the Dusuns and the Chinese, since the latter were frightened to move far away from the coasts and Government protection; but peace having now been established for several years, the Bajaus have gradually lost this lucrative form of employment. Apart from damar, the only other native product in which there is any considerable export trade from the Tempassuk is tobacco, which is grown to some extent on the valley slopes around Kiau, a village overlooking the Tempassuk river, situated on the slopes of Mount Kinabalu, and round many of the villages of the interior.

The chief markets of the Tempassuk district are Tamu (market) Timbang, held every Wednesday a couple of miles or so down-stream from Kotabelud, the Government post, and Tamu Darat (*i.e.* the up-country market), the site of which is located some seven miles up-stream from the same place. Tamu Darat is the more important of the two markets, and is held once in every twenty days, but a smaller market called Tamu Sesip (*i.e.* the market which is slipped in between, since it takes place between the large markets), which is held on the same ground on the tenth day after Tamu Darat, often fairly bids to rival it. Tamu Timbang is, however, coming more and more into favour, since a native who brings jungle produce from up-country can obtain slightly better prices there, and is enabled to make a selection of any articles he may require at the Kotabelud shops before returning home.

Among the natives a great part of the trade in the

markets is, as elsewhere, carried on by barter, though small articles are often paid for in money. The Chinese, too, vastly prefer bartering goods with natives to paying cash, as by this means they are enabled to obtain a double profit.

The scene in a large market like Tamu Darat is most animated. The first arrivals on the ground are usually the Chinese traders from the shops, and the Bajaus and Illanuns from the coastal villages. Both Chinese and natives ride up to market, the usual mounts being buffaloes, bulls, cows or ponies. On arrival the Chinese busy themselves in arranging on their small palm-leaf-roofed stalls a choice assortment of such articles as are likely to attract Dusun customers: cloth, matches, beads, gambier, buttons, small tin lamps, cheap tobacco-boxes, looking-glasses, knives and scissors, cotton-thread, needles, kerosene oil, cooking-pots and an assortment of various odds and ends, nearly all of which are cheap, nasty, and made in Germany. The Bajaus and Illanuns unload from their buffaloes sacks of small dried fish which look like white-bait, shell-fish, fresh fish of various kinds, packages containing native-made salt, native-woven head-cloths, and cooking- and water-pots of reddish-coloured clay, partly varnished over with damar gum.

The Chinese, Bajaus and Illanuns, being more sophisticated than the Dusuns, need to be kept strictly in order to prevent them from plundering or cheating the latter; consequently they are given one half the Tamu ground to themselves, and are separated from the Dusuns by a rope stretched across the market until the signal to begin trading is given by the native chief in charge, who hoists the Government flag on the flag-staff to declare the market open.

While the Chinese and the Bajaus have been making their preparations, the Dusuns have been arriving; those from the villages near by come in first, but those from a distance usually time themselves to arrive at a point about a mile and a half on the up-stream side of the market ground on the previous evening. Here they meet together and exchange news, discuss the prospects of the padi crop, plan buffalo-thieving expeditions and cook their evening meal. The next morning they again cook and feed, and then come leisurely down to market.

The weapons which nearly every man carries, usually a native chopping-knife and a spear, are left outside the market ground proper in charge of the policeman who assists the native chief in preserving order.

On entering the Tamu each group of Dusuns, men, women and children, goes to the spot assigned by custom to their particular village. Near a fallen tree by the river you will find the Tiong people from the Ulu Tuaran, who bring with them the ornamental brass rings which Dusun women wear on their rattan-cane girdles, and which they are adepts in casting. Under each tree are the people of a different village, some bringing tobacco in the large carrying baskets known as *bongwn*, others with piles of native hats made of split and woven bamboo or rattan, tastefully ornamented with coloured patterns. Others, again, have brought great loads of white or amber-coloured damar gum; a few women are arranging cooking-pots for sale, made of a coarse greyish-looking clay mixed with sand; and perhaps in the hands of one of the up-country natives, who has brought down tobacco, may be seen one of those curious and sweetly toned Dusun "organs" (*sempatan*), made from a gourd fitted with bamboo pipes.

When everyone is ready the signal to trade is given. Dusuns staggering under big loads of damar make their way across to the shops of the Chinese, where pandemonium is let loose owing to the huxtering cries of rival stall-keepers, each of whom tries to obtain the goodliest share of the trade for himself. Bajaus and Illanuns rush across and thrust their, often unwanted, wares upon up-country Dusuns, nearly snatching any articles they require out of the vendors' hands; and all over the market arises a babel of tongues, Dusun, Bajau, Chinese, Illanun and Malay. This animated scene, the smells of dried fish, *blachan* (a paste composed of small pounded shrimps—it only needs to be smelt once to be remembered), tobacco and fruit, the bright-coloured head-cloths, the brown limbs and bodies of Dusuns, the shining river, and the graceful trees which shade the market, make a visit to Tamu Darat a sight not easily forgotten.

The Chinese, fortunately for the Dusuns, are no longer allowed to leave their stalls, as in former days a Chinaman would rush out like a spider from its web and "collar" some wretched Dusun who was weighed down under a heavy load of jungle produce, drag him to his stall and "buy" his goods before the Dusun had quite realised what was happening. Now the Dusun picks his way down the miniature street to the stall where he thinks he can obtain the best value for his goods, regardless of the blandishments of the store-keepers by whom he has already been cheated once.

Occasionally the Dusun "gets one back" on the stall-holder, as witness the wails proceeding from the Chinaman in the corner stall who has just cut open a couple of large balls of jungle rubber which he bought from a Dusun a few minutes ago: these he now finds have nothing but rubbish inside them. The Dusun gentleman who sold them has meanwhile recollected that he has an important engagement at home. Dusun tobacco, too, is often not above suspicion. Strips of the cut and dried article are wound into bundles about nine inches long by four or five inches wide, a bundle of this kind being technically known as a *pĕrut* (stomach). In buying a basket of tobacco it is usual for a purchaser to take several *pĕruts* of tobacco from below as well as above and open them, as it is by no means an uncommon trick for a Dusun to place good tobacco on the top of his basket, while all the rolls below have a core of rubbish and a mere wrapping of tobacco on the outside.

The chief in charge of the market now generally makes a round of inspection among the tobacco sellers, with a view to detecting such swindlers; and this has had a salutary effect, adulteration of tobacco having become comparatively rare. A good deal of this native-grown tobacco finds its way through the hands of Chinese or Malay middlemen to Brunei, whence no doubt it is distributed to the adjoining territories. Native tobacco is smoked in the form of a cigarette, the wrapper being made from the leaf of the *nipa* palm. Bundles of these wrappers, ready cut, can be bought in all the markets, and are known as *kirai*.

In coming down to market the Dusuns still use the old-time track, which chiefly follows the bed of the Tempassuk river, and it is as a rule only in times of flood that they will make use of the Government bridle-path to the interior, which they consider much longer—I have tried both and know which I think the best, the large, round and slippery stones in the bed of the river making exceedingly unpleasant going.

A fair amount of trading in buffaloes takes place at some of the larger markets, but in order to put down buffalo thieving as far as possible the bargain has to be completed in the presence of a Government chief, and the animal must be marked with his brand. Very often a Dusun who has brought down a heavy load of jungle produce is enabled to take home a buffalo, which he has obtained in exchange for it from one of the Chinese stall-holders.

Before bringing this chapter to a close, perhaps a few remarks may be made about the old beads which appear to have passed as currency to a certain extent. All old beads are considered valuable by the Dusuns, to whom age is quite as much synonymous with beauty and value as to the veriest virtuoso at home. Of course, in many cases, there is a great deal to be said on the practical side for the Dusuns' passion for old things; for instance, modern gongs are much inferior in workmanship and tone to those which the Dusuns treasure.

Most of the old beads of paste, porcelain or glass which

A MARKET SCENE IN THE TEMPASSUK DISTRICT.

The chief article on sale in this corner of the market is Indian corn, of which two or three heaps of cobs can be seen. The market shown is held weekly.

are seen in Borneo are, I should think, of Chinese origin, and some of them are valued at from fifty cents to one dollar each (1s. 2d. to 2s. 4d.). The most interesting kinds of beads to be met with are not, however, of these materials; they are called *bongkas* and appear to have been made by cutting small discs out of some kind of fairly thick marine shell, and piercing them with a drill. I have frequently made inquiries to try and find out where these beads were formerly obtained, but always without result, the Dusuns saying that they did not know, as they had come down to them from their ancestors. At present *bongkas* are reckoned by the string, a string consisting of a loop long enough to reach from the fork of the thumb to the point of the elbow. In most parts of the Tempassuk four strings (sometimes only three) of *bongkas* go to the dollar.

Bongkas beads are chiefly used for decorating the fringes which are worn by women around the tops of their skirts, or sometimes a broad band of this beadwork is seen on the edges of the cowl-like hoods which they wear for field-work (the same kind of cap is also worn in the Tempassuk on ceremonial occasions). These beads are now becoming rare in the Tempassuk owing to the tempting prices offered for them by the Chinese shopkeepers, who, I understand, dispatch them to Sarawak, where they obtain quite large sums for them from the wilder tribes. In fact so keen is the demand that I have known a party of three Dyaks to come to the Tempassuk specially to collect *bongkas* in order to re-sell them in their native country. Shell-bracelets are made to the present day by the Tempassuk Bajaus, but I have never been able to hear that they made shell-beads, which indeed are not found among them.

CHAPTER XVI

MANUFACTURES

THOUGH Dusun manufactures are well worth studying, they do not come up to the high standard of those of several of the other tribes of Borneo, notably the Kayans. The production of certain articles, such as cloth, is carried on in almost all villages, but in the case of others there is a tendency, without any apparent reason, for each village to have a speciality of its own.

For instance, Penelabu (or Kinalabu) makes a very neat type of knife with a handle of pig-tusk, usually putting two in a case; and Kaung in the Ulu Tempassuk a particular kind of woman's hat, which I have never seen worn locally, though it is traded to, and finds favour in, Tuaran. In Tambatuan and in Pinasang, a village on the right bank of the Tempassuk above Tamu Darat, they make a particular kind of carrying-basket (*bongun*); at Tiong in the Ulu Tuaran, brass rings for women's girdles, and so forth.

One of the first things which strikes a visitor to the Tempassuk is the curious hat worn by both pagan and Mohammedan natives. The makers of these hats are the up-country Dusuns, who trade them with their lowland brothers, and also with the Bajaus and Illanuns. The materials employed in their manufacture are strips of natural or dyed rattan and bamboo, while some types show exceedingly skilful workmanship.

The types of hats made by the up-country Dusuns, and

worn by both men and women in the Tempassuk, are peculiar and varied; they are made in the up-country villages, and an up-country Dusun will tell you at sight from which village a particular hat comes, as there are slight local differences in shape and also certain small marks in black and red rattan woven in near the edge of the hat, which, to one who knows, are sure guides to the place of its origin. There is a large hat worn by women of the kind made at Kaung and at Tamis in the Ulu Tuaran. These when sold at Tuaran fetch as much as two dollars each, though locally they can be bought a good deal cheaper. There is another peculiar type of woman's hat made, and worn, only at the village of Saiap, near Mount Kinabalu.

Two kinds of hat are worn indifferently by both men and women, though hats are not so frequently used by the latter; in the Tempassuk a cowl-like hood of native cloth protects the head against the heat of the sun during work in the fields. Another kind is made by the people of Bundu Tuhan, a village of the Interior, just outside the Tempassuk boundary. Occasionally conical hats may be seen, which are cut out of a single block of light palm-wood, but they are distinctly rare. Hats are much more commonly worn by the women of the villages round Tuaran than by their up-country sisters of the Tuaran river or those of the Tempassuk district.

Dusun cloth is woven on a very simple type of loom, a specimen of which is well illustrated in Ling Roth's *Natives of Sarawak and British North Borneo* (vol. ii., p. 30). The apparatus has a belt attached to one end of it, and when the other end has been tied to an upright of the house the weaver adjusts the band round her waist and by throwing her weight slightly backwards makes the loom taut for weaving. Needless to say, the apparatus is without frame of any kind, while the treadles, cloth-beam and warp-beam are all of the very simplest description, and consist of round wooden sticks of varying diameter pushed through the warp. A wooden sword is used for beating up the cloth, the shuttle being also made of wood and of simple type.

The materials from which Dusun cloth is made are *lamba*, the fibre of a species of wild banana, cotton, or thread made from some kind of tree-bark. These may either be mixed —*e.g.* a cloth may have a warp of *lamba* and a woof of cotton or bark-thread—or used singly.

When finished, the cloth is dyed with native indigo and is then ready for making up into the skirts, hoods or trousers for which it is chiefly intended. There is a slight tendency for native cloth—and European cotton thread for weaving is coming into use to a certain extent—to be displaced by European goods, but it still is much in favour owing to its splendid wearing qualities. Cloth is not woven in the villages around Tuaran, but cloth-weaving is general in the Dusun villages of the Tempassuk, and also, I believe, in the upland villages of the Tuaran district. Some very fine cloths are made by the Rongus Dusuns who live outside the Tempassuk district in the direction of Kudat; these have elaborate patterns in white on a black background and are sometimes further ornamented by the insertion of a few strands of red thread.

Pottery is made in many villages, the only type of vessel I have ever seen being a rather squat, wide-mouthed pot with a rounded bottom, which can be used either as a water-jug or for cooking purposes. The pots are made of a mixture of clay and sand, and when fired are of a greyish colour.

Most Dusun villages have a blacksmith, who, if not capable of turning out fighting weapons, is at least able to make very effective blades for working-knives, especially for the large chopping-knives called *parangs*. These knives are kept in a state of almost razor-like sharpness, and every native wears one by his side. The blades are so forged that they do not last for a great number of years, as only the actual cutting edge is of steel, the back and sides being of soft iron. The method of manufacture is to weld a narrow strip of steel between two broad pieces of iron, the steel being so placed between the edges of the latter that the greater part of it projects beyond them. Thus the steel cutting edge, which the natives constantly rub down on sharpening stones, is finally worn away, and only the iron remains, when the *parang* cannot be used any longer.

Reaping-knives, toddy-knives for slicing across the flowering shoot of the coco-nut palm, knives for splitting rattan and small cased knives for general purposes are other products of the Dusun blacksmith's forge, but in a few villages he has higher aspirations than the mere manufacture of workaday tools. Most excellent fighting *parangs* with beautifully carved handles of stag's horn are turned out by the smiths of Kiau, the art of making them having originally been learnt from a Dyak settler. The blades of these *parangs*, which are locally known as *gayang*, resemble in shape the Dyak *parang ilang*; but both faces of the blade are alike, and are not, as in the case of the *parang ilang*, respectively convex and concave. Weapons of similar type, but usually of somewhat inferior workmanship, are made in several other up-country villages, chiefly outside the Tempassuk district. In the case of the ordinary working-knife, a Dusun can generally tell you at sight whence it comes, as each village turns out a slightly different type of blade to that of its neighbours; and I believe that *gayang* can also be ascribed to the village where they are made owing to slight differences in the engraved scroll-work on the faces of the blade near the back.

Very creditable spears are made in several villages, Kiau again probably turning out the best. The blades are protected from wet by a sheath made from two pieces of wood fastened together and bound with strips of rattan cane. The small sheath-knives mentioned above have handles of wood or natural boar's tusk, and the sheaths, like those of fighting weapons, are made of two pieces of wood fitted to the blade and fastened together with bindings of natural or coloured rattan cane.

One of the arts at which the Dusuns are adepts is the making of baskets; some of these are of true basket-work, made from strips of rattan or bamboo; others are formed from the red skins of leaf stalks of the sago palm pressed out and sewn together. The carrying-basket is one of the most important of the Dusun's possessions; he takes it with him to his garden and brings home a heavy load of *kaladi* roots or padi, and in it he brings down to market the damar gum which he has collected in the jungle, or the tobacco which he has grown to sell.

Two types of large back-basket are in common use in the Tempassuk, each kind being, as a rule, fitted with a board some foot and a half wide running from top to bottom along one side, and with three loop-straps of tree-bark. The board rests on the carrier's back; and of the straps, one is worn around the forehead or over the top of the head towards the front, while the other two go over the shoulders. Both types of basket are somewhat in the shape of a truncated cone and are carried apex downwards. One of them, a most excellent kind, is chiefly manufactured at Tambatuan and in a village above Tamu Darat—if I remember rightly, the village is Pinasang. This basket, which goes by the name of *bongun*, has a body made from sago-palm-leaf stalks, which are bound with a wooden or tree-bark rim at top and base, the actual bottom being of wood. It is further fitted with a wooden cover consisting of a round top with a rim made out of a strip of tree-bark. These baskets are splendid for holding personal belongings when on the march, since they are cheap, light and strong, are absolutely rain-proof and are built for the very purpose for which they are required.

The other type, called *basong*, is similar to the *bongun*, with the exception that it has a much broader mouth and no cover. The *basong* is chiefly used for carrying jungle and agricultural produce. When a native is travelling light he generally uses another and smaller type of basket fitted only with shoulder-straps. This kind of basket, which is called a *bariet*, stands about two and a half feet high, has a circular mouth with a wooden cover and a rectangular base with an edging of wood: the material of which it is constructed is rattan cane. A *bariet* will hold sufficient articles for a native who is going for a few days' journey—a change of clothes, a betel-box, some *sireh* leaves, a little rice, some dried fish and possibly a bundle of charms to protect him from the hidden dangers which lurk in the forest.

Brass-casting on a small scale is carried on in at least one village in the Ulu Tuaran, the chief articles made being the small brass rings and cylinders which are threaded on women's rattan girdles. I have never had an opportunity of seeing the casting carried out, but newly cast rings are frequently on sale in Tamu Darat, to which market they are brought down by Tiong or Tamis men. The metal for them is obtained by melting down old betel-boxes or gongs.

I have dealt in another chapter with the making of such articles as fish-traps and also with the subject of house-building and the manufacture of various domestic utensils.

CHAPTER XVII

RELIGION & SUPERSTITIONS

THE Dusuns are by religion animists—that is to say, they believe that all objects, whether animate or inanimate, have, or at any rate may have, an indwelling spirit in them. Stretches of jungle, deep pools, mounds whose shape is out of the ordinary, points jutting out into the river, trees of peculiar growth, especially the species of *Ficus* which is called *kayu ara* by the Malays, are all thought to be the abode of spirits. To propitiate these and to ward off by means of offering or otherwise the evil spirits which cause sickness and disease is one of the chief objects of Dusun ceremonial observances.

In addition to the propitiation of spirits, there are many omen-animals to whom attention is paid; some of these, if met, betoken good luck, but woe betide the man who sees an animal of evil omen and disregards its warning! he will be killed by a tree falling on him in the jungle, or a crocodile will seize him as he crosses a river; his padi crop will fail, or will be destroyed by rats and monkeys, or his wife or children will sicken and pine away.

Apart from the belief in spirits, most of whom are evilly disposed to man, the Dusun has a somewhat hazy belief in a Supreme Deity called Kenharingan, who, with his wife Munsumundok, created the world and everything in it.[1]

Both the Creator and the Creatrix are beneficent, though they are to the Dusun mind too far away to take much interest in human affairs, but they have a son, Tawardakan, who is by no means well disposed towards humanity. One Dusun legend tells how when Kenharingan created men he

[1] The story of the creation will be found in the following chapter.

made them all equal; there were no rich and no poor, and everyone was happy. Tawardakan, however, who was of a jealous and discontented disposition, disliked seeing mankind in this easy condition, and brought it about that some men should become rich and others poor, which unfortunate state of affairs persists until the present day.

In addition to the beliefs mentioned above, in the valleys of both the Tuaran and Tempassuk observances in connection with head-hunting and the propitiation of the trophies of skulls are still carried on to a small extent, though of course actual head-taking has been stopped for some years past. At Tuaran also we find the various customs connected with the cult of sacred jars, one kind to which reverence is paid being called the *Gusi*.

The Dusun's conduct, needless to say, is largely regulated by his belief in spirits and omens, and, in addition to the influence exercised by these, he is further hampered by the prohibitions and tabus which restrain his actions in many of his daily occupations. There are war tabus and birth tabus, house tabus and tabus for the padi-field, tabus to be observed in speaking and tabu days when no work must be done. But we must go into the Dusun beliefs in detail.

One of the first things that strikes an observer on seeing Dusun religious ceremonies is the great part played by the women. They are the chief performers in all the more important religious rites—the men only undertaking the office of musicians, to accompany the women's chants—and are, in fact, priestesses, or at least such of them as have undergone the requisite training. They are said, and this would form an interesting subject for further investigation, to conduct their ceremonies in a tongue unknown to the men, learnt during their period of instruction, which at Tuaran extends over some three months and costs the novice a considerable fee, at the present day generally paid in hard cash.

In the Tempassuk, and probably in the valley of the

Tuaran as well, though I do not know this for certain, each village has its own presiding deity or genius, who is known as the *Kenharingan Tumanah*, the second word being, I think, of the same derivation as the Malay word *tanah* = earth, or soil. Perhaps this statement is a little too positive. I make it owing to the phrase, "I am your *Kenharingan Tumanah*," frequently occurring in folk-stories. It is possible from what I have learnt since writing the above that the *Kenharingan Tumanah* may be nothing more than the Earth Spirit (*Hantu Tanah*) of the Malays. There are Dusun legends of men of old having encountered their Kenharingan Tumanah under various guises. In swearing to speak the truth as witnesses in court Dusuns at the present day recite an oath which runs somewhat as follows:—"I swear by Kenharingan above and by the earth-god that I will speak the truth. If I do not do so, may a crocodile seize me as I cross a river, may my padi wither, or a tree fall on me in the jungle." A Dusun on changing his place of residence will generally sacrifice in his new home to appease the local spirits, and I remember meeting some Dusun coolies who were going up-country to work on the bridle-path and were taking fowls with them to sacrifice—possibly to the Kenharingan Tumanah; but according to Dusun ideas the whole world is full of spirits, most of whom are malignant. Doubtless the birds would be eaten afterwards, but the spirits would have been called upon to drink the blood first, and so might be considered appeased.

Not only do people going to live in a new place have to make offerings to propitiate the spirits of the soil, but natives of a village returning home after a stay in another district require to undergo a sort of "religious disinfection" in order that any evil influences they have brought back with them may be dissipated, this work being done by some of the women shamans. One of these performances occurred while I was stopping in Kampong Tambatuan. Similarly an ex-policeman who had returned to Tuaran, and was reported to have taken a head somewhere or other, had to have a ceremony performed over him to prevent the spirit of the dead man causing him trouble.

The religious rites performed by the women priestesses are denominated by natives, when speaking Malay, by the general term *menghaji*, a word apparently derived from the Mohammedans, as a *haji* is a man who has performed the pilgrimage to Mecca (Malay: *naik haji*=to go on a pilgrimage). The word means to recite or read out or learn anything connected with religion (e.g. *menghaji Koran*=to learn to recite from the Koran). It is, as far as I know, only used by Dusuns when speaking Malay. The word used by up-country Dusuns of the Tempassuk, which means to perform a religious ceremony, is *memurinait*. There are, of course, *menghajis* for many different purposes, the most important being that connected with the annual expulsion of evil spirits from the village. This ceremony, which at Tuaran is called *mobog*, is carried out by a procession of initiated women, who go the round of all the houses in the village, attended by men who act as drum- and gong-beaters. The celebrants stop here and there, while offerings are made and posturing dances performed in time to the chants of the women and the musical accompaniment of the men. When the circuit of the village has been accomplished the procession wends its way to the river-bank, where a raft laden with such things as evil spirits may be thought to delight in —food, models of men and women, buffaloes, deer and other animals—is moored in readiness. The spirits, who are supposed to have followed the procession to feed on the offerings—at Tuaran they are attracted by the squeals of a sucking pig which the women beat with little wands—pleased at the abundance of gifts before them, crowd on to the raft, which is then pushed off into mid-stream and carried away by the current. Needless to say that if the raft comes to shore anywhere near the village it is launched again as quickly as possible. The raft-builders do not seem to worry if it goes aground near some village farther down-stream; they have got rid of their objectionable "hangers-on," and that is all they care about.

Other *menghajis* are performed at Tuaran, the most important of which are the the *menghaji* for rain, called *menawar* (Malay: *tawar* or *menawar* = to neutralise?), when offerings of rice and eggs are thrown into the river as a sacrifice to the water spirits; the *menghaji* after harvest, called *menomboi*, when offerings of rice are said to be placed on large stones; the *menghaji* of the young rice, *masalud*, at which a cock is sacrificed among the growing crops, a rough image of the bird made with its feathers set up on the spot, and water thrown over the rice, probably with the object of ensuring sufficient rain; and the *menghaji* of the sacred *Gusi* jars, *mengahau*.

A *Gusi* is a large jar of ancient Chinese porcelain. It is usually greeny-brown in colour, and, as far as I remember, a fairly large specimen would stand about three and a half feet high. At Tuaran, where these jars are venerated—they are not found at the present time to any extent in the Tempassuk, nor, I believe, in the up-country villages of the Tuaran district—the *Gusis* are kept in a railed-off enclosure in an inner room. According to native ideas each jar has an indwelling spirit, which if not propitiated by an annual sacrifice of a buffalo, will bring misfortune upon the heads of its owners. Usually a jar is not owned by an individual, but by the members of a family, each of whom is entitled to its use for any religious rites they may wish to perform. At one time there used to be a great deal of litigation with regard to the ownership of *Gusis*, but at length this became so troublesome that a proclamation was issued which forbade a case with regard to the ownership of a sacred jar to come to court, but at the same time stipulated that anyone who had contributed a share of the purchase money was entitled to free access to and use of the *Gusi* whenever it might be required. Recourse may be had to the law to enforce the rights of *waris*. According to native estimates, the Tuaran people are extremely well off, and from 2000 to 3000 dollars ($1 = 2s. 4d.) is by no means an out-of-the-way price to pay for a single specimen.

The Tempassuk Dusuns, as my friend Sirinan of Kampong Piasau told me, take a very prosaic and business-like view of the worship of sacred jars. When I was talking the matter over with him and asking him if there were *Gusis* in any of the down-country vlllages, he replied: "Oh no! there are none left now; we used to have some, but Brunei traders came along and offered us high prices for them, as they could sell them profitably at Tuaran and Papar, where they are very highly valued; so we reflected that it was better to have the cash than keep jars which were the habitations of evilly disposed spirits, who required expensive sacrifices to keep them in a good temper, and we sold them off."

I am inclined to think that there is a good deal of snobbishness behind the sacred-jar cult, as a family who can afford to buy a *Gusi* and offer the annual sacrifices is rather inclined to put on airs about its possession. An incident in connection with a *Gusi* illustrates rather well the natives' tolerance, if not reverence, for mad people. There used to be an old madman at Tuaran who was constantly stealing small articles from people's houses and making himself a general nuisance. One day he took it into his head to carry off the family *Gusi*—I am not sure it was not someone else's family *Gusi*; anyway he tied a rope round its neck, threw the jar into the river and attached the other end of the cord to a tree which overhung the water. The owners of the jar, having found out that he had taken it, made him disclose the place where it was hidden, but when they had got it back in safety they neither punished him nor took any steps to prevent his doing further mischief. This story was told me by Mr H. W. L. Bunbury, who at the time was

District Officer, North Keppel. I knew the old man myself, and he once sold me a shield which I afterwards found out he had "lifted" from a neighbour.

Before leaving the subject of religious ceremonies I ought to say a word or two about the special dress which is worn by women at the Tuaran *menghajis*, and also about certain instruments which are used in all religious rites. The dress of a Tuaran priestess consists of a short, tight-fitting jacket of blue or black Chinese cloth, and a ceremonial skirt of a kind of old cloth of variegated colours. The latter is said to have come originally from Brunei, and specimens are at the present time valued at about a hundred dollars each. The jacket is swathed with a long scarf of somewhat similar design and colour to that of the skirt, which is wound diagonally across the body. The scarves, which are also old, are called *chandei*, and cost somewhere about thirty dollars a-piece.

The front of the jacket over the scarf is decorated with a number of strings of old beads, each loop having two cone-shaped silver ornaments plugged with wood strung upon it. The cones are so arranged that they hang in pairs with their points directed downwards to form a sloping series on each side of the body. The whole ornament is called a *kamuggi*, and the points of each pair of cones are as a rule connected by a chain of snake-scale links. Long bugle-shaped beads of cornelian are frequently threaded on the more expensive *kamuggi* and on the *okob*, another kind of ceremonial necklace, which has a roughly crescent-shaped ornament of embossed silver on a copper background in front, and a number of small plates of similar materials depending from it at intervals.

The hair, which is piled up into a mass on the top of the head, rather towards the back, has a row of four bamboo pins stuck into it running from back to front. The heads of these are ornamented with shuttle-cock-like bunches of feathers, generally those of the peacock pheasant or domestic fowl, while two of the bunches, those at the front and back of the head, are decorated with hanging strings of green beetle-wings or bits of tin-foil.

In all religious ceremonies the Tuaran priestess carries in her hand a peculiar rattle, called *tetubit*, which consists essentially of two discs of metal perforated at the edge and joined together by a string that is attached to a handle made from a single section of the carapace of a fresh-water turtle. Slightly varying forms are used for different ceremonies. With this instrument a clanking accompaniment is kept up during the chants and dances.

In the Tempassuk the *gunding*, an instrument which corresponds to the *tetubit*, and is there usually made of several small rectangular sheets of brass, with some bunches of charms tied to the end of a short stick, is regarded with great veneration, one native even going so far as to call it the Dusuns' Koran. It is kept in a bamboo receptacle which is hung up against the wall of the house near the door in order that it may scare away any evil spirits who may wish to effect an entry. No man may handle it, and only those women who have been initiated as priestesses. In the Tempassuk the *menghaji* dress is much the same as that of every day, except that the curious cowl-like hood of native cloth which the women sometimes put on for field-work is always worn, and clothes used for religious ceremonies are sometimes profusely decorated with old shell beads. In addition to the jacket, skirt and hood, a long cape is sometimes worn.

To turn now to head-hunting in its religious aspects. Apart from the sporting side of the pursuit, where the heads are considered merely as trophies and signs of the prowess of the warrior, there is to a certain extent an undercurrent of meaning. According to the old custom of many countries, the killing of a human victim was considered necessary to ensure the success of the crops, and at the erection of a new house a head was buried under the central post in order to pacify the outraged genii of the soil, who had been disturbed by the operations of the house-builders. Sir Charles Brooke, in speaking of the Dyaks, says that feasts in general are "to make their rice grow well, to cause the forest to abound with live animals, to enable their dogs and snares to be successful in securing game, to have the streams swarm with fish, to give health and activity to the people themselves, and to ensure fertility to their women. All these blessings, the possessing and feasting of a fresh head are supposed to be the most efficient means of securing."

It is easy to understand how a people with such beliefs as these would become attached to the custom of head-hunting, quite apart from any ideas of prowess or sport.

I do not think that the low-country Dusuns of the Tempassuk have been addicted to the practice within recent times, and I have never seen any skulls hung up in their villages, but in the up-country head-hunting is still remembered, and old heads are to a certain extent venerated. Head-hunting was never so popular among the Dusuns as among the Kenyah Kayans of Sarawak and the Muruts, since they are essentially a peaceable race of cultivators, who have always been the oppressed rather than the oppressors, their wives and children in former days being frequently seized and sold into slavery by bands of raiding Bajaus and Illanuns from the coast. Still, a certain amount of head-hunting did go on between village and village, and occasionally a Chinaman paid the penalty for his temerity in following the pursuit of gain too far up-country.

It is now very difficult to collect information with regard to head-hunting, especially if you are a Government officer and start asking questions in villages where the people do not know you very well. Most of the small amount of information I was able to get was gathered from Yompo, a young Dusun of Kiau with whom I was very well acquainted. After the return of a party from a successful head-hunting expedition all the participants are regarded as unclean until

DUSUN PRIESTESS OF TAMBATUAN IN CEREMONIAL DRESS.

Among the Dusuns, initiated women play a prominent part in religious rites, which they conduct in a language which is not supposed to be understood by the men. The woman in the picture is holding a divination-stick in her hand.

they have undergone a purificatory ceremony—in this some of the older women officiate, and ceremonial bathing forms a part.

There was one small recrudescence of head-hunting shortly before I went to the Tempassuk, the murderers—two young Dusuns of Wasai in the Ulu Tuaran—being executed at Jesselton shortly after I first took up my residence in the district. They, apparently being wishful of distinguishing themselves, went and hung about the jungle near Kiau village, with which Wasai in the old days had been at feud, and seeing a woman working alone in one of the gardens, killed her. They were about to take the head, when, thinking that they heard someone coming, they ran away and made for Wasai as fast as they could. After a long time sufficient evidence was obtained to bring the two offenders to trial, and they were in due course convicted.

Three mementoes of the affair came into the hands of Mr H. W. L. Bunbury, then District Officer, North Keppel—namely, two little wooden models of a human head and a hat, which was of an ordinary Dusun conical type, except that its top was decorated with a short wooden pillar to the apex of which was tied a bunch of cock's tail-feathers. According to Yompo, these wooden models, which he said were called *tenumpok*, represented the head which the men were unable to obtain, two models being made in order that each man might have a memento of the exploit. He further told me that a freshly taken head was put on a stone set in the ground.

With regard to head-hunting customs at Tuaran I was informed by Adu, a middle-aged Dusun of that place, that the ceremonies performed on the return from a successful raid were called *domali*. At Tuaran, where many of the dwellings are communal houses, the skulls are hung up in the common verandah and are decorated with bunches of the long dried leaves of a plant called *silad*. In one case I was lucky enough to see a portion of a ceremony connected with head-hunting at this place. It appears that a policeman, a native of Tuaran, who had been serving away from home had taken a head, probably in some small skirmish with a rebellious tribe, and had returned home on leave. Thereupon it was determined that a ceremony must be performed and a buffalo killed, partly in order to celebrate the event and partly in order that the spirit of the deceased might be pacified, so that the head-taker might suffer no evil consequences.

The portion of the ceremonies that I witnessed was a procession of seven or eight men walking in single file near a village, while they kept up a continual cry which had a peculiar whistling sound. Each man was wearing one of the brass-hilted swords known as *pedang* (see Chapter XIX.), but this was sheathed in a scabbard about four feet long, which broadened out to a width of six inches at its farther end. The lower edges of the scabbard were profusely decorated with human hair and its outer face with carved patterns, the whole weapon being called a *tenumpasuan.* The leader of the party carried a conch-shell trumpet, on which he blew occasional blasts, and all wore attached to their belts large bunches of *silad* leaves. One man had a human vertebra to which was tied a triangular plaited ornament of the same kind of leaves.

It is now unusual to see Dusuns with much tattooing on their bodies, as this was usually connected with head-hunting, but I have been informed that Tempassuk Dusuns who had participated in a successful head-hunting expedition used to tattoo their bodies with two bands of patterns running from the shoulders to the hips, though I have never seen a man so decorated. Sir Spencer St John corroborates the information given to me, as he says that he saw men with "a tattooed band two inches broad, stretched in an arc from each shoulder, meeting on their stomachs, then turning off to their hips; and some of them had a tattooed band extending from the shoulder to the hand." According to Mr Whitehead, "some of the men are slightly tattooed with a few parallel lines on the forearm."

Connected with war and head-hunting are certain tabus to be observed by the women left at home while their men-folk are away on an expedition. Probably my small collection of these is by no means complete, as other tribes have also tabus which the warriors must keep when on the war-path; however, I give below such as I obtained:

War Tabus—

1. When the men are on the war-path the women must not weave cloth or their husbands will be unable to escape from the enemy, because they will become uncertain in which direction to run. In the weaving of cloth the backward and forward movements of the shuttle represent the uncertain movements of a man running first to one side and then to another in order to escape from an enemy.

2. Women may not eat from the winnowing basket, for the edges of it represent mountains, over which their men would not be able to climb.

3. The women must not sit sprawling about or with their legs crossed, else their husbands will not have strength for anything.

On the other hand:

4. It is lucky for the women to keep walking about, for then the men will have strength to walk far.

In addition to war tabus there are many others which regulate conduct on special or general occasions—for example:

1. If a person dies in a newly built village within six months of its completion it must be abandoned and another site chosen.

2. Nobody but the owners may enter a new house before a religious ceremony has been performed over it.

3. No one must hold or wear anything white, yellow or red where a religious ceremony is in progress.

4. Nothing white, yellow or red must be brought into a house where women are dyeing cloth.

Taking into account the Dusun's fear of evil spirits and the trouble which he takes to propitiate them, it is only natural that he should set great store by all kinds of objects which he considers useful as talismans. Charm-belts are very generally worn, and are made either of string network or of cloth, each talisman being netted or sewn into a separate compartment. Any object out of the common which a native finds is considered to have a magical value, and I have seen fossil shells, so-called bezoar stones, quartz crystals, rhinoceros' teeth and pieces of wood used for this purpose. The pieces of wood used as talismans are usually tied up into little bundles and are probably the fossil (?) wood which Burbidge calls *kayu lagundi* (tree of youth) in *Gardens of the Sun*, p. 256. These charm-belts are always put on when a native leaves his house. Small brass bells are frequently worn by children: these are regarded as a protection against spirits, and possibly the little bells attached to the tops of Dusun women's skirts may also serve the same purpose.

To turn now to the subject of sacred trees. In the Tempassuk a certain tree, called the *limpada*, is much venerated and feared by the Dusuns: it is by no means uncommon, grows to a fair height, has large leaves and a long, smooth-skinned, red fruit, which is of oval shape and about a foot long. According to Dusun legendry, Kenharingan has put a curse upon anyone who shall violate a tree of this species, the punishment being that the offender shall die of incurable ulcers. When, however, one of these trees is found growing on a piece of ground which is required for a clearing it may be felled, but not until a religious ceremony has been performed.

I remember that once when walking along the bridle-path which leads to the Interior, with Lengok of Bengkahak and Gumpus the headman of Tambatuan, I turned to the latter, who was wearing a sword (*gayang*), and told him to cut away one or two branches of undergrowth which were overhanging the path. He replied that he was afraid that he would blunt his weapon, but as he had been using it pretty freely all the way along for a similar purpose I did not quite see the force of his remarks; however, I said nothing more about the matter, as the branches did not really block the road. When we arrived at our destination, which, if I remember rightly, was Gumpus's own village, Lengok, who was alone with me, said: "Tuan, do you remember that when we were coming along the path you told Gumpus to cut some branches and he said he was afraid of blunting his sword?" "Yes," I said, "I remember it; but what about it?" "Well, that was not the reason he would not cut the branches," said Lengok; "it was because it was a young *limpada*-tree you wanted him to chop down."

Another tree which is regarded by the Dusuns with some reverence is the banyan, and according to the people of Tuaran a tree of this kind is the dwelling-place of a spirit who keeps a large number of *Gusi* jars among its branches. Natives who have gone into the jungle are said to have seen these jars arranged in rows under a banyan-tree, which they have come upon suddenly; but on taking a second look the jars have vanished, for the spirit has seized them up again into the tree.

Trees on rivers, especially those near river mouths, are frequently hung with shreds of cloth as propitiatory offerings to the water spirits, one special tree being generally set aside for the purpose. Another matter which plays a very important part in the everyday affairs of the Dusuns is the belief in omens. Omens may be either good or bad, but most of those to which the Dusuns pay attention seem to belong to the latter class. A flying swarm of bees is considered a bad omen, and to hear the *kijang* (called *paus* by the Dusuns) or muntjac (*Cervulus muntjac*) bark when on a journey is considered such a bad sign that a native will either stop for the night at once or else go straight back home. The large millipede (*Iulus* sp.) may be either a good or a bad omen if met with on a journey: if it is going in the same direction as the traveller it is a good portent, but if it is proceeding in the opposite direction, or crossing the path, some piece of bad luck is sure to happen to anyone who persists in continuing on his way. I remember being much amused, when we met a millipede which was walking across the path, at watching old Lengok trying to coax it into going in the same direction as ourselves.

In addition to the fact that the Dusuns pay great heed to omens when working in the fields or on journeys, they have a peculiar monthly calendar of good and bad days which regulates their work in the padi-fields. On bad days no work must be done among the rice, or perhaps work may be done in the hill-rice fields but not among the swamp-rice. The month consists of two periods of lucky days, and two of unlucky, the last day of each of the good periods being called *kopopusan* (finished). With regard to the good days, *ka-in-duoh*, *ka-in-teloh*, etc., these are merely the Dusun ordinal numbers, 2nd, 3rd, etc. I have to thank Father Duxneuney of Putatan, British North Borneo, for elucidating a difficulty I had in connection with the meaning of these words.

The disease which the Dusuns most greatly fear, and not without good reason, is small-pox. Consequently resort is had to magic in order to keep this dread foe at bay. When news is brought that a neighbouring village has become infected, wooden models of spears and men are made and set up on the side of the village facing the source of infection. The idea is that protecting spirits are called up into the models by a religious ceremony which is performed, and that these fight with the spirits of small-pox.

I have already made mention of the Dusuns' respect for mad people, madness being attributed to possession by a spirit. In one case, when in residence at Kotabelud, I remember hearing gong-beating going on during the whole of a day, the sound being the continual boom, boom, boom of a *tetawag* or *tawag-tawag* (a deep-toned gong), which when beaten in this fashion always denotes trouble. On sending to find out what was the matter, I was informed that a man had suddenly been seized with madness and had run away into the jungle; so the people of his village were trying to drive out the evil spirit which possessed him in order that he might return home.

On another occasion when coming down from up-country on the day of the large market known as Tamu Darat, and nearing the market ground, I noticed an object which looked like a human body lying in the middle of the bridle-path. All the Dusuns who passed the object—there were many of them on their way to market—seemed to give it as wide a berth as possible. On coming close up I saw that I had not been mistaken. A Dusun youth, who was in some kind of a fit, or had fainted, was lying in the middle of the path. He was wearing a small carrying-basket of the kind called *bareit*, and as he was on his back with his legs doubled up under him, and with his head bent right back, owing to the basket being between his body and the ground, he looked as if he was in danger of suffocation. I noticed that his eyes were open and that the coloured parts of the eyes were rolled so far up as to be almost hidden.

I was just going to a ditch at the side of the path to get some water in my hands to throw over him when a Dusun who was with me called out: "Don't go near him, Tuan! He's *gila babi* [*i.e.* pig mad, the Malay term for epilepsy], and he'll bite you, and then you'll get it too." However, I got the water, and just as I was splashing it over the patient three Bajaus came up, who, not being frightened like the Dusuns, helped me to unfix the back-basket. In a few minutes the fellow had recovered, and stumbled off to the nearest water for a drink, remarking that he was hungry and he supposed that this had made him faint.

In sickness offerings are made to appease the spirits which are supposed to be the cause of the disease: small offerings are made at first, and if these do not have the desired effect then something more expensive is tried. "First of all we offer a fowl," said a Dusun to me, "and then, if that does not appease the spirit, we kill a pig."

Before bringing this chapter to a close there are one or two other subjects about which I should like to say a little. One of these is with regard to the Dusun's belief in an after life. According to general ideas the spirits of the dead find their way to the top of Mount Kinabalu, which is their final abode. From the accounts given me, souls both of the good and the bad seem to reach this land of the dead, though de Crespigny says that "the wicked ones are left unsuccessfully trying to struggle and scramble up the rocky sides of the mountain." I intend, however, to say something more about the soul's passage to Kinabalu in the chapter which deals with burial customs.

There is one class of tabu in force among the Dusuns of which I have up till now omitted to make any mention, that dealing with the telling of personal names. According to Dusun custom it is tabu to mention your own name, that of your father or mother, your father-in-law or mother-in-law. If a European asks a Dusun his name he will usually give it, but he would not think of doing so to another native. A man who wishes to know a person's name must seek the information from a friend of his, who may speak the name without committing any breach of custom. The Dusuns say that if they were to mention the name of their mother their knees would swell. These tabus seem to be more strictly observed with regard to female relations than in the case of males.

The making of blood-brothers is by no means uncommo

among the Dusuns. Omboi, a native of Tuaran, told me that when two men were wishful to become blood-brothers each made a cut in his wrist and then the other drank a little of the blood from the cut. After that, presents are exchanged, either fowls, tobacco or rice. In the Tempassuk a fowl is sacrificed in the making of blood-brothers and each man says: "If I cheat you, may I become as this fowl, which has just been killed."

There is among the Dusuns a peculiar custom called "paying *sagit*." *Sagit* may often be merely compensation or damages for some offence committed. For instance, if a man's wife is insulted, he may demand *sagit* from the offender, the guilt of the latter and the amount of compensation being decided by the elders of the village. There are frequent cases of this kind of *sagit* at Tuaran. However, *sagit* occasionally takes quite another meaning, of which I became aware through buying some human hair to redecorate the scabbard of a sword. Having found a man with long hair, I asked him if he was willing to part with it, and, if so, how much he wanted to let me "crop" him. He answered that he would sell his hair to me for sixty cents, but that I must give him a fowl in addition to sacrifice as *sagit*. This was for the purpose of warding off any evil which might happen to him owing to his hair, a part of himself, passing into my possession. Needless to say, I gave him his fowl, a matter of only another ten cents.

CHAPTER XVIII

LEGENDS

SHORTLY after my return from Borneo I happened to remark to a certain learned ethnographist that I had made a rather large collection of native folk-tales. From what he said I gathered that he thought I would have been better employed had I devoted myself more to the study of sociology and other matters. With all humility I cannot say that I agree with him in this opinion. The folk-tales of a primitive people are, I think, one of the first things that should be collected, as through them we obtain an insight into the native's religion, his way of thinking and his methods of accounting for natural phenomena: besides this, in folk-tales we often come upon casual references to customs and beliefs of which we should probably never have heard under ordinary circumstances, and through these is opened a field for investigation which would otherwise have remained closed.

Of course it may be objected that folk-tales are somewhat similar almost the world over. To this I would answer that if we find that the people among whom we are living have similar tales to those of a people elsewhere, we have established a possible connection with this second people, and we may then search and see whether there are any other resemblances. Comparative religion and comparative study of customs are always interesting, whether beliefs and customs of a like nature have arisen independently in different places through the similarity of men's minds, or whether they have originated at some remote period in the history of man before our primitive ancestors had become far dispersed from that quarter of the world in which they were evolved.

Again, though it may be said that the counterpart of a tale can very often be found among some other race or tribe, yet there must always be minor differences from country to country, these being often extremely important as throwing light on the methods and manners of the people we are studying.

Sir J. G. Frazer, in his most useful little book of questions published by the Cambridge University Press, instructs the budding inquirer not to try so much to obtain information from natives by constant questioning as "to start the savage talking on some topic of interest, say on birth or death customs, to let him run on till he has exhausted himself, and then to jog his memory by asking him about points which he has either imperfectly explained or entirely omitted." This is excellent advice so long as the savage will fulfil his share in the matter by starting to talk about a subject which has been suggested and running on until he has exhausted himself.

Unfortunately my experience among the aboriginal tribes of Borneo and of the Malay States is that in the ordinary way this is exactly what the savage will not do. Even if you are certain that he has every wish to help you, the probability is that when you ask him a question he will answer it to the best of his ability, and then sit mumchance until you question him again as to some point in his answer. The faculty of being able to give a connected account of any ceremony or occurrence seems generally very poorly developed. Occasionally exceptionally intelligent natives are to be met with. Where Sir J. G. Frazer's "instructions" cannot be followed for such a reason, the folk-story is often an excellent substitute.

Apart from this, it is by means of the folk-tale that we are often enabled to become good friends with the native. If a man has told you a story and he sees that you do not laugh at him, or show contempt, he will very likely tell you about other matters which he would be chary of mentioning to anyone who had not gained his confidence. One folk-story often leads to others, as the following little episode will show.

In the course of a journey up-country I once put up in a small hut not far from a village which I had never visited before. As is usual, the village headman, accompanied by several followers, came down to meet me. After talking for a short while on local matters, the hut meanwhile becoming rapidly filled with natives, I soon became aware that the people were very suspicious and sulky. They sat and glowered, and would hardly answer the most innocent questions. I was able to guess without much difficulty the reason for their attitude, as an important man among them had recently been tried and sentenced for complicity in a head-hunting outrage.

Having tried to show them, as far as possible, that I had not come to make any fresh trouble, I began to talk to them about folk-tales, and to ask if they did not know any which they could tell me, only to be met with the answer: "Oh yes, the old people of long ago knew stories, but we, their descendants, have not heard them." "Why is that?" said I. "I expect we did not ask for instruction from them," replied the man who was answering me. "Well, if that's the case," said I, "you ought to be ashamed of yourselves, for in every other Dusun village where I have been they had no lack of stories. However, if you won't tell me a story, suppose I tell you one instead." So I told them a short tale that I had heard a few days before at Kampong Piasau. When I had finished, one of the old men said, with a chuckle at having been found out: "Why, Tuan, how long have you been in the country that you know so much about the Dusuns' affairs?" That night I got as many stories as I could take down.

Very often a village has one or two folk-tales peculiar to itself, the incidents related being said to have happened to some man of the village in ancient times. Of this kind are the stories of "Why the Dusuns of Tempassuk do not eat snakes," peculiar to the village of that name, "The Orang-Utan of Kiau," and "The Man of Nabah." Roughly speaking, I think that Dusun folk-tales may be said to fall into six or seven classes: of these the local story, those concerning religion or customs, those which account for various natural phenomena, those which relate to the doings of people of old times and the marvellous adventures which befell them, those which tell how the Dusuns became acquainted with useful inventions and articles of diet, and those of a humorous character are the most important.

The classes, however, often shade off into one another, particularly in the case of the first four. To the Dusun his folk-tales are in most cases much more than mere stories told to while away the time, for in them are enshrined his religious beliefs, his ideas with regard to the things of nature which affect him, his explanation of the origin of various customs, his astronomy and his history.

Concerning folk-tales dealing with native religion I have already said something in a previous chapter, and if any of my readers should wish to read a large number of the stories which I collected they will find them in *The Journal of the Royal Anthropological Institute*, vol. xliii. (1913). The usual time for telling folk-stories is during harvest, both in the fields and after work is finished, this being the season for rejoicing, toddy-drinking and feasting. I am enabled by the courtesy of the Royal Anthropological Institute to reprint below a tale of each type. The stories were told in Malay, the *lingua franca* of Borneo, and were taken down straight from the lips of their narrators.

The Orang-Utan (*Orang-Utang*)

A legend of Kiau on the slopes of Kinabalu, told by Yompo

Long ago some men went into the jungle carrying blow-pipes, and when they got near to the River Tenokop they heard someone singing verses among the trees. Then they looked and saw an Orang-Utan (*Kagyu*) sitting on the ground singing, and this was his song: "First of all I lived at the River Makadau, but I went to the River Serinsin; from there I went to the River Wariu; from the Wariu to the Penataran; from the Penataran to the Kilambun; from the Kilambun to the Obang, and from the Obang to the Tenokop. I cannot go up into the trees again for I am old and must die upon the ground. I can no longer get fresh young leaves to eat from the trees; I have to eat young grass."

Then the men who had been listening said to one another: "This *Kagyu* is clever at verses, let us shoot him with our blow-pipes." One man was about to shoot when the *Kagyu* saw him and said: "Do not shoot me, but make me a hut and let me live here till I die. When you have made my hut, bring your sisters here and I will teach them magic, for I am skilled in it." So the men made him a hut and they brought their sisters to him, and the *Kagyu* instructed them how each sickness has its own magical ceremony. He taught them the spells for snake-bite and fever, and for the bite of the centipede.

Then the men went home, about three days' journey, to get rice for the *Kagyu*, but when they came back with the rice the *Kagyu* was dead; and from that day whenever there was sickness in Kampong Kiau they called the women who had been instructed by the *Kagyu*, and those who were ill recovered, and if a man was wounded and was treated by the women no blood came from the wound.

A Legend of the Beginning of the World

Told by the headman of Timpalang, a Tuaran Dusun

At first there was a great stone in the middle of the sea. At that time there was no earth, only water. The rock was large, and it opened its mouth, and out of it came a man and a woman. The man and the woman looked around, and there was only water. The woman said to the man: "How can we walk, for there is no land?" They descended from the rock and tried to walk on the surface of the water, and found that they could. They returned to the rock and sat down to think; for a long time they stopped there; then again they walked upon the water, and at length they arrived at the house of Bisagit (the spirit of small-pox), for Bisagit had made land, though it was very far away.

Now the man and his wife were Kedharingan and Munsumundok (chief gods of the Dusuns). They spoke to Bisagit and asked for some of his earth, and he gave it to them. So going home they pounded up the rock and mixed Bisagit's earth with it, and it became land. Then Kenharingan made the Dusuns and Munsumundok made the sky. Afterwards Kenharingan and Munsumundok made the sun, as it was not good for men to walk about without light. Then Munsumundok said: "There is no light at night, let us make the moon," and they made the moon and the seven stars, the *blatek* (spring-trap) and the *kukurian* or constellations. The seven stars are the Pleiades; the *blatek* or *blantek* is, I believe, the constellation known as the Hyades.

Kenharingan and Munsumundok had one son and one daughter. Now Kenharingan's people wept because there was no food. So Kenharingan and Munsumundok killed their girl child and cut it up, and from the different portions of its body grew all things good to eat: its head gave rise to the coco-nut, and you can see the marks of its eyes and mouth on the coco-nut till this day; from its arm-bones arose sugar-cane; its fingers became bananas and its blood rice. All the animals also arose from pieces of the child.

When Kenharingan had made everything, he said: "Who is able to cast off his skin? If anyone can do so, he shall not die." The snake alone heard and said: "I can." And for this reason till the present day the snake does not die unless killed by man. (The Dusuns did not hear or they would also have thrown off their skins and there would have been no death.)

Kenharingan washed the Dusuns in the river, placing them in a basket; one man, however, fell out of the basket and floating away down the river stopped near the coast. This man gave rise to the Bajaus, who still live near the sea and are skilful at using boats. When Kenharingan had washed the Dusuns in the river he performed a religious ceremony over them in his house; but one man left the house before Kenharingan had done so and went off into the jungle to search for something; and when he came back he could not enter the house again, for he had become a monkey. This man is the father of the monkeys.

The Origin of a Dusun Custom

Told by Sirinan of Piasau, Tempassuk District

Once there was a woman who had newly given birth to a child. The house she lived in was a large one, ten doors long. One day the women of the other rooms were dyeing cloth with *tahum* (a kind of indigo), and the men of the house were away hunting, some in one place, some in another. About midday it began to rain, and with the rain came much thunder and lightning. While it was still thundering, the woman who had newly given birth performed a ceremony in the house, and while she was performing it she saw a woman chasing a boy outside on the ground below, and their appearance was as if they had been quarrelling, for the boy was weeping and the woman kept snatching up sticks to throw at him. But she did not manage to hit him, and she kept calling out: "Stop, stop, for the people here do not know the custom."

So the woman who was in the house stopped her performance and going to the door called out: "Why are you treating your boy like that?" The other woman stopped, and said: "I am treating him like this because you people do not know the custom." "What sort of custom?" said the first woman, and while she still spoke the thunder stopped, and the boy also stopped running away. The woman outside answered her: "In this you do not know the custom, and that is why my son is fighting me. It is because you women are dyeing cloth when your husbands have gone to hunt, and it would be good if they, your husbands, were all together in one place in the jungle. See when they come back, some will bring white, some red and some yellow; these women are dyeing their cloth *black*."

Then the women of the house said: "We did not know of any custom like this. What is it?" The woman answered them: "This is the custom: when you wish to dye cloth (black or blue) you must not take hold of anything white, red or yellow." Said the women of the house: "Instruct us in this custom." And the woman outside said: "You must keep this custom, and it would be good if men did not get hit by things thrown by my son [*i.e.* thunderbolts]. If the things he throws about only hit a coco-nut-tree it does not matter, but if they hit a man, there will be trouble for that man. Another time your husbands must not be seeking for things to eat, red, white or yellow, when you are dyeing your cloth black. And do not bring these colours into the house while you are still dyeing cloth." Then the woman and the boy vanished.

After a time came the men who had been hunting; four had got a deer (red blood), and the other six had brought tumeric (tumeric is yellow), and the young white shoots of the *bĕluon*-tree. When the women saw the men coming, they called out: "Whatever you have brought from the jungle, do not bring it into the house this night." So the men slept outside with the goods they had brought from the jungle. On the morrow they brought their deer and other things into the house, and the women of the house told them how the woman had chased the boy. And to the present day women may not touch red, yellow or white when they are dyeing cloth.

["I think that the boy who was being chased by his mother was the Spirit of Thunder."—SIRINAN.]

Note.—The colours mentioned would appear to be symbolical of a thunderstorm:

Black or dark blue . .	The clouds
White	The rain
Yellow and red . . .	The lightning

THE MAKING OF THE BLUNTONG (RAINBOW)

Told by Sirinan (low-country Dusun) of Piasau, Tempassuk District

Long ago the rainbow was a path for men. Those who lived up-country used the rainbow as a bridge when they wished to go down-country in search of wives. For though there were women up-country, the up-country men were very fond of the down-country women. Because of the men's desire for wives from the coast they made the rainbow as a bridge, and you can see the floor and hand-rail of the bridge in the rainbow to the present day. The men when they had first made the rainbow walked on it to the women's houses. When the men had fed, the women followed the men along the rainbow to their homes. When they arrived up-country the marriages were celebrated with a feast, and the men became drunk. Then came a headman from another village and said to them: "You men are very clever; how long have I lived in this country, but never yet have I seen anything like your rainbow. Do you intend to leave it there or not?" The men replied: "When we want to go down-country with our wives we will put it in place, but when we do not want it we will take it away," and thus they do to the present day. What the men were I do not know, but they were more than ordinary men. It is an old-time tale of our people. Perhaps it is true, for just now, as you saw, the rainbow vanished.

How the Bajau came to the Tempassuk and the Dusun learnt the Use of Beeswax

Told by Serundai, Orang Tua of Kalisas, Tempassuk District

There is a tree named *kendilong* which has a sap white as water, and this sap is very irritating to the skin. The *kendilong* is a home for bees, and if men wish to take the honey they cut steps in the tree up to the bees' nest.

Once there was a poor man, and every night he dreamed that if he found a *kendilong*-tree he would become rich. So he set out to look for one, and when it was near night he found a *kendilong*, and slept the night there. Now there were bees' nests in the tree. The next morning he went home and brought two companions back with him. Two men climbed the tree, and one stopped below by the trunk. They took the bees' nests, but did not know to whom to sell them. Now there was a Bajau who had come up the river in a boat, for at this time there were no Bajaus living in the country. This man met the Dusun who had got the bees' nests, and going home with him he saw four sacks of nests and bought them for a little cloth, saying that he did not know what they were. He said that he would try and sell the nests, and that he wished to become the Dusun's brother. So they swore brotherhood, and sacrificed a hen, and the Bajau promised to give the Dusun his share if there were any profits from the nests, at the same time telling him to collect any more that he might find. Then the Bajau sailed away, and the Dusun searched hard for bees' nests.

Now the Bajau had promised to return in three months' time, and, when he came, he brought a *tongkang* (a kind of small junk) full of goods, while he found the Dusun's house full of bees' nests. So the Dusun got much goods from the Bajau, and became rich, and that is how the Dusun got to know about beeswax.

The Legend of Nonok Kurgung

Told by Orang Tua Lengok, a low-country Dusun of Bengkahak, Tempassuk District

Long ago, when there were no people in this country of the Tempassuk, there were two people at Nonok Kurgung, a man and his wife. The woman became with child and gave birth to seven children at one time, both male and female; four were females and three were males. When these children were grown up they wished for husbands and wives, and asked their father and mother how they were to get them, as there were no other people in the country. Their father and mother said to them: "Wait, and if your dreams are good you will get your wish."

When the woman was asleep Kenharingan came to her in her dreams and said: "I have come because I have pity on you that you cannot get wives or husbands for your children. Your children must marry one another, as that was the reason I gave you seven children at one birth." In the morning the woman asked her husband if he had had any dreams, and he said: "No." Then he asked his wife if she had dreamed, and she said that Kenharingan had come to her and told her that their children must marry one another. So they consulted together and ordered their children to marry, and after they had been married for some time all the women gave birth to twenty children each at a time, and these children in their turn intermarried.

Now at this time the people had no plantations, and they got their rice by cutting down bamboo stems, the rice coming out from the inside of the stem. There was a river with many *nonok*-trees near the village, and the children used to go and bathe there and lie under the trees. Every day they went to bathe there, and every day a child was lost. This went on until twenty children had been lost, and the fathers decided to try and find out what was happening to them. They searched the river and they searched the banks, but could find nothing, and there were no crocodiles in the river.

After they had hunted in vain for three days they went home, and when they met together they decided they would run away from the place. So they collected all their goods to start. One night all was ready, and the next morning they started out, taking with them their wives and children, their baggage and bamboos to give them padi. After they had journeyed for a day one man and his family stopped behind to make a house, a second man stopped on the second day, and so on till there was nobody left to journey on. These families which stopped formed villages, and from their bamboos came all sorts of food-plants, vegetables, rice and *caladium*, and these they planted in their gardens. This is how this country became peopled with Dusuns to as far away as Marudu.

The Origin of the Blatek, the Ror and the Puru-puru (Three Constellations)

Told by Sirinan, a low-country Dusun of Piasau, Tempassuk District

Long ago men planted only tapioca, *caladium* and beans; at that time there was no rice. When they had planted them they fenced them round, and after a time they cleared away the weeds in the crop. At weeding-time they found that wild pigs had been getting in and had eaten all their *caladium*. "What use is it," said they, "our planting crops? The wild pigs only eat them." In the evening the men went home to their houses, and when it was night they went to sleep.

Now one man dreamed, and in his dream an old man came to him, and he said to the old man: "All my *caladium* and tapioca and beans which I planted have been eaten by wild pigs." Said the old man: "You must make a *blatek* [Malay, *blantek*] [spring-trap] at the edge of your fence where the pigs enter." Then the man awoke, for it was near morning, and thinking over the dream, he resolved to make a *blatek* near the edge of his garden. So he ate, and when he had finished he went out to his clearing and started making a *blatek*. When he had finished it he set it and returned home, and on the fourth day after he had set the trap he went back to his plantation to look if it had caught anything. When he got there he found a wild pig in the trap, but it had become decayed and was not fit to eat. He poked it with the end of his walking-stick, and found that its head was separate from the body, and that the under jaw and teeth had fallen away from the head.

The man went home, and at night he went to sleep and dreamed that the same old man came to him and said: "What about your *blatek*? Did it catch a wild pig?" "Yes," said the man, "I caught a pig, but it had become rotten and I was not able to eat it." "Did you take a walking-stick with you?" said the old man. "And did you prod the wild pig's head with the stick?" "I did," said he. "Very well," said the old man, "do not plant *caladium* and beans this year; plant rice instead." "But where shall I get rice from?" said he, "for there is no rice in this village." "Well, search for it in other villages," said the old man. "If you only get two or three measures that will be enough. The marks where you thrust your stick into the pig's head shall be called the *puru-puru*. The lower jaw shall have its name of the *ror*, and the *blatek* also shall keep its name, and all these shall become stars."

Then said the man: "I want instruction from you, for if I get rice how am I to plant it?" Said the old man: "You must watch for the *blatek*, the *ror* and the *puru-puru* to appear in the sky, and when, shortly after dark, the *puru-puru* appears about a quarter way up in the sky, that is the time to plant rice. The *puru-puru* will come out first, the *ror* behind it and the *blatek* last of all." When the man woke up he found that the old man's words had come true, and that the *puru-puru*, the *blatek* and the *ror* had become stars. To the present day they follow this custom, and the rice is planted according to the position of these stars as seen shortly after dark (about seven o'clock).

THE LAZY WOMAN AND HER "BAYONG"

A Dusun story, told by the Orang Tua of Kampong Tarantidan, Tempassuk District

Long ago there was a very lazy woman; she would not work, and as for bathing, she was so lazy that she only washed herself once in ten days. One day she went to the bathing-place and a *nipa* palm called to her from across the river. The palm-tree kept on calling her, but she was too lazy to answer or to cross the river to see what it wanted. At last the *nipa* said: "Why are you so lazy that you will not cross the river? There is a boat there on your side of the water and you can paddle across and take my shoot." So the woman went very slowly and got the boat, and going very lazily across the river in it she took the shoot from the palm. Then said the *nipa*: "I called you because you are so lazy. You must take this shoot and dry it a little in the sun, and make a *bayong* from it." (A *bayong* is a large basket for carrying, made from the *nipa* shoot; it has no cover.)

Now the lazy woman nearly wept when she heard that she was to make a *bayong*; however, she took the sprout home and made a *bayong* from it. When this was finished it spoke to the woman, and said: "You must take me along the path where people are going to market and put me down near the side of the road where everybody passes; then you can go home." So the woman took the *bayong* and left it near the road where people were going to market. Many people passed there, but no one noticed the *bayong* until a rich man came along and, seeing it, said: "I will take this *bayong* to market, as it will do to hold anything I buy there, and if the owner is at market I can give it back to him."

Presently the rich man came to the market, and he asked everyone there if they had lost a *bayong*, but nobody acknowledged it. "Well, then," said the rich man, "it is my gain, and I will put what I have bought into it and take it home; but if anyone claims it they can come to my house and get it." So the rich man put all his goods—*sireh*, lime, cakes, fish, rice and bananas—into the *bayong* until it was full, and while the man was talking to some of his friends the *bayong* started off on its own accord to go home to the lazy woman's house. When it was still some little way off from the house it began calling to the lazy woman: "Come here, come here and help me, for I can't stand the weight!" Then the woman went to the *bayong*, though she was nearly weeping at having to go and fetch it home, but when she saw that it was full of all sorts of good things she said: "This is a splendid *bayong*, but perhaps it will want some payment. At any rate, if it is always like this, I shall get an easy living by just leaving the *bayong* on the road to market."

So on market days the woman always placed the *bayong* near the side of the path, and it always came home full; but it never met any of the men who had found it before until it had cheated six men. Now at the seventh market the men who had filled the *bayong* on the six previous occasions, and had thus lost their property, happened to be going to market all together, and when they saw the *bayong* left near the road, they all recognised it as the one which had cheated them. So the six of them collected buffalo dung and filled the *bayong* to the top—"For," said they, "this *bayong* is a proper rascal!" Then the *bayong*, being full, started off straight for home and did not go to the market. When the lazy woman saw it coming she rushed to help it home, but when she found it was full of buffalo dung she began to cry —"For," said she, "if the *bayong* does not bring me food surely I shall die." As for the *bayong*, it would never bring food from the market again.

CHAPTER XIX

WARFARE, HEAD-HUNTING & WEAPONS

THOUGH the Dusuns may be said to be head-hunters, this cult never seems to have attained the same popularity with them as among the Kenyah-Kayans and Sea Dyaks of Sarawak. In the Tempassuk the villages of the plains do not appear to have indulged in head-hunting since they have been in contact with Europeans. The lowlanders of Tuaran, on the other hand, have at the present day some fairly large collections of skulls in their long houses, and how these were obtained I will explain later. In the hill country of both districts head-hunting has only ceased since the Chartered Company has acquired a firm hold, and one case has even occurred within the last few years, the principals in the affair being executed at Jesselton shortly after I went to the Tempassuk.

The reasons for head-hunting among Bornean tribes in general seem to have been threefold: firstly, the practice was not without religious significance; secondly, it was considered a sport and the heads regarded as trophies; and thirdly, among some tribes no youth was considered fit to rank as a man until he had obtained a head, the women taunting those who had been unsuccessful as cowards. With regard to Dusun head-hunting in particular, it certainly had a great deal of religious significance—this side of the matter I deal with in another chapter—but it could scarcely be considered a sporting pursuit, the methods employed in obtaining heads being the very reverse of fair fighting.

The usual procedure was for some of the "braves" to set out from home and proceed to hang round another village with which they were at feud, taking care to hide themselves well in the jungle, preferably near to some of the villagers' padi-fields. When an unarmed straggler or two, very likely women or children, came out to work in the fields, they made a sortie, killed them, cut off their heads and made off as fast as their legs would carry them back to their own village, where they shivered in fright at the thought of a counter-attack. Anyone who had been present at the head-taking, even if he had, as someone once said, "only danced around and yelled 'Hurrah!'" considered himself entitled to decorate his body with the particular tattoo pattern which denoted a man who had taken a head. The head of a woman or child was considered of just as much worth as that of a full-grown man.

I think that a little story with regard to some skulls illustrates very well the Dusun's sharp powers of observance with regard to matters in which he has an interest. On one trip I made up-country I took with me old Lengok, the Orang Tua or headman of Bengkahak; and during our journey we paid a visit to Tambatuan. Here, when walking round the village, I noticed a basket containing a couple of old human skulls hung up against the side of a small hut which was used as a store-house for padi.

Turning to Lengok, I said in jest: "Well, Lengok, whom do you think those heads belonged to, Bajaus or Dusuns?" He went up to the basket, took out the skulls, and after turning them over for a minute in his hands replied: "These are Dusuns' heads, Tuan." "Oh, don't talk nonsense," said I. "How on earth can you tell what tribe they belong to?" "Well, you see, Tuan," said Lengok, "the Bajaus have got round heads, while the heads of Dusuns are a good deal longer." The old fellow had thus found out for himself that length and breadth of the skull were important characters in determining race, a conclusion which was only arrived at by anthropologists after long and serious study. His diagnosis was undoubtedly correct, as the Dusuns are dolichocephalic (long-headed) Indonesians, while the Bajaus are a Proto-Malayan and brachycephalic (short-headed) people.

The village of Kaung still has a head-house, but I was unfortunately never able to visit it, as on the couple of occasions when I was near the village the Tempassuk was so badly in flood as to be impassable, and I was unable to cross from the resting-hut which lies close to the bridle-path on the opposite bank of the stream. I, however, visited the village in 1915. There were then three head-houses, each containing two or more skulls; one of the huts had, however, fallen down. Mention is made by Burbidge of a "little flat-topped head-house at Kiau containing about fifty skulls," but though it may still exist, I have never seen it.

According to tales told by the natives, regular battles between village and village did occasionally occur in former days, but they were admitted to have done so very rarely. Except for his sneaking penchant for head-hunting, the Dusun is a man of peace, if not a coward; and, being a keen agriculturist, he dislikes war extremely, as it interferes with his chief pursuit. In head-hunting regular scores of heads were kept between villages which were at feud. For instance, if Kiau had got eight heads from Kaung, and Kaung only four heads from Kiau, it was "up to Kaung" to get at least an equal number, and, if possible, one or two more. If both villages wished to close the account, this could be done by the village which had taken most heads paying for the balance at a rate agreed upon by the elders of both parties.

This method of settling old feuds was a good deal used when the Tempassuk was brought under proper control by the Chartered Company, after the defeat and death of Mat Saleh, and when the subsequent operations against his lieutenants Kamunta and Langkap had been brought to a successful conclusion. It was in the final battle against Mat Saleh at Tambunan that the Tuaran Dusuns are said to have got most of the heads which can now be seen in their villages. At the time that the Government was preparing for the expedition which ran him to earth, the Tuaran Dusuns, who were terrified at the mere name of Mat Saleh, were very much against their will pressed into service as carriers.

After the battle, the Tuaran men, who by this time felt quite courageous, ran about with drawn *parangs*, cutting off the heads of the enemy who had been shot by the Sikh military police—whence these skulls. No doubt on their return to the bosom of their families the "warriors" represented themselves as being the conquerors of the much-dreaded Bajau leader. I heard a story that one of the men cut the top off a skull that he took, picked out the dried brains, and made it into a drinking-cup, but as he died very shortly afterwards it was thought that he had been killed by the dead man's spirit for his impiety, a skull taken in head-hunting being a thing which will bring good luck if propitiated and sacrificed to at regular intervals, but a very unlucky possession if not treated with due respect.

Dusun weapons of offence are largely procured from other tribes; indeed probably the majority of those found in the extreme north of Borneo have not been locally made, many of them being of Sulu type. The cutting weapons found among the Dusuns are the *pida* (or *barong*), a very broad-bladed knife which tapers to a sharp point and is capable of inflicting a most dreadful wound—I had a Dyak lance-corporal who had once had his face laid open from the bridge of the nose to the angle of the jaw with one of these weapons; the *pedang*, a sword with either a straight or cutlass form of blade and a cross-shaped handle; and the *parang ilang*, a sword with a blade narrow towards its handle and broad towards the point, with one side of the blade concave—that on the left when the sword is held back upwards—and the other convex. The peculiar form makes it necessary to give a sort of scooping cut in using it, which renders the *parang ilang* a very awkward sort of weapon in the hands of a tyro. Probably most of the *pedangs* found in North Borneo were made in Brunei. The weapon has a wide distribution and is largely used in the Malay Peninsula.

The type of hilt is said—I should think quite correctly—to have been derived from the swords used by the old Crusaders. Not only is the hilt in the shape of a cross, but the upper limb of the cross is converted into a small round chalice, which is, of course, entirely meaningless to the native. No doubt the *pedang* was introduced into the East Indies by Arab traders. The *parang ilang* itself is not so common in North Borneo as a variant of it which is often called the *gayang*: this is of similar shape, but the blade has not got convex and concave sides. The handles of both the *gayang* and the *parang ilang* are generally made from the base and brow-tine of a stag's antler, and are highly carved, but wood is occasionally used as a substitute.

The *gayang* is manufactured in one or two villages in the Tempassuk, the best specimens coming from Kiau. In this case I know that the smiths learnt how to make the weapon from a Dyak who was for a long time resident in the district. With regard to the much rougher specimens turned out in other villages, I am not quite certain if they are truly native products or not, but I rather suspect that they are copied from weapons seen in the hands of wandering Dyaks, though they differ from the Dyak type in several small particulars.

Apart from spears, the only stabbing weapon in use is the large sword-like dagger known as *sundang* or *serundang* to the Malays of the Peninsula, but locally called a *kris*, which can also be used for cutting. This, again, is, I believe, really a Sulu weapon: it may have either a waved or straight blade, and the hilt, which is made of wood, ivory, elephant or sperm-whale tooth is always cut to represent a perched bird. The true Malayan kris with a hilt in the shape of a squatting human figure is rarely seen in the Tempassuk, and has never been made locally.

Spears are manufactured in many Dusun villages, and are used both for fighting and hunting. An up-country Dusun, when going out to his rice-field, which is often some way from his house, almost invariably carries his spear with him, partly in case he may meet a pig on the way or in the crop, and partly, I think, because he has not yet forgotten the days when attacks used to be made by the gangs of head-hunters or Bajau ruffians from the coast. Spears are also useful as walking-sticks, and they are always used in this way by natives going on long journeys.

The Dusun shield is circular and is made either of wood or rattan cane. The wooden shield is made in one piece and may be either of hard or soft wood; the rattan shield is formed from a long piece of cane wound in a flat spiral form, the coils of the spiral being woven together with fine basket-work of the same material. Every shield has two hoops at the back, into which the left arm as far as the elbow is slipped when the shield is required for use.

One very curious specimen which I bought in the Tempassuk was a round hat made from a piece of light palm-wood; on the under side of this, and some distance from the brim, was a raised ring of wood which was for the purpose of fitting the hat to its wearer's head. This wooden rim was bored with two holes on either side, which communicated with one another. A separate string was passed through each couple, with the ends knotted together. When the hat was being worn, two short loops thus hung down on each side of the man's face, the idea being that, should the owner of the hat meet with any trouble in the course of his wanderings, he could snatch it off, run his left fore-arm through the loops and immediately be provided with an effective buckler.

The only other weapon which requires much notice is the blow-pipe. This instrument is not now used to any very great extent in either the Tuaran or Tempassuk districts, and is only, as a rule, to be found in up-country villages, though probably it was much commoner in former days. So much has been written about the Bornean blow-pipe and the methods by which it is manufactured that I do not think it worth while to go into the matter again here, as the Dusun blow-pipe, except in a few unimportant details, is exactly similar to that used by the Kenyah-Kayans and other tribes. It consists of a cylindrical tube of hard wood, while the muzzle end is fitted with a small wooden sight above and with a flat spear-blade attachment below, which is said to be of use in guiding the dart on leaving the muzzle, but can if necessity arises be also used as a weapon.

The short darts, of which the points are covered with *ipoh* poison, have a conical head made of pith, the upper or larger end of which closely fits the bore of the weapon. In discharging the dart from the blow-pipe the weapon is not held like a gun as might be expected, but is gripped with both hands close to the mouth-piece, the knuckles being upwards.

The dart-quiver is a bamboo box made from a large internode, with one of the adjoining nodes left untouched to form its bottom. It is usually covered with a cap made from the same or a similar bamboo, which consists of an unbroken node, with a few inches of an adjoining internode to form the sides. A slight shaving down of the outside of the quiver at the top allows for the fitting of the cap. The blow-pipe is at present used for hunting monkeys, though in former days it was largely used as a weapon of offence.

Mention may be made here of the working-knife, which is carried by every native. This is worn on the left side of the body, being attached by two cords around the waist which are fastened by a loop and toggle. Though the *parang* is not primarily intended for a weapon, it is very often put to this use, and is generally kept in a state of razor-like sharpness.

Before bringing this chapter to an end I must make mention of Dusun war coats and helmets. The former are

A DUSUN MAN OF TAMBATUAN IN WAR DRESS.

He wears a thick coat of closely-woven fibre, which is fringed at the bottom and trimmed with cowrie shells. The round shield is made of wood, and the sword, suspended rom a cowrie-covered bandolier, has a tail of human hair inserted in the pommel.

A HEAD-HOUSE AT KAUNG "ULU," TEMPASSUK DISTRICT.

The basket which the man has removed from the little house, or hut, contains several human shulls and also some of the Orang-utan. When a man was wounded in a fight, but his head not secured, the Kaung people added an ape's skull to the basket as a substitute for the man's.

very thick and heavy and act as a protection against sword-cuts. They are fringed at their lower edges and sometimes are decorated with cowrie shells. The material of which they are made is *lamba* fibre. Of the helmets, I have only seen two specimens; one of these, which was ornamented with cowrie shells, had a brim, the other not. They were rough, but, I should think, fairly serviceable in native warfare.

THE BAJAUS & ILLANUNS

CHAPTER XX

RACES OF THE TUARAN & TEMPASSUK DISTRICTS

THE Bajaus resemble the Dusuns in speaking a language belonging to the Malayo-Polynesian group, but are racially nearly allied to the Malays proper, while the Dusuns, if they are related at all, are only distantly so. Scientifically speaking, the Bajaus are Proto-Malays, but this practically only means that they are an early evolved Malay people. They have, I believe, the rounded skull of the Malay, and they also conform to type in other respects, though their features are more roughly cut than those of the Peninsular or Sumatran Malay. These remarks apply equally well to the Illanuns, except that they are, perhaps, a better-looking people. These two peoples dwell, as has been already remarked, on the sea-board and lower river reaches. In religion they are lax Mohammedans, but their customs are slightly different; yet, owing to their being of the same faith and of very similar habits, they may be conveniently described together. In personal appearance, dress and character they are almost identical, while it is generally impossible for a European to distinguish between members of the two tribes. A native, of course, can do so, but then he would listen to see which of them were talking Illanun and which Bajau; besides this, he would probably be able to make a fairly good guess by taking into account small differences of facial type or of dress—such as the tying of the head-cloth—which a European would not notice.

The Bajau man is rather a dark-skinned person of low stature. His cheek-bones are fairly high and his eyes small, hard and bright. St John says in speaking of the tribe: "No one can accuse the Bajaus of being a handsome race; they have generally pinched-up, small faces, low foreheads, but bright eyes. . . . I never saw a good-looking face among them, judging even by a Malay standard"; and this description is, on the whole, not unfair.

In character the Bajau is a lazy spendthrift, a liar, a cheat, a thief, a wheedler, a blusterer and a swaggerer. Some Europeans have the same idea about the Bajaus that the Western American is said to entertain with regard to Red Indians—"the only good Injuns is dead 'uns"; but still the Bajaus have some redeeming features, which are not without their appeal to me. Firstly, the Bajau is above all things a sportsman: organise a deer-drive, a pony- or a buffalo-race, and the usually lazy Bajau becomes a different person. I do not think that the Bajau's love of hunting is by any means to be solely ascribed to the desire for meat, or that of racing to the wish to win a wager. No doubt both these matters add to the zest with which he pursues the sport, but sport he loves for sport's sake. Excitement of any kind is the Bajau's delight, and excitement he must have. Piracy, raiding and burning Chinese shops, which is the Bajau's idea of the highest kind of pleasure, gambling, buffalo- or pony-racing, cattle-thieving, cock-fighting or hunting—all these are, or used to be, indulged in with the greatest ardour.

Like the Malay, the Bajau is incapable of properly performing work which requires long and continuous effort; but if he can be interested in a task he will work at it well so long as the interest lasts. The Bajaus, having been undisciplined free-booters and rovers for many generations, did not take kindly to the rule of the Chartered Company, under which they were forced to give up their amusements of this kind. The consequence was that both they and the Illanuns, having found a leader in the so-called rebel, Mat Saleh, proceeded to resist the threatened restraint of the Company's rule to the best of their ability; but the Mat Saleh "rebellion" was the only serious trouble which the Chartered Company have had with the natives from the time that they first began to tighten their hold on the country.

Piracy and pillage having been now suppressed, the Bajau has to make shift to content himself with such amusements as remain to him. Buffalo-thieving is still a popular amusement, while gambling, cock-fighting, and horse- and buffalo-racing receive their fair share of attention. To these relaxations many Bajaus have now added the sometimes profitable pursuit of trying to extract advances from estate managers pretending that they are going to recruit labourers and give them advances. With money so obtained a Bajau generally retires to a gambling shop, and has a splendid time until the day of reckoning arrives.

The character of the Illanuns is somewhat similar to that of the Bajaus, "only more so." The Bajau is a truculent swaggerer; the Illanun can outdo him at his own game. The Bajau is a braggart, a liar, a spendthrift and a gambler; the Illanun is a bigger one. The Illanun's chief idea of pleasure is to swagger about in fine clothes and do no work, unless an occasional piracy or inland raid can be so described.

In the days of old the Illanun pirates must at any rate have been fine seamen, for their name was feared throughout the Archipelago, and even around the coasts of the Malay Peninsula. They still cling to the memory of their former prowess, and show their fancied superiority in their independent bearing and truculent demeanour. The best that can be said for them is that, though their deeds are evil, they are gentlemanly rascals. Their worst actions are often partly redeemed by some humorous touch or plausible excuse, which makes one want to laugh even when extremely angry.

The Illanuns are a rather better-looking people than the Bajaus, though they certainly cannot be called handsome.

Mongolian characteristics are, I think, more developed among the chiefs than among the common people. The aristocratic type of face is rather long and thin, with fairly high cheek-bones, light, yellowish skin, a somewhat delicate nose, and long almond eyes set at a considerable angle from the horizontal. St John's description of the Illanun Raja Muda would answer well for one of the chiefs of that tribe with whom I was acquainted. He says: "The Raja Muda, the Illanun chief, came on board and was very civil. He is a handsome-looking, manly fellow and extremely polite. From what I have heard and seen he is a type of his countrymen —a different race from the Bajau: a slight figure, more regular features than the Malays, a quiet, observant eye; he wore a delicate moustache." This description of an Illanun noble is good, but I am not sure that it would answer for the Illanuns in general.

As I have remarked in an earlier chapter, the Illanuns are comparatively recent arrivals from Mindanao in the Philippines. The Bajaus, though older settlers along the north-west coast, appear to be also invaders, and according to Dusun legendry first came in trading prahus from the direction of Kudat. Some of the Bajaus claim that their ancestors came originally from Johore.

Both tribes are nominally Mohammedan, but are not fanatical; indeed they are very lax in the observance of matters of ritual. Owing to the two tribes being of the same religion, a considerable amount of inter-marriage takes place, and possibly the fate of the Illanuns, who are comparatively few in numbers, will be absorption into the preponderating mass of the Bajaus. The Illanun villages in the Tempassuk district, which only number about seven all told, are situated some near Fort Alfred, not far from the mouth of the Tempassuk river, and some around and beyond Pindasan, formerly the great stronghold of Illanun pirates.

The women of both tribes are allowed a degree of liberty almost equal to that of their Dusun sisters. They do not veil themselves except at festivals, not even wearing a scarf over the head as does the Malay woman—the scarf being used to veil the face whenever the wearer has a fit of modesty. Bajau and Illanun women frequent all the low-land markets and prove themselves excellent saleswomen of fish, fruit, native-made cloth, betel nut, *sireh*, lime, etc. They even join in dances with the men, and respectable women will play musical instruments before mixed company.

The ladies are usually anything but beautiful, and are rendered even less attractive than necessary by their unlovely methods of dressing their hair and the clumsy fashion of their dress. In addition, a large quid of *sireh* stuffed into one cheek or partly protruding from the mouth, with trickles of blood-red saliva running down the chin, scarcely adds to the charms of even the most attractive face.

The character of the Bajau and Illanun women is, however, I believe, a good deal higher than that of their menkind. Scandals are comparatively rare, though considerable liberty, if not licence, is allowed to widows and divorced women. Prostitution is unknown.

Both Bajau and Illanun women are expert cloth weavers, and those of the latter tribe often support their menkind in idleness by selling the products of their looms.

Unfortunately nearly all the money on which either a Bajau or an Illanun man manages to lay his hands is lost in his favourite pursuit of gambling. Probably in the old days, when native gambled with native, the effect was not so bad as it is at present. For though losses and gains no doubt had an unsettling effect, the money or valuables at any rate remained in the tribe. Since the Chartered Company's rule has been established, however, the monopolies for liquor-selling, pawnbroking and gambling have been put up for auction to the highest bidder. The farmer, invariably a Chinaman, has shops in every place of the least importance, and into them he put his agents or sub-lessees. In each shop there are two doors opening in the frontage, one giving entrance to the gambling-room, the other to the shop proper, where pledges are taken, liquor sold and, in out-stations, a considerable business done in general goods.

At Kotabelud the gambling shop used to be crowded all day long by a crowd of lazy Bajaus apparently engaged in ridding themselves of all the property in their possession in an attempt to make money without exertion. When a man had been "cleaned out" of all his ready money he would return next day with some family heirloom, a dagger with an ivory hilt, a fine old brass betel-box or a silver ornament, and pledge his property in the pawnshop, so conveniently under the same roof with the gambling establishment. With the money thus obtained he would again tempt fortune, probably with no better luck than he had experienced on the day before. Even then his appetite for gambling would remain unsatisfied, and frequently Bajaus gamble till they have stripped themselves and their houses of every scrap of valuable property.

The very best of the pledged articles comparatively seldom find their way to the shelf kept for unredeemed pledges, as the Bajau or Illanun owner manages to keep paying interest on his most treasured heirlooms, but they are frequently left in pawn for long periods, and if redeemed find their way back to the pawnshop almost at once. To do the pawnshop-keepers justice, they are usually fairly good to the natives, and do not declare their goods forfeit even after the legal period has expired without payment of interest, being willing to allow old customers time to scrape together the necessary money to renew the ticket.

The chief harm done to the coastal people by the licensed gambling shops is not so much that the Bajaus and Illanuns are encouraged to gamble—they would do that anyhow—but that all their wealth is passing into the hands of another people—the Chinese. The Government of the Federated Malay States has recently closed all the gambling shops in the states of the Federation, but some few years ago, when they were allowed, it very properly forbade Malays to stake any money in them.

A Chartered Company which has to try and earn dividends for its shareholders and controls a poor country cannot, however, afford to be quite so nice in these matters as the Government of a rich country like the Federated Malay States, though I should scarcely say that this was an argument in favour of the continued existence of chartered companies in general. What the fate of the Bajaus will be in the future it is difficult to say, but though they are economically an almost useless people, I am inclined to think that they will continue to exist, if only because they are such rascals. In most cases it seems to be the simple and inoffensive tribes and races who are crushed out in the struggle for existence, while nobody can accuse the Bajaus of being either one or the other. The Illanuns will, as I have remarked above, probably become absorbed by the Bajaus, owing to their small numbers, common religion and similarity of customs and methods of living. Even at the present day there are many natives who have a Bajau father and an Illanun mother, or *vice versa*.

Drying Padi in a Dusun Village.

The round trays, ordinarily used for winnowing, contain the grain, which is being dried. The old woman sitting on the boulder has a stick beside her with which to drive away the fowls.

CHAPTER XXI

AGRICULTURE, HUNTING & FISHING

THE Bajau man is but a poor agriculturist. There is nothing intrinsically wrong with his methods, but to him agriculture seems to be a comparatively modern development, to which he has not taken very kindly. It is seldom that enough rice is planted to last the family till the next harvest, and through his indifference and laziness he is often late in ploughing the land and setting out the young seedlings. Since all the Bajau villages are in the lowland districts, they chiefly plant wet padi, but a little dry padi is also grown on land which it is difficult to irrigate. Their methods are similar to those already described for the Dusuns, but less ingenuity is usually shown in irrigating the soil. Each group of fields is surrounded by a strong bamboo or wooden fence in order to keep out wandering buffaloes and cattle.

Near harvest-time, when flocks of small birds collect to feed on the ripening grain, scarers similar to those used by the Dusuns are erected, and also windmills on tripods of tall bamboos, the bamboo "sails" of which make a creaking and a humming noise as they revolve. From the back of the sails, at the centre, there usually projects a long tail, made, I believe, from a leaf of the coco-nut palm, the pinnæ of the leaf hanging downwards. The tail is supported by a cord attached at one end to the top of the windmill frame and at the other to the leaf at a distance of about three-quarters of its length, so that the inner portion is slightly raised from the horizontal, while the tip falls downwards. The vibration caused by the sails makes the tail quiver and jerk, and adds greatly to the effectiveness of the windmill as a bird-scarer.

When the land is lying fallow, buffaloes are turned loose in the fields and help to manure the ground to a certain extent.

A considerable amount of sugar-cane is planted, and both Illanuns and Bajaus make rough sugar-mills which are worked by a buffalo, which walks round and round in a circle, yoked under a movable horizontal beam which operates two vertical rollers. These interlock at the top and base with rudely cut worm-gear. The lengths of cane are thrust between the rollers and the expressed juice runs down and percolates, through a strainer of sheet bamboo, into a receptacle below. The juice is taken from this and cooked in large iron pans until it attains the consistency of thick molasses, when it is ready for use.

Of late years some Bajaus in the neighbourhood of Kotabelud have taken to growing a considerable acreage of ground-nuts, having, I believe, learnt how to do this from a few Javanese settlers who first started planting them. The crop appears to pay well, and there seems to be a possibility that more land may be utilised for this purpose in the future. Indian corn is planted to a small extent, as are also certain vegetables, chiefly French beans, cucumbers and brinjals. Coco-nut palms, which bear well, and fruit trees, such as belunoes, mangoes, memplums, pawpaws, limes, langsats and bananas, grow round most villages, but receive little attention.

Large herds of cattle and buffaloes roam the plains and marshlands between Kotabelud and Pindasan, but no sort of attempt is made at mating or breeding suitable animals, and the herds are to all intents and purposes wild, except that every animal has an owner. Young animals are ridden down on ponies, caught with nooses and marked by nicking the ear, or ears, each man having his own particular sign. Cattle-catching affords an opportunity for a very fine display of horsemanship, and shows the Bajaus at their best, for they are, above everything, fine riders.

When an animal is required for riding, one is selected from the herd, and a professional cattle-catcher is given the task of catching it and breaking it in. If the animal is sold, the breaker-in, according to custom, receives half the value it fetches. Young bulls which are to be trained for riding are tamed by being fastened up in the village with their necks in a wooden pillory, consisting essentially of a couple of posts, which allows fairly free movement of the head vertically, but very little sideways. The same kind of wooden saddle is used by the Bajaus as by the Dusuns. A switch of three or four small rattans bound together at the handle-end is used by both Dusun and Bajau riders.

Epidemics of cattle-sickness, possibly rinderpest, occur occasionally, but I have never known one to attain very serious dimensions, though I have had to isolate infected villages once or twice. A few goats are kept in some villages and quite large animals can be purchased for a couple of dollars or so.

In the Bajau villages of the coast and of the river estuaries fishing supplants padi-planting as the chief industry, and an excellent supply of fish of all kinds is to be had for the taking. The usual methods of catching sea-fish are by small stake-traps (*bĕlat*), lines, seine-nets, casting-nets and fish-spears.

Bĕlat are light stake-traps usually set close to the shore in the shallow water of estuaries, many of them being left dry at low tide. They consist of wallings of bamboo (?) laths strung together and attached to short poles driven into the mud.

The casting-net is very similar to that used in the Fen counties of England for catching live-baits for pike-fishing. It consists of a bell-shaped net weighted round the edge with a chain of lead or tin and having a cord attached in the centre which ends in a loop. In using it the fisherman slips this loop over his left hand, and draping his right shoulder and arm with a part of the net gathers up the rest of it in orderly folds, partly into his left hand, partly into his right.

In casting the arms are held almost horizontally, and bent so that both hands are close together, the left being slightly lower than the right; both arms are then swung quickly to the left in a horizontal direction, the body following them with its weight thrown on the left foot. The part of the net held in the hands is released and the arms are dropped slightly. The net flies out, and falls on the water in a perfect circle, but still remains attached to the fisherman's left hand by the cord from its centre. The chain round the edge sinks quickly, enclosing the fish within the net, and if these are only of small size the net can be withdrawn slowly from the water with the catch in it, for the fish are prevented from escaping by the drawing together of the heavily weighted net edges.

Large skates are often speared with a barbed fish-spear consisting of an iron head, shafted with bamboo or wood, the fish being visible at the bottom as the fisherman's light dug-out canoe glides over the clear water of the shallows.

One kind of small fish much resembling the European white-bait, which is called in Malay *ikan bilis*, is a favourite delicacy among the Dusuns, and up-country natives come in numbers to the coastal markets to purchase these fish from the Bajaus at the season when they visit the shores. King-crabs (*Limulus*) are frequently on sale in the markets, and are sought after for their eggs.

A good variety of fresh and dried fish, molluscs—chiefly kinds of clams and cockles—crabs and prawns are always on sale, while turtles' eggs are not uncommonly seen. The last-named are dug out of the sandy beaches where the turtles lay them. "Giant clams" (*Tridacna*) of fair size are found among the coral reefs in clear water and are eaten by the Bajaus, but as I do not remember having seen them brought to market, probably they are not considered sufficiently good eating to be saleable.

Shells producing mother-of-pearl are obtained in small quantities, and fetch a very fair price when sold to the local Chinese traders, but among them there are usually very few specimens of the pearl oyster (*Meleagrina margaritifera*), the majority of the shells being those of species of *Trochus* (*Trochus niloticus*) and *Senectus* (*Senectus argyrostoma*). These shells are collected more by the Orang Bernadan (Tawi Tawi Islanders), who visit the coasts, than by the local Bajaus. Quite large pearls are often found in the shells of *Tridacna*, and I brought one back from Borneo which is almost as large as a sparrow's egg; but they possess little beauty, being merely white and shiny, so that they are, I believe, almost worthless, except as curiosities. It is of those pearls that the wonderful stories of breeding small ones are told by the peoples of the Malayan region, it being often asserted that if one of them is placed in a small box together with some grains of rice, after a time the mother-of-pearl will be found to have produced young, while the rice grains will have been broken at the ends as if they had been nibbled by mice.

The Bajau regards agricultural pursuits and the trade of fisherman—especially the former—as necessary evils to be endured with stoicism, but it only requires the magic word hunting to be whispered to rouse him to a state of wild enthusiasm. Whatever may be his sins of omission and commission, and they are many, he is certainly a sportsman, and takes part enthusiastically in hunting, horse-racing and other sports. It is this quality which, in spite of his otherwise more or less undesirable character, finds him a warm corner in the hearts of many Englishmen, and makes them cherish a sneaking regard for him of which they are half ashamed.

To see a Bajau mounted on his sturdy little pony, and armed with a throwing-spear, galloping over the most breakneck country in pursuit of a muntjac, locally sometimes called the Bornean roe-deer, is a sight not easily forgotten.

This style of hunting is fairly frequently practised on and around the grassy and scrubby foot-hills near Kotabelud. Though not numerous in such open country, an odd deer or two of this species can generally be found in the folds of the hills wherever there is scrubby cover, and especially where a small stream of water is shut in by clumps of trees and bushes.

Probably at a remote date all these foot-hills were forest-covered, but felling for clearings and continual fires, both intentional and accidental, have now, in the lower reaches of the Tempassuk, driven back the forests from the foot-hills, while virgin jungle is only found on the mountains which tower above them. The lofty forest trees which once occupied this area are now replaced by the very coarse and persistent grass known as *lalang*, bushes of the so-called Straits rhododendron (*Polyanthema melastomum*), and other shrubs—indeed, except near springs and water-courses, it seems doubtful whether the trees could ever assert themselves again even should fires be prevented.

Some of the destruction of timber must, I imagine, have been fairly recent, as several old men of the Dusun village of Bengkahak, which lies in the foot-hill region between Kotabelud and Pindasan, were agreed that the forests had retreated considerably since their youth. I imagine the constant grass-fires which the Dusuns light in the dry season are partly responsible for this, as no doubt they sometimes reach and attack the edges of the forest zone. Clearings for hill-padi planting had, and have, also a great deal to do with the denudation of the forests, but much less in the foot-hills bordering the plains of the coastal districts than up the valley of the Tempassuk, though here, when a clearing is abandoned, a secondary forest growth, chiefly of soft-wooded trees, rapidly springs up again. The *lalang*-grass, as remarked before, is periodically fired, chiefly, I believe, with the view of affording fresh pasturage to the herds of cattle, which obtain more nutriment from the fresh young grass-blades than they could from the old and wiry leaves; but the fires also serve to clear the country of the tall grass which makes travelling uncomfortable off the beaten tracks, and to destroy the refuges of poisonous snakes, especially cobras.

But to return to the Bajaus. A hunter is almost invariably followed by one or more mangy and starved curs, his hunting dogs, and in spite of neglect and ill treatment these are often marvellously clever at driving out the game. Guns being rare among the Bajaus, they are exceedingly keen on joining a European, as hunting on horse or on foot, armed only with a throwing-spear, though an exciting sport, does not invariably result in a kill.

One common method of hunting is to surround a couple of sides of a projecting and roughly triangular strip of jungle with hunters on horse and foot, and to put in a line of beaters, accompanied by dogs, at the base of the strip where it joins the main body of the forest. The beaters work down towards the apex and drive the game before them, timely notice of the starting of a deer being afforded by their curs, which give tongue freely. According to native custom, the actual slayer of the animal is entitled to certain tit-bits: his claim being satisfied, the rest of the hunters set to work in a mob, slashing away the skin and meat with their knives as if for dear life, and in a marvellously short time little remains but the larger bones, from which the meat has been cut away. For once in a way the wretched curs eat their fill on the scraps, and then the hunters make their way homeward laden with the spoil.

Nominally a Mohammedan should not touch the meat unless a prayer is said and the animal's, or bird's, throat cut while it is still alive; but a few muscular twitches would be considered a sign of life, and I have heard of natives saying that when shooting it is only necessary to say "*Bismillah*" to sanctify the flesh for their use, thus avoiding the necessity for throwing away game which has died immediately on receiving the charge.

When a cow is killed for the feast the Bajaus can sometimes scarcely restrain their impatience until the wretched animal has gasped out its last breath, and I have seen lumps of flesh hacked from the bones and thrown into a heap which still twitched and quivered for some seconds after they had been severed from the carcass.

Snares and traps very similar to those made by the Dusuns are also used among the Bajaus for trapping game. Guns are now almost unknown in their hands, as since the Mat Saleh and Kamunta troubles the British North Borneo Government has absolutely prevented any natives, with the exception of a few favoured chiefs, from obtaining weapons of precision, while they were deprived of those they possessed when the rising was put down and the country brought properly under control.

CHAPTER XXII

DRESS, DOMESTIC AFFAIRS & GOVERNMENT

BEING by nature a somewhat truculent and swaggering scoundrel, the Bajau or Illanun is by way of feeling that his clothes should give some indication of his sentiments towards the rest of the world. The young men especially like to add to the boldness of their appearance by wearing brightly coloured head-cloths, stiffened with rice-starch, and so tied that two or three peaks stand out abruptly from the head. Gaily coloured trousers of narrow-striped native cloth are also to be seen, which are baggy around the waist and as far as the knee, but very close-fitting in the calf, while long enough partly to cover the instep. This kind of garment, which is without buttons, is, I believe, of a type much worn in the Sulu Islands. It is secured under the belt by folding over a portion of the baggy top.

A bright-hued scarf, often made of two long strips of differently coloured cloths, is thrown negligently over one shoulder, and is used as a handkerchief, or for carrying small articles. The full dress of young Bajau men is the tightly fitting short jacket with embroidered facings and two rows of silver buttons, the native-woven head-cloth and *saputangan* (around the waist), the short and baggy blue or black trousers, and the loose cloth worn over one shoulder.

The elder men do not sport the bright colours in favour among the young bloods. Their usual dress is a pair of loose Chinese-pattern trousers, often of black or dark blue cloth, or of white calico, and a rather short coat of the same material, which fits somewhat tightly in the arms and around the chest, but is cut loosely below.

European singlets have of recent years come very much into fashion among the natives, and are often worn without a coat. The head-cloths of the older men are also usually darker in colour than those of bachelors. Cheap foreign-made belts are now in very general use, while the cloth which is frequently worn over the shoulder, or a handkerchief (*saputangan*) of native manufacture, wound round the waist above the belt, contains the brass betel-nut box which a native man invariably carries.

Personal jewellery worn by men consists of silver rings, often of striking, though somewhat crude, design, set with cornelians, rock crystals, or glass, and sometimes with what I believe are natural crystals of iron pyrites. Coco-nut pearls and those from the giant clam (*Tridacna*) are also mounted in rings, as well as bezoar stones, reputed to have the property of absorbing the poison from snake-bites and scorpion-stings. Hanging silver tobacco-boxes, shaped like a watch, and possibly really derived from the old fat Dutch watches, are rare, but are still sometimes worn, being attached to the belt by a chain. Shell-bracelets, the manufacture of which I have described elsewhere, are affected by both men and women, and bracelets of silver also adorn the arms of both sexes.

I learned, on the authority of a Bajau named Si Ungin or Sungin, that in the days of yore long hair was commonly worn by Bajau men, at any rate until they married, but it is now exceptional to see a man with long hair in the Tempassuk or Tuaran districts, and I can only recollect once having done so. This was on the Sulaman Inlet, the man in question being one of my boat's crew.

Bajau men are seldom handsome, and the same can usually be said of their women, but what looks the women *do* possess are spoiled by their fashions in clothes and hair-dressing. Except, perhaps, on feast days, when clothes of bright colours are worn, it would not be far wrong to say that Bajau and Illanun women always look untidy. This impression is given by the loose, shapeless and generally sombre-coloured clothes which they wear, and the unbeautiful way they have of drawing their hair tightly back from the front of their head, tying it in a sort of knot behind, and leaving a ragged-looking tail depending from the knotted or coiled mass.

The everyday garments of the Bajau women of the Tempassuk are a sort of bottomless sack of some sad-coloured cloth reaching from under the arms—it is rolled up and tucked in tightly over the breasts—almost to the feet, and a pair of loose under-trousers, gathered in just above the ankles. The bottoms of these can be seen when the *sarong* is held up, or rolled upwards for walking. In the Tuaran district the sack is worn without the trousers.

The freedom granted to the women is remarkable considering that the Bajaus and Illanuns are Mohammedans, though this is probably partly due to the unorthodox behaviour of their menkind, and their lack of knowledge of Mohammedan custom. The women are even more untrammelled in their liberty than their sisters of the Malay Peninsula. They seldom, except on high days and holidays, wear any cloth which can be used to veil the face, and respectable women dance with men before a crowd of onlookers. I believe, however, in spite of the freedom which they enjoy, their morals compare very favourably with those of other Mohammedan women, who are more closely guarded.

Native-woven cloths are seldom worn by the women. The articles made in native fabrics are men's head-cloths, handkerchiefs, cloth for coats and trousers, together with garments called *kain ampik* and *kain moga*, which are of thick material and in the form of the Malay *sarong*, though they are used, not as the Malay garment generally is, as a covering for the body between the waist and the ankles by day or night, but as wrappers for the whole body either at night or during chilly weather.

Gold ornaments are seldom worn by Bajau or Illanun

women, since neither tribe is by any means rich, and wives are kept in a state of poverty by the laziness and gambling habits of the husbands. Round ear-studs, usually of silver, more rarely of gold, are worn by unmarried girls, and these are often remarkably pretty examples of goldsmiths' work. Many of the old silver ornaments, *sireh* and tobacco boxes and other articles, are of very fine design, and are, I believe, the work of Illanun silversmiths, who at one time established quite a reputation for themselves. Some of the old articles, which can even now be occasionally picked up by a collector, were, however, almost certainly made in Brunei.

Nowadays the Chinese silversmith is finding his way into the out-stations and is beginning, or in many cases has already managed, to shoulder out the native craftsman, who is unable to compete with a specialist. Some silver-work still finds its way from Brunei to the Tempassuk by the hands of Malay traders, but the specimens are usually trumpery in the extreme, the workmanship being rough, the patterns degenerate and the silver of paper-like thinness. The modern silver articles which I have seen brought for sale by Brunei Malays were small, hollow silver buttons in the form of a flower bud, and the somewhat coronet-like head ornaments worn by brides.

In addition to the head-cloths which I have mentioned above, Bajau and Illanun men, and sometimes women, when on a journey or working in the fields, wear large sun-hats, which they obtain from the Dusuns of the interior. I fancy that one type of hat used by the Mengkabong Bajaus is made by themselves. To these they frequently attach a chin-cord of twisted yellow and red wool, the material for which is obtained from the Chinese shops.

Perhaps the working-knife should be mentioned as part of the native outfit, since, when he leaves his house, every native, Bajau, Illanun or Dusun, almost invariably girds himself with one of these useful weapons. The knife, in its wooden sheath, is worn on the left side of the body, being attached to waist-cords fastened in front by means of a toggle, a Chinese cash or a Sarawak coin generally fulfilling this purpose, or more rarely a disc cut from a *Trochus* shell. The uses to which the *parang* is put are various indeed, among them being clearing away weeds and undergrowth, cutting firewood, opening coco-nuts, cutting up deer or cattle for food purposes, and preparing materials for house-building, while, if necessary, it becomes a weapon of defence or offence.

Bajau villages may be built on land, over the water of some estuary or salt-water inlet, or on the sea-shore, either above or below high-tide mark. All the Illanun villages that I have seen have been built on land. In any case the dwellings of both peoples, like those of the Dusuns, are raised on posts. Bajau or Illanun houses are never of the communal type. Much of the household refuse is thrown down through a hole in the floor, this being quite a sanitary method of disposing of it if the house is over the water or on the shore below high-tide mark, but by no means so on land.

In spite, or perhaps because, of the absence of pigs, those scavengers of Dusun villages, Mohammedan (Bajau or Illanun) villages are usually a good deal cleaner than those of the pagans. Nor do I think, though it breeds disease-carrying flies, is the accumulated refuse directly responsible for sickness among the villagers, since there is always a current of air under the house.

A Bajau village is generally situated in a coco-nut grove, where the trees belong to various owners. Scattered about, too, are other fruit trees, such as mangoes and *bĕlunoes*. The rice-fields will probably be just outside the grove of trees which shelters the village, and here, after the harvest, the buffaloes roam about or wallow in the deep mud-filled excavations that they make for themselves.

The houses of the village are walled and roofed with palm-leaf attaps, and before some of the larger dwellings is a platform—reached by a ladder from the ground—on which clothes are dried and various household work is performed. Male visitors to the house ride up to the steps, dismount and, before entering, tie their buffaloes, bulls or ponies to one of the posts supporting the platform. A Bajau house usually consists of a single room with perhaps a cook-house built out behind. A passage or gangway leads from the door, which is near one corner, to the opposite end of the building, the rest of the room being slightly raised above the level of this to form a sort of sitting and sleeping dais.

Here is stored the family property, boxes containing clothes, brassware (trays, *sireh* boxes, gongs, etc.), and here also are placed the sleeping-mats and pillows, covered in with mosquito nets suspended from some of the cross-beams. In the houses of well-to-do men the top of the mosquito curtains are sometimes ornamented with patchwork hangings. The blending of colours in these is often quite pleasing, not at all like the horrible patchwork articles so often seen at home.

Brightly coloured dish-covers made of strips of pandanus-leaf are placed over plates of cakes or other food set aside on the dais, and perhaps some old brass cannons will be seen tied up or supported against one wall of the house, cannon in the old days having passed as legal tender, so that the possession of a number of them indicated that their owner was a man of wealth. A kris, a *pida* or some other native weapon will very likely be hanging up against a post of the house, and some of the women will be occupied in weaving on their rather primitive looms the brightly coloured waist- or head-cloths, for the manufacture of which the Bajaus and Illanuns of the Tempassuk are held in such high repute.

The houses of the poorer peasants are often small and wretched in the extreme, especially in the villages built over inlets of the sea, such as the Sulaman or Mengkabong. The type of house I have been so far describing is that of a native chief, or of a man in easy circumstances; such a dwelling sometimes has a small upper room close under the thatch. Here the girls of the family sleep, and during the day-time occupy themselves in weaving cloths.

The flooring of Bajau houses is made of sheet-bamboo, that of the outside platform—if there is one—of slats of *nibong* palm wood; the thatch and walls are of palm-leaves, those of the *nipa* or the sago palm being generally used. Two or three small windows illuminate the building, and are closed at night by wooden flaps or shutters hinged with rattan bindings to the upper part of the window frame.

Villages of any importance possess a mosque; though, except for the fact that the walling does not reach the thatch, but is only carried half-way up, this does not usually differ much in external appearance from an ordinary house.

The Bajau or Illanun villages are not so full of animal life as those of the Dusuns, particularly those of the up-country people, where grazing ground is limited, and buffaloes and cattle make their way into the villages and even under the houses. The Bajau's cattle, unless they are trained animals, will be found among the herds which roam around the bases of the foot-hills or on the grass plains of the Krah. The absence of pigs, which I have remarked above, also detracts from the liveliness of Mohammedan villages, and numerous pariah dogs exist—I was going to say are kept—and on moonlight nights give themselves up to the congenial employment of baying the moon. No more mournful sound can be imagined than this chorus of curs all yowling together upon the same note, and natives believe that when the dogs thus "break forth into song" it presages the death of some inhabitant of the village.

Some fowls are reared by most villagers, but they are not usually so numerous as in Dusun villages. A few goats crop the grass around the houses, and these, with some half-starved cats with short tails bent round almost at right angles a few inches from the tip—a variety peculiar to the Malay region—complete the animal population.

In the villages built over the waters of estuaries or inlets of the sea the small dug-out canoe or *gobang* replaces the buffalo or pony as a means of conveyance from place to place, and the visitor to a house ties up his canoe to a post just as a man on land does his buffalo. Owing to the position of their settlements, the Bajaus of these villages, as is only natural, look to the sea and to the brackish water of the inlets to provide them with a living rather than to the land, though many of them have a few rice-fields.

Their chief occupations are, therefore, fishing, salt-making and the cutting of *nipa*-palm leaves for use as attaps to thatch and wall their houses. Where fishing is undertaken on a large scale, boats of fair size (*pakerangan* or *perahu lembu*) and seine nets are used, and the greater part of the catch is preserved by drying it in the sun. A good deal of this dried fish finds its way to market, where it is sold or bartered to the Dusuns. Where less wholesale methods are employed, the fish are either consumed at home or sold fresh to the Chinese shopkeepers or to other natives.

Though making pretty pictures in photographs, especially in the case of Mengkabong, where the houses are not arranged in a regular line, these villages built over the water prove on close inspection to be assemblages of most crazy and dilapidated hovels. Still, here and there may be seen a larger and better-built house, denoting that it is the dwelling of some more prosperous native.

The Mohammedan natives have a great deal scantier menu than the pagans, since their religion forbids them to eat pork; and such game as snakes, rats, squirrels, monitor-lizards, monkeys and other Dusun delicacies are also tabu to them. On the occasion of a marriage or other ceremony, or at a religious festival, a buffalo or an ox may be killed, otherwise the natives seldom eat meat, unless they can hunt down a deer or a muntjac. Excellent fish is obtained on the sea-coast, and the river fish are also quite eatable, so the Bajaus and Illanuns probably do not feel the lack of meat; but they are very keen about it if they can get it for nothing, either by hunting or by attending some feast. Rice forms the staple article of diet, eked out with a little fish, some salt, chillies, and possibly a few spices.

Cookery is most primitive, but the women know how to make a few kinds of cakes. Coco-nut oil, generally made by boiling the kernels in water and collecting the oil which rises to the surface, is used for frying sweets, in native medicines, and also for dressing the hair. Cane-sugar, or rather molasses, is used for sweetening in native cookery; this is obtained by pressing the fresh canes between two upright rollers in a mill worked by a buffalo and boiling down the resulting liquid. Coarse salt is also made locally, and I have described the processes of manufacture elsewhere.

Nowadays life in a Bajau or Illanun village is very humdrum compared with what it must have been formerly, for since the young bloods are no longer at liberty to go on plundering expeditions, which provided them both with excitement and a livelihood, they are reduced by necessity to the unpleasant task of having to do a little work in order to live. The monotony of their lives, however, is somewhat brightened by visits to the gambling farm, an occasional hunting or racing party, cock-fighting, or perhaps a small buffalo-stealing expedition. Their natural dislike for work makes them but indifferent agriculturists, but they are much better fishermen, partly because they are essentially a maritime people, partly, I believe, because fishing, with its uncertainty, contains some elements of sport and excitement.

A fair number of Bajaus make a little money by transporting on buffaloes goods for the Chinese shopkeepers, the main traffic of this kind being to and from Usakan Bay, the fortnightly calling-place of the local steamer. Many young men from the Tempassuk, attracted by the prospects of handling ready money and change of scene, go to work on rubber estates at Beaufort or elsewhere, and often do not return for several years.

Crime in the Mohammedan villages is not serious, except in regard to buffalo-stealing. Most of the cases coming to court are trivial cases of cheating and petty stealing. While I was at Kotabelud there were some rather ingenious thefts committed from the Chinese shops, by means of a long and slender rattan cane to which a few thorns were left adhering near one end. An opium-sodden Chinaman would be lying fast asleep at night in his shop on a bamboo platform behind the counter, with a number of native-made head-cloths, varying in price from two to twenty dollars, hanging on a line above his head. A thief who has observed the position of the cloths during the day-time crawls under the shops at night—they are slightly raised from the ground on posts—and making a small hole in the bamboo floor, or utilising one already there, pulls down the cloths from above the Chinaman's head, and, having landed his catch safely, quietly takes his departure, leaving his "fishing rod" behind him as a souvenir of his visit.

Another method is sometimes used in stealing rice. The thief, having observed that a sack of rice is stored in a certain house, makes his way under the dwelling at night, breaks away a little of the flooring—not a difficult task—immediately under the sack of rice, and, cutting a hole in the bottom of the sack, lets the rice off into a receptacle held below—his canoe if the house he is stealing from is built over the river.

Offences against the person, assaults, woundings and murders, are rare, though I once had to deal with a case in which a man was stabbed through the floor of the house, his assailant temporarily escaping. He was, however, eventually discovered by having all the weapon sheaths in the village opened and examined for blood-stains. On doing this, it was found that the inside of a kris-sheath belonging to a young Bajau was caked with dried blood—the weapon itself had been cleaned. When the prisoner saw that there was strong circumstantial evidence against him he at once confessed that he was guilty. The reasons he gave for revenging himself on his victim were peculiar, but were of such a nature that I can scarcely set them down here.

The Bajaus and Illanuns of the Tempassuk at the present day still acknowledge a number of chieftains, the highest in rank being the Dato Takopan (Bajau) and the Dato Temengong (a chief of importance among the Bajaus). On the Mengkabong, and on some of the rivers along the coast in the direction of Brunei, Pangerans (chiefs of the royal blood of the Sultans of Brunei) are acknowledged as overlords. In the old days petty chieftains were accustomed to adopt very high-sounding titles, and to style themselves rajas, but since the establishment of the Chartered Company's rule the power of the majority of the native chiefs has declined considerably, since the Company now appoints "Government chiefs," who receive a monthly salary, and are selected from the most trustworthy and energetic of the native headmen. Thus, although a candidate of high rank would be selected in preference to a commoner, all other things being equal, there are now among the Government chiefs men who have risen to the position owing to merit rather than birth.

The head Government chief in the Tempassuk at present is Haji Orang Kaya Kaya Mohamed Arsat (or Arshad), a Banjarese, for long a Government clerk, who by many years of faithful service, and by his conduct at the time of the Mat Saleh rebellion and afterwards, won himself the position which he now holds. He has very wisely strengthened his authority over the Mohammedans, who are always ready to respect a *haji* or Mecca pilgrim, by marrying the sister of the principal Illanun chief. Futhermore, his influence with the pagans is almost as strong as it is with the Mohammedans, and his knowledge of native customs, and of native ways, makes his assistance invaluable to a young Civil servant fresh from home.

Another class of people who have a good deal of influence with the Mohammedan tribes are Sarips, men partly of Arab, partly of native extraction, who claim descent from the Prophet of Islam. They are on account of this claim naturally looked upon with great respect, and are considered entitled to wear yellow, which is the royal colour.

In the old days, as far as I can ascertain, the majority of the chiefs exercised but little authority over their lawless followers, and any man who had gained a reputation by his bravery, or by bluster and cajolery, was sure to attract to himself a following of reckless freebooters.

The Illanun head chief traces his origin from the Illanun magnates of Mindanao and is a descendant of Sa Tabok, the pirate, concerning whom I shall say something in a later chapter. Illanun chiefs have a peculiar custom of taking (or receiving) more high-sounding titles as they advance in years, thus a Dato may eventually end up with the title of Sultan.

Some of the Bajau titles, such, for instance, as that of Dato Temengong, seem to have been bestowed by the Brunei royalty on petty chiefs, or men of some capacity who made themselves useful to the Brunei Court, or to Brunei officers who visited the country to collect *duit buis* (tribute)—exacted by threats from some of the Bajau villages. The *duit buis*, a sort of poll-tax, was given in kind, and in addition, when the boat with the Sultan of Brunei's representative on board cast anchor, the village had to contribute two pikul of brass, and the same amount when anchor was weighed again. Mengkabong, Inanam, Menggatal, Tuaran and the Sulaman villages acknowledged the Brunei potentate as their lord (chiefly, I expect, when they were overawed by a display of force). According to Haji Arsat, who is my informant with regard to these matters, one pikul of cannon (brass) was at that time reckoned as being worth fifty dollars (Mexican).

CHAPTER XXIII

FOOD & INTOXICANTS

THE Bajau's staple food is rice, as is the case with the majority of the peoples inhabiting the tropical and some of the sub-tropical and temperate regions of Asia. Rice by itself would, however, be but a poor diet, and so it is supplemented with vegetables, fish or flesh, while in the tropics it is further helped out with seasonings of spices, red peppers and other condiments. The Bajaus, being dwellers on the sea-coasts and the lower reaches of the rivers, are not unnaturally great consumers of fish; and they also supply the inland tribes from their superfluity, fish being one of the chief articles they barter with the hill people. Various vegetables are eaten, the commonest being a kind of stringy French bean, brinjals, gourds and cucumbers, as well as leaves of various wild plants.

The Bajau's women-folk make a few kinds of delicacies, one of the commonest being *penjaron*, small round cakes of native sugar, or molasses and rice-flour, which are sold in the markets and, if fresh, have a not unpleasant taste. *Tapai* cakes I shall mention below, and in addition to these I have seen pierced rice-flour cakes in fanciful shapes taken to the mosques at the end of the fasting month.

In spite of owning large herds of cattle and buffaloes, the Bajaus, like the majority, if not all, of the peoples of the Malayan region, do not drink milk, nor do they use it or its derivatives (butter and *ghi*) for cooking. Animals are but rarely killed for eating, and then only on such occasions as marriages or feast-days. Venison when obtainable is eagerly sought after, but pork, both from wild and tame pigs, is of course forbidden to them as Mohammedans.

Coco-nut oil, obtained by boiling the kernels of old nuts with water and skimming off the oil which rises to the surface, or by pressing them, is used for cooking and for many other purposes. In former days coco-nut oil was burnt in the old Grecian-shaped standard or hanging brass lamps, which can still be sometimes purchased in the villages, but are now only used on occasions of ceremony.

Sugar-cane is planted to a fair extent, and from it is obtained the brown molasses which enters into the composition of so many kinds of native cakes; but it is largely eaten raw, especially by the children. Indian corn is also grown, and is baked or boiled for eating. Fruit is an important article of native diet; fruit trees, especially mangoes, *impalum*, *bĕlunoe*, limes, jack fruit and others, are to be found in most villages, while pine-apples are occasionally to be seen on sale in the markets, together with pommeloes, large orange-like fruits, which have been introduced, and are, I believe, grown in one of the Illanun villages around Fort Alfred. Red peppers of various kinds form an important condiment in both Bajau and Illanun cooking.

Tapai cakes, made from fermented rice, are commonly eaten, and balls of rice-flour mixed with the substances used instead of yeast are often to be seen hanging on a line outside Bajau houses, where they are left until fermentation has set in. *Tapai* cakes are not unpleasant to eat, the liquor from the fermented rice-flour tasting something like brandy sauce.

Unhusked rice is prepared for cooking exactly as among the Dusuns—that is to say, by pounding the padi, as rice in the husk is called, in a wooden mortar until the grain is separated from the chaff, winnowing away the latter in an open tray-like basket, and washing the rice before cooking in two or three changes of water.

Intoxicants are of course forbidden to both tribes as Mohammedans, but though infraction of this ordinance of their religion is not very common, a few Mohammedan natives do, as I have already related, obtain drink from their pagan neighbours on one pretext or another. Sophisticated Mohammedans, both in the Malay Peninsula and Borneo, even if observant of religious matters, will drink beer if they can obtain it, and say that their religion allows them to do so. I have heard them give various reasons for their indulgence in this liquor; all of them seem rather flimsy, and suggest an adherence rather to the letter of the law than to its spirit.

One man who likes it says that beer, not having been invented in the Prophet's time, could not have been forbidden (the same might be said of whisky); another that it is only forbidden to drink liquor made from any large plant, such as the vine (on this assumption whisky would again be exempt from prohibition); another that beer does not contain enough alcohol to come under the interdict. The beers to be bought in Chinese shops being usually different brands of light lager, the third reason for not abstaining is probably the best.

Stimulants in the form of *sireh*, betel and tobacco for chewing purposes are freely used by both sexes. Tobacco purchased from the up-country Dusuns is smoked by the men in the form of leaf-covered cigarettes, which taste more of the smouldering wrapping than of the tobacco.

Opium is smoked by some Bajau and Illanun men, but the smokers form a very small percentage of the males of either tribe, though the Illanuns are more addicted to the vice than the Bajaus: even in their case it is usually only the chiefs who are opium smokers. Opium seems to have a much more harmful effect on Malays and on other native peoples of the Archipelago than on the Chinese. A Malay opium smoker is almost invariably an absolutely hopeless person to deal with, but the Chinaman, unless he be a very old hand, who indulges heavily in the drug, seems to experience very little damage in so far as his capabilities for doing business are concerned, though an opium-smoking

Chinaman can usually be detected by certain bodily signs. What the reason for this is I do not know. Possibly the Malayan peoples have naturally more weakly constitutions than the Chinese; or the vice, being of more recent introduction among these peoples, has a greater demoralising effect on them than on the inhabitants of far Cathay; or the Malay is more reckless in his indulgence than the Chinaman.

CHAPTER XXIV

LOVE, COURTSHIP & MARRIAGE

COURTSHIP and marriage among the Bajaus are not subjects about which I can write a great deal, though I was once present at a Bajau marriage, or at any rate at the ceremonies performed on the final day. The number of wives which a Mohammedan native may take unto himself—namely, four—is limited by Mohammedan law, based, I presume, on the teachings of the Koran.

As among the pagans, Mohammedans pay a *bĕrian* at marriage, though this, instead of being looked upon as a perquisite of the woman's relations, is frequently put by for the benefit of any children who may be born, and held in trust by the mother and father of the girl. The usual *bĕrian* mentioned in the case of a commoner is three pikuls of brass (cannon). The pikul is 100 katties (1 kattie is equal to 1⅓ lb.). A pikul of brass was formerly valued at $50·00 Mexican. The present value is about $20·00 according to Orang Kaya Arsat. At the present day cannon may not be actually included in the *bĕrian* given, cattle, buffaloes, gongs or other brass-ware, reckoned to be their equivalent in value, being received instead.

The portion, or portions, of the marriage ceremony which I saw was the procession of the bridegroom to the bride's house, escorted by a number of young men wearing krises, and the whole, or part, of the actual wedding ceremony. As I made no notes at the time I have to rely on my memory of an event which happened some five years ago, hence there may be errors in my description. The first part of the ceremony that I witnessed in the house was a general meeting of all those interested in the marriage, except the bride, who was not present. The terms of the contract were recited and the husband publicly instructed in his duties as a married man by one of the elders of the mosque—the Imam, I believe. The rest of the performance consisted of ceremonially putting the couple to bed and the momentary appearance of the bride in order to sit with the bridegroom before the assembled company; but I cannot clearly remember which part of the ceremony came first—I rather think the putting to bed.

The Bajau bride and bridegroom are lucky in not having to endure the lengthy *bĕrsanding* (ceremony) which Malay couples have to undergo, both bride and bridegroom sitting almost motionless, perhaps for hours together, while their relations and friends come to pay their respects and make presents of money. The glimpse we obtained of the Bajau bride was fleeting, and I was told that she would not have stopped as long as she did had I not expressed a wish to see the bridal costume. I do not remember that the bridegroom's dress differed in any important particular from that worn by the average young Bajau on occasions of ceremony, with, perhaps, the exception that he wore a kris, but the bride's head was crowned with a kind of silver tiara, and she wore a set of silver ornaments exactly like the guards used by rich Chinamen to protect their long finger-nails. As far as I can recollect, these are used on the right hand only, and three of them form a set, the points of the thumb and second finger not being covered. At any rate two sets which I purchased comprise only three guards each.

Of course a Bajau wedding is an opportunity for a feast, which is not likely to be ignored, hence there is always a large gathering of villagers at every wedding. Matriarchy obtaining to a certain extent among the Bajaus, the bridegroom does not take his bride home to his father's house, or immediately settle down in a dwelling of his own, but stops for about two months with his wife's people, employing his time, perhaps, during this customary domicile with his mother-in-law in building a house for himself. Before marriage opportunities for courting are, I believe, not very numerous, in spite of the fact that Bajau women enjoy a great deal of freedom. The arrangements for a marriage and the manner in which the *bĕrian* is to be paid are made by the parents of the contracting parties.

The theory of matrilineal descent is not carried to such lengths among the Bajaus as among some of the Malays —*e.g.* the Malays of Negri Sembilan and, I believe, of Menangkabau, where all land descends in the female line. The male children inherit the land, cattle, buffaloes, ponies, gongs, etc., while the women receive the household goods, perhaps a little brass-ware—anything, in fact, which is used by women only, such as sets of *kulintangan* or dulcimer gongs, essentially women's instruments.

If a man dies leaving a wife and only young children, the deceased's brother often makes an attempt to obtain some of the property, and is frequently successful.

A rough wooden coffin is used at funerals, and, if I remember rightly—I may, however, very possibly be incorrect in this statement, as I write from memories of five years ago—this has no bottom, being merely placed over the body, which rests on a bier. Rough standing stones are set up over graves, or sometimes wooden posts are used instead. One post, or stone, is placed at the head of the grave, another marks the position either of the middle of the body or of the knees. In the case of Illanuns of high rank—for instance, the family of the head chief, the Dato Meradan—a new grave has to be continually guarded, night and day, for a period of a hundred days after the death has taken place, a hut being built for the purpose of sheltering the watcher.

While I was stationed at Kotabelud the wife of Orang Kaya Arsat, the sister of the Dato Meradan, died, and the Orang Kaya had to conform to this Illanun custom, though he himself is a Banjarese. The watching must have been a very trying experience, and he seemed comparatively seldom to install a substitute. The reason for this practice is that a body-snatching spirit, the *Berbalan*, is thought to be continually on the prowl to plunder newly made graves, and, judging by the Illanun's procedure, he has a particular desire to disturb those of persons of good family.

Divorce among the Bajaus and Illanuns is given according to Mohammedan custom, the third or final divorce being absolute. In the Malay Peninsula a man who has finally divorced his wife can take her back by getting her nominally married to another man, known as a *China buta* (blind Chinaman), who then divorces her before she re-marries her former husband. This absolute divorce may be given in the first place. First divorce or second divorce (*talak dua, talak tiga*) are less severe forms, and the husband may take his wife again without ceremony, provided that this is done within a stated time, while during that time his wife may not marry another man. Should the allotted period have expired, and the husband, having thought matters over again, wish to take his wife back, he can do so, but must re-marry her. Divorce does not, however, seem to be very frequently resorted to.

CHAPTER XXV

MANUFACTURES

THE Illanuns, and especially their women, are makers of articles of considerable beauty. The Bajaus of the Tempassuk are much less skilled, but the women are fairly expert cloth-weavers, an art which they seem to have learnt from their Illanun sisters. Formerly the Illanuns had a great reputation as silversmiths, but unfortunately the Illanun silversmith is now extinct, having been ousted by the enterprising Chinaman. The native worker in Malaysia is, owing to his methods, always at a disadvantage as regards the latter; for the Chinese craftsman is a specialist, who, when he is not working on orders he has received from customers, is turning out goods for stock, so that he may have something to sell when a possible purchaser comes along.

Supposing you want an article made by a native craftsman, the following sort of experience probably befalls you, the article you want being, say, a brass betel-box. First of all you must find out where there is a brass-worker. After many futile inquiries you hear that there is one in a village three miles away. Setting out for this place, and having taken several wrong turns, you at last arrive at his house, only to find that he is out catching a buffalo or has gone to a village a mile or so away in order to visit a sick relative. A messenger is sent to fetch him, and after a wait of a couple of hours he arrives.

The next trouble is that he has no ready-made boxes in stock, no metal from which to manufacture even one, and no money to buy it with. This makes it necessary to give him a money advance, and he then has to search for someone who has some broken brass articles suitable for melting up. The metal once obtained, he will work upon your order in the intervals between padi-planting and fishing, therefore you must not expect to receive the completed article for a month or more; but if you give him a free hand and pay a good price, so that he is interested in showing you what he can do, he will probably turn you out a really beautiful piece of work. Unfortunately, unless native craftsmen can be taught to specialise, it seems likely that as a class they are doomed to extinction, owing to the competition of the Chinese worker, and of the cheap and shoddy imitations of native-made articles which are manufactured in Europe.

Probably cloth-weaving will be carried on in the Tempassuk long after brass-casting, wood-carving and weapon-making have become lost arts. The Bajau or Illanun young man is extremely fond of dressing himself up in fine clothes, and the article of clothing by which he sets most store, if he possesses one, is an expensive native-woven head-cloth. Some of these cloths, especially if they contain much "gold" thread, are priced at anything up to thirty dollars, though the cheaper kinds can be purchased for a dollar or a dollar and a half.

Tempassuk cloths have a considerable reputation outside the district, and are exported to some extent to Tuaran, where the Bajaus do not weave cloth, or even farther afield. Many of the Bajau and Illanun women of the district spend a great deal of their time in weaving these cloths; and in some villages, especially the Illanun settlements near Pindasan, the clack-clack of the weaver's sword as she beats up the last-placed threads of the cloth can be heard issuing from every house. The man whose wife is a good weaver need do very little work, but can live on the proceeds from the sales of her manufactures, which she herself often peddles in the local markets.

In former days native-spun cotton thread and native dyes

for colouring it were the rule, but now ready-dyed thread, bought at the Chinese shops, is generally, if not universally, in use. Since aniline dyes are used as the colouring matter, and the thread is of rather inferior quality, the cloths now produced probably do not compare favourably with those formerly made from native materials, but even the modern cloths have wonderful lasting powers, although the colours are apt to fade and do not stand washing well.

Head-cloths and sleeping-cloths, about which I shall have something to say presently, are artificially stiffened, in the case of the former to make the ends stand up when tied. To produce the stiffening, the dyed thread is immersed in water in which rice-starch has been dissolved, and is then wound on to a drying wheel of split bamboo. When it is thoroughly dry it is ready for weaving. Thread for making scarves for tying round the waist (*saputangan*—*i.e.* handkerchiefs), or the cloth for coats and trousers, is not usually stiffened.

The head-cloth (*justar* or *dustar*) is always a square, but its patterns vary according to the kind and quality; some of the most expensive varieties are profusely decorated with flower and geometric patterns of different colours in raised weaving, which at first sight might easily be taken for embroidery; others, generally the cheaper varieties, have lines of different colours running through a red or black ground. Nearly, if not quite, all head-cloths are differentiated into a centre and a border region, while in the cheaper cloths the former is usually ornamented with bands of narrow lines of different breadths and colours running parallel along each side and intersecting near the corners. These bands give the cloth a look which is rather reminiscent of a Scotch tartan, and the resemblance is often further strengthened by the central part being cut up into big checks by fine parallel lines running through it. Even in the cheaper cloths the small piece contained between the corners and the intersecting bands of the borders is usually filled in with floral patterns in raised weaving, while in the more expensive specimens the whole of the border and central portions is almost solid raised weaving.

Two varieties of sleeping-cloth are made: one, the *kain noga*, is composed of either two or three pieces of cloth placed edge to edge and stitched together. The majority of these cloths are striped, and the stripes are worn horizontally across the body, the longitudinal edges of the compound cloth being sewn together so that it forms a sort of bottomless sack like the Malay *sarong*: the wearer usually draws the garment on over his head and slips it off over his feet. When sleeping the whole body is wrapped up in the cloth.

I was lucky enough to obtain one magnificent specimen of the other type of sleeping-cloth, the *kain ampik*, of a most unusual kind, which, considering the time that it must have taken to weave, was a bargain at the price I paid for it —four dollars, or about seventeen shillings. The borders of the cloth were ornamented with a solid band of raised weaving in different colours and gold thread; the body of the cloth was black relieved by a somewhat sparse arrangement of yellow and white star-like flowers in raised weaving, except for a strip of solid raised weaving about a foot wide running from top to bottom. There are several varieties of the *kain ampik*, but this band of pattern down the back is its distinguishing feature.

This, a most wonderful piece of work, was decorated with small geometrical and other patterns in red, yellow, white and gold thread. As every colour and division of the pattern requires its own small needle-shuttle, or is simply worked in by hand, it will be realised that the skill necessary for weaving such a cloth must be of no mean order, and the time taken to complete it many months.

Illanun cloth is of better quality than that produced by the Bajau women, the weaving being finer and the texture closer. This is, I believe, partly due to greater skill in weaving and partly to the threads of the woof being better beaten up with the weaver's sword. The loom used by both peoples is only a little less primitive than that of the Dusuns, there being no loom-frame proper beyond the cloth- and warp-beams. The treadles are worked by strings; there is a hard-wood sword for beating up the warp threads, and a comb for keeping the woof threads in proper order.

Two other handicrafts in which the Bajau and Illanun women are experts are the making of mats and baskets. Both are manufactured from the leaves of the screw-palm or pandanus, cut into long strips, and some of the best mats are of extremely fine texture. The round, squat and open-mouthed baskets used chiefly for holding padi are also excellent specimens of work, and are sometimes ornamented with patterns in colours. Small two-piece wallets for holding tobacco, gambier, etc., where one section slips over the other, and which somewhat resemble cigar-cases in shape, are made from the same materials, and these too are decorated with patterns in various colours.

Embroidery is not much used for ornamenting articles of clothing, but I have seen some long mats with very nicely worked embroidered corners at their heads, and embroidered ends are sometimes found on the round and rectangular pillows which are in general use. Small breast-pockets on men's coats are occasionally embellished with foliate patterns in red thread or silk, as also are ornamental false lacings on the fronts of jackets.

Allied to basket-work is the making of covers for dishes. These are in the shape of a truncated cone and consist of a wooden framework, covered with broad strips of pandanus (?) leaves running perpendicularly, which are dyed in various colours and sewn to the frame. Ornaments, cut out of pandanus leaf, either geometrical or in the shape of flowers, are often stitched on the outside of the cover, especially if the covers are used on the occasion of feasts.

The Bajau men of several villages near the sea, notably

those of Kampong Kolambai, near the Pangkalan Abai in the Tempassuk district, are experts in making shell bracelets and armlets. The cheapest kind is made from a species of giant clam or *Tridacna*, which the natives call *kima*. A single valve of a large *Tridacna* shell will have a thickness of an inch or more except near the edges. From the selected shell—which must be an old one, as new shells are said to be too brittle—a piece of suitable size is cut, and a large hole is then roughly chipped out in the centre of the piece. After this the edges of the embryo bracelet are rubbed down with sand and water on a large stone. The same block of stone, and the same part of it, being always used for this purpose, a deep groove is worn in it, which helps materially in the forming of the bracelet. The article, having been brought to a regular shape, is smoothed and polished, and when finished fetches about a dollar in the local markets.

The finer kind of bracelet is made from a species of large *Conus* shell, locally called *sulau*. The top of the shell is cut off and treated in a fashion similar to that already described for making *Tridacna* bracelets; but as shells of sufficient size are difficult to obtain, and the material is brittle, and therefore more difficult to work, full-sized bracelets of this kind are sold for as much as three or four dollars.

Brass-casting and silver-work have already been mentioned; the former industry is still carried on by a few Illanuns, the method employed being the *cira perduta* process. The chief articles now made are heavy rectangular *sireh*-boxes, often quite plain, or with only a few slightly engraved floral patterns on the cover; but I have seen some modern pieces ornamented with large lozenges of copper inlay. The art of brass-working is rapidly dying out, and very probably will be actually dead in another twenty years' time. The prices asked for large pieces of modern work are prohibitive, and this probably militates against the chances of the art ever being revived.

Very fine old brass boxes can be often picked up for a dollar or two in the out-station pawnshops, these being unredeemed pledges. The cast and chased ornamentation on them is often extremely artistic, and their shapes are pleasing. Certain types of these boxes were made in Brunei, others, I believe, in the Sulu Islands and Mindanao, but probably some few were the work of the Illanun craftsmen of Borneo.

Most villages have a blacksmith, who is capable of turning out very fair knives, spear-heads and other small articles, but the making of waved or straight kris and *sundang* blades is now a lost art, if indeed such articles were ever made in either district, of which I have no proof: in fact I am rather inclined to think that the two commonest forms of sword to be found in the hands of the Bajaus and Illanuns, the *barong* or *pida*, and the *sundang*, which is locally called kris, were mostly imported from Sulu. The long Illanun sword, the *kompilan*, may have been made locally to a small extent.

The Bajaus of the coastal villages carry on the manufacture of salt by rather a curious process, and trade the finished product with the Dusuns of the interior. The salt-maker collects large quantities of *nipa*-palm roots, which contain a good deal of salt, together with other drift-wood gathered along the shores. These he heaps together into a pile near his salt-making hut and sets fire to them. When the fire is burning brightly he damps it down with sea-water and heaps on more wood. This process is repeated again and again for a couple of days or so, until a large heap of wood-ash has been obtained. The ashes are then gathered up and pressed down into large funnels made of palm spathes, which are placed in a row in a rack fastened between two posts of the hut. Underneath the row of funnels is placed a small dug-out canoe.

When everything is ready sea-water is poured slowly

into each funnel and allowed to percolate through the ashes and down into the canoe. The process is repeated several times till it is considered that all the salt mixed with the ashes has been carried off, and an almost saturated salt solution has filled the canoe. The salt-maker then starts a fire in a fireplace consisting of two long parallel mud walls, set near together and about three and a half to four feet high, one wall being pierced at the base with holes set at regular intervals, which allow of the fire being attended to, and perhaps make a draught. The salt solution is then poured out into shallow rectangular dishes made of palm spathes, each about one foot six, or nine, inches long by a foot broad. These are placed in rows transversely on top of the walls of the range and the contents cooked until all the water has been driven out. Just before the salt becomes dry it is marked out into bars with a knife in order to facilitate division of the cakes into smaller pieces. The finished product is greyish white in colour, and each cake has a browned or blackened crust at the bottom where it has been in contact with the dish.

The making of pottery is in the hands of the women and, though no potting wheel is used, very creditable cooking-pots and water-gourds in reddish-coloured ware are turned out. Some pieces are slightly decorated with patterns produced with the aid of small wooden stamps, and are given a coating of damar gum.

One other small industry is perhaps deserving of mention; this is the making of lime for mixing with the *sireh*-chew. Lime is made by burning coral, the shells of saddle-back oyster, or of other marine molluscs. At Tuaran pink lime is often to be seen on sale in the local markets, but I am unable to say by what method it is coloured. Both lime and salt are largely traded with the up-country Dusuns, but the latter sometimes make an inferior quality of lime for themselves by burning fresh-water shells.

The amount of trading carried on by the Bajaus of the

Tempassuk is now not large, and is chiefly limited to the bartering of fish, salt, *sireh*, lime, Bajau cloths and a few other articles with the peoples of the interior. In former days they seem to have acted as middlemen between the Chinese buyers of jungle produce and the Dusun collectors; but as the country is now in a peaceful state the Chinese are no longer afraid to attend the markets, and so deal directly with the Dusuns, without employing an expensive and generally untrustworthy go-between. Occasionally a Brunei trader who does not wish to make a prolonged stay in the district will commission a Bajau to buy a large quantity of Dusun tobacco for export; but as the Bajau generally is minus both money and most of the promised tobacco when the Brunei man's boat puts in again, the transaction rarely has a very satisfactory ending for either party, the Bajau being harassed by the law, which is set in motion by the Brunei, and the latter, if he ever sees his money again, probably having to be content with somewhat irregular instalments.

As the Bajaus have large herds of cattle and buffaloes, and a fair number of ponies, quite a trade in them is developing as the country becomes more opened up. A large number of cattle for killing purposes are embarked on the small local steamer for shipment to the towns every time she calls at Usakan. Buffaloes are exported to the Marudu district, where they can be sold at a good price for work on the estates; but a fair number are also purchased by up-country Dusuns either directly from the Bajaus or from the Chinese, who buy animals from the Bajaus in order to barter them to the Dusuns for jungle produce. The best of the Tempassuk-bred ponies are in fair demand locally, and also among the Europeans of Tuaran and Jesselton.

CHAPTER XXVI

COCK-FIGHTING, GAMBLING & OTHER AMUSEMENTS

COCK-FIGHTING and racing, together with hunting, which I have described elsewhere, are probably the three amusements most in favour among the Bajaus. The first is largely practised on every occasion when matches can be arranged. During my residence at Kotabelud there used to be cock-fighting every Sunday afternoon at the Chinese shops. Here used to assemble numbers of local Bajaus, some of the more sophisticated Dusuns, Chinese shopkeepers and native policemen.

The matches had usually been fixed in advance and, in most cases, the merits of the respective birds were fairly well known. I have never seen artificial spurs among the Bajaus, though they are used by the Dyaks of Sarawak; consequently the sport was not so cruel as it would have been with these aids. Charms are largely employed by the owners of fighting cocks to ensure the invulnerability of their champions, and to cause them to inflict serious wounds on their opponents. Ancient stone implements are thought specially potent for this purpose, if the bird's beak and spurs are rubbed with them.

An umpire presides at cock-fights, he and the owners of the birds being the only persons admitted to the ring, which is sometimes enclosed within a bamboo fence. The two owners squat opposite to each other, holding their birds on the ground between their hands, and after an involuntary peck or two on either side, which they are forced to give by their masters, at a signal from the umpire the combatants are released and the battle begins. It is necessary for a bird to run from its opponent three times before it is declared vanquished, while it is comparatively seldom that a bird who has once turned tail wins the fight. Each match thus comprises three rounds, a round being terminated by the temporary defeat of one of the birds.

On the umpire declaring the round at an end, each bird is seized by its respective owner, and various measures are taken to help it to recover its breath and strength; the head and comb are washed; the beak, mouth and throat swabbed out with a feather moistened with water; the crest blown upon with the mouth, and charms surreptitiously applied to the feet and beak. Both birds having been fettled up, they are set facing one another for the next round.

Sometimes a combatant which is very hard pressed will run its neck between the "shoulder" of its opponent's wing and its body, so that the birds are looking in opposite directions over each other's backs, neither of them being able to do any damage to his opponent. A "clinch" of this kind is not considered fair fighting, and should it continue for long the birds are seized by their owners and again set facing one another. Accidental locking of this kind often occurs, the birds looking most foolish and confused, each trying in vain to get at his opponent, and neither having the wit to extricate himself.

Yells of applause from the spectators greet the victor at the end of each round, and on the conclusion of the match; while any clever piece of work with spurs or beak is also greeted with a chorus of approbation. Bets are made freely, but the giving of odds seems to be almost or quite unknown, all wagering being in even money. Though it is not really allowed at such meetings, as it sometimes leads to quarrelling, a good deal of cock-fighting goes on at some of the smaller markets, which are seldom visited by the police; but the most important matches and the largest number of them are fought at Kotabelud, where some supervision can be exercised.

Probably gambling takes rank even before cock-fighting as a Bajau amusement. Since the establishment of the Chartered Company's rule, gambling, as was the case until recently in the Straits Settlements and the Federated Malay States, has been made a monopoly, the right to erect gambling-houses in townships and out-stations being knocked down to the highest bidder, invariably a Chinese "towkay." With the gambling monopoly go the monopolies for dealing in opium or spirits and pawnbroking: in small settlements like Kotabelud or Tuaran all three businesses are often conducted under one roof, though a separate part of the house or an adjoining shop is reserved for the gambling establishment.

I have always been very much opposed to grandmotherly legislation, passed by cranks and faddists, usually a small but very active minority, who sometimes manage to impose their will on the people of Britain and other countries, owing to the majority being too lazy to band together to defend its liberties. Furthermore, I believe that attempts to make people good by law are seldom permanently successful, the usual result being that a vice which has been rigorously suppressed, instead of being controlled within decent limits, is supplanted by another whose effects are even more disastrous.

This does not, however, imply that I look upon the gambling shops, where the Bajau squanders his wealth, with any friendly eye; but the reason for my dislike is not based on Puritanical grounds. When Bajau gambled with Bajau affairs were probably quite bad enough, and the discomfort and damage caused to the community at large undoubtedly severe; but the loss of one man was the gain of another, and the property or money staked still remained within the tribe.

A much worse state of things is now prevalent; the Bajau's property and money go to enrich the owners of the gambling monopoly; his goods are pledged in order to

Dusuns of Tempassuk Village, near Kotabelud.

Four typical lowland Dusuns in holiday costume. The two men in the centre, Bengali and Gimbad, are old friends of the author.

provide money to gratify his passion, the money obtained from the pledging being lost in the gambling-shop, while he often continues to pay interest on the valuable articles pawned for years without ever being able to redeem them, except that he may possibly take them out with borrowed money, renew the ticket, and then immediately put them back again. The property and wealth of the Bajaus thus find their way into the hands of the Chinese, without their receiving any benefit in return. The best that can be said of the matter is that the gambling-shops are fairly conducted, though, of course, the bank always, or nearly always, wins in the long run. The pawnshops, too, in out-stations are often extremely lenient with their customers, and I have frequently come across instances where the broker has waited for a considerable time after he had a right to foreclose on a valued article of property in order to give the owner a chance of paying up the interest. But this was probably not entirely due to kindness, as it would be more profitable for the pawnbroker to allow the customer to keep the article in for several years, perpetually paying interest on it, than to foreclose on the pledge and sell it out of hand for a comparatively small amount.

One game which is in great favour is played on a board ruled into twelve squares, each of which has a different character marked on it. Round this squat the gamblers and the banker. The latter then spins a teetotum, which has characters on its sides corresponding to those of the board, on a plate, and while it is still spinning shuts it in under a tin cover. The players, when the teetotum has ceased to spin, put their stakes on the square or squares they fancy, and when all have finished the cover is lifted and the winning character—*i.e.* which is uppermost as the top lies in the plate—is announced. The bank pays ten times the stakes placed on the winning square; the others are raked in.

Various kinds of card games are also played in the gambling-farm, but these are private affairs among the natives themselves, a small fee being paid to the manager of the gambling-shop to allow them to use it.

Among the chief articles which find their way into the pawnshop to supply money for gambling are heavy old brass betel-boxes—often very beautiful specimens of the brass-caster's art—old silver-ware and various types of weapons. The very best weapons, with fine blades, large ivory bird-shaped tops to the hilts and silver mountings, are somewhat rarely to be found exposed for sale among the unredeemed pledges, since they are regarded as heirlooms by the natives; and though there may be many of them in the pawnshop, their owners nearly always manage to keep the interest on them paid up and to renew the tickets periodically. Nevertheless the pawnshop is a happy hunting-ground for those who have sufficient insight to be able to admire the beautiful old brass-ware, while the less highly priced native weapons and betel-boxes can be picked up ridiculously cheap.

To obtain a good collection, perseverance, time and trouble are as necessary for success as in most other matters. It is quite useless to go once to the pawnshop and come away grumbling that there is nothing nice in the place. Visits must be paid periodically, say every fortnight, and before long some beautiful specimen will be obtained which will be more than sufficient reward for the trouble taken.

The very best weapons, even if obtainable, are, according to European ideas, extremely expensive. The large ivory hilt of one of these alone may, according to native ideas, be worth anything from twenty to thirty dollars; and sixty dollars (about £7 English) would not be at all an out-of-the-way price for a fine kris (*sundang*). *Parang ilang*, really Dyak or Kayan weapons, so-called krises with fine blades but wooden or very small ivory hilts, and heavy-bladed Sulu *pida* (sometimes called *barong*) can, however, be frequently bought for anything from one to three or four dollars.

The gambling-house in an out-station with a Bajau population is generally crowded with natives the whole day long, and I am afraid that besides the Bajaus some of the low-country Dusuns, especially those of Tuaran, are rather badly infected with the gambling fever.

Racing on ponies, buffaloes or cattle is also a very favourite amusement among the Bajaus. When I was stationed in the Tempassuk regular race-meetings used to be got up (if I remember rightly) every Thursday on an open space near the bridle-path which leads from Kotabelud to Usakan Bay, while native sports arranged by Europeans, especially if they include pony-races, are most enthusiastically welcomed. The little native ponies, though extremely hardy, are given practically no attention; their rough coats are never brushed or groomed, and great patches of hair are often destroyed by the ravages of numbers of large cattle-ticks.

A saddle is frequently absolutely dispensed with; the reins are of rope and the bit is a curious native-made brass snaffle. I have seen natives riding in the most reckless way during a race, apparently intoxicated with excitement: they yelled, threw their bodies and arms about, and apparently guided their ponies almost entirely with their knees, though they now and then belaboured their steeds with a rattan switch, a very effective little instrument consisting of three or four small round canes bound together at one end to form a handle.

An account of Bajau and Illanun amusements would not be complete without some reference to native dancing, and especially to the *bĕrunsai*, a form of dance which is, I believe, peculiar to the Bajaus. In the ordinary native dances, in which only one or two male performers take part, the posturing motions so much in favour in Java and other islands of the Archipelago are much in evidence.

In dances illustrating warfare a sword of the type called *sundang* is placed on the floor, the blade and the sheath being crossed. Round these the solitary performer, a man, revolves to the music of gongs and drums. His arms, wrists and hands are constantly in motion, and his body turns slowly, while his feet keep time to the music with curious half-stamping, half-shuffling steps. He is showing the audience how strong and how bold a man he is; the stretching of the arms in tense positions, the slow upward turning of the palms of his hands, the defiant stamping of the feet and the fierce air of the dancer all being calculated to convey these impressions. The onlookers by this time have become stirred up to a tremendous pitch of excitement, and yells of applause greet every fresh posture of defiance. Suddenly the performer shades his eyes with his hand—he has spied an enemy. He seizes the weapon from the ground and manœuvres to gain an advantage over his approaching adversary. He sinks to the ground and stealthily crawls towards his imaginary opponent, who presumably is using identical tactics. Finally there comes the dash into the open, the quick stabbing of his enemy and the conqueror's dance of defiance and victory. A clever dancer can so work the natives up that they seem to lose all sense of the unreality of the performance, while the air is rent with yells and war-cries.

I once saw a very amusing monkey-dance performed by two men who had stuck pieces of raw cotton on their eyebrows and chins, the make-up being intended to give them the appearance of *kra*-monkeys. Their antics were so ridiculously comic that they "brought down the house," the natives, another European and myself, being absolutely incapable with laughter.

The peculiar Bajau dance called *bĕrunsai* is preceded by a musical entertainment, and sometimes by other dances, which may last for anything up to a couple of hours, the performance starting at about eight or nine P.M. and lasting till daylight. At one *bĕrunsai* which I witnessed the musical instruments consisted of three large, broad-edged gongs with large and projecting bosses of the kind called *tawag-tawag*;

two flat-faced gongs of the variety known as *chenang* or *chanang*; two double-ended drums; and a set of nine *kulintangan*, small gongs arranged in a row on two strings stretched from end to end of a long frame and played with two little club-shaped pieces of wood in the manner of a dulcimer. All these instruments were used in the preliminary musical entertainment, the performers on them, with the exception of the *kulintangan*, being men.

These gong dulcimers appear to be regarded as women's instruments, and as every lady who considered herself an accomplished musician took a turn at them, the performance became somewhat wearisome. The large gongs, *tawag-tawags* and *chenangs*, beaten by men or boys, are hung from cross-beams of the house, the note of the former being changed by grasping and releasing their bosses with the left hand. The two drum-beaters sit cross-legged opposite to each other, with their instruments upon their knees. One end of each drum is struck with a small stick held in the right hand, the other with the wrist and open palm of the left hand. The music produced is by no means unpleasing, but a little of it goes a long way.

When all the women have had their turn at the *kulintangan* the *bĕrunsai* proper begins. Some three or four men, one of whom is the leader of the dance, make their way to a space in the centre of the room which has been cleared in readiness. They begin by walking round and round in a circle, chanting slowly meanwhile, and inviting the women to come out and dance with them. The circling is from left to right, and there is no reversal of this motion throughout the dance. More men join the circle, and after a decorous interval, in which they make a pretence of overcoming their diffidence, three or four women leave their sisters who are sitting at the back of the room and bashfully approach the men.

The latter then join hands, but the circle remains open between the leader and the man following him. The women enter the circle by this gap, and the leader of the women grasps the scarf which hangs from the left shoulder of the men's leader, the other women attaching themselves behind her in single file. The men then begin to pay the women all sorts of extravagantly Eastern compliments, each verse being chanted by the men's leader and taken up by his followers, to which the women reply that the men are making fun of them. The pace becomes increased, a regular step taking the place of the walk; the circle is entirely closed and the women move farther into the centre, but retain their position with regard to the men's leader. The men press their attentions on the women only to meet with a sharp rebuff; and as the fire of sally and retort becomes hotter and hotter, so the dance increases in pace until the men are (supposedly) worked up to a great pitch of excitement and the whole circle is revolving at a tremendous rate, almost every step of the dance becoming a terrific stamp.

Then the women, feigning to be frightened at the angry passions they have stirred up in the men, relent somewhat, and as their answers become less provocative, so the ardour of the men also lessens in degree, till at length the dance falls away into a slow step and finally into a walk, though a slow chanted interchange of compliments and replies is still kept up. Presently the dance again increases in intensity with a quicker exchange of pleasantries, but only to die away gradually as before. Thus the performance continues till the early hours of the morning.

CHAPTER XXVII

RELIGION & FOLKLORE

NOMINALLY both the Bajaus and the Illanuns are orthodox Mohammedans of the Sunnite sect, but actually they are extremely lax in the observance of the precepts of their religion; not that their belief in its truth is any way weak, but their ideas are somewhat similar to those of the Peninsula Malays, who seem to reckon on late repentance as a means of ridding themselves of the burden of their sins. The Bajaus have the further excuse that Mohammedan teachers of any erudition are extremely rare among them.

The great mass of the people is illiterate, and therefore not even books on religious subjects, written in Malay, can be read by them. Of course even the literate Malay of the Peninsula is unable to understand the Koran, although he can read the Arabic, since the characters in which Malay is now written were originally introduced by the Arabs who converted so many of the tribes of the Archipelago to the religion of the Prophet. He has to rely on the expositions of Koran teachers, and on pious commentaries in the vernacular. So far as I know, no attempt has ever been made to translate the Koran into any language used in the Eastern Archipelago, and I believe that anyone making an attempt to do so would be "excommunicated" for impiously daring to tamper with the sacred book by translating it into the common tongue.

The average Bajau man, at any rate in his young days, seldom attends mosque on Fridays or keeps the fasting month of Ramadan. All Mohammedan youths undergo circumcision, but beyond this, and abstention from pork, and generally from intoxicating liquor, their religion seems but little to affect their daily life. The five daily prayer-times are neglected, except by such as aspire to be considered pious, and by old men who are preparing themselves to pass into the next world.

Sharips—alleged descendants of the Prophet, of partly Arab blood—of whom there are a fair number in the Tempassuk, are, however, regarded with great respect, as are also *hajis* or returned Mecca pilgrims, a fact of which unscrupulous impostors have not been slow to take advantage. In one case a bogus holy man travelled about the country, presenting the simple inhabitants with spurious gold dinars (a Turkish gold coin), which he was careful to inform his hosts were extremely old, valuable and sacred, as he had brought them all the way from the holy city of Mecca. As in the East a present calls for a present, and usually a larger one than that received, the good man was soon loaded with valuable property presented to him by his grateful admirers. Unfortunately for him, someone at last found out that the valuable coins were only gilt, and the good man was arrested. The plea that he had given away the coins, on which he depended for an acquittal, should his trick be discovered, did not avail him, and, as far as I remember, he involuntarily retired to a cell to meditate on matters religious or otherwise.

Another form of imposition, which would flourish were it not firmly suppressed, is the collection of alms (*sedekah*) by religious impostors for the nominal purpose of enabling them to perform the pilgrimage to Mecca. This sort of cheating is not usually done by natives, but by scoundrelly wandering Pathans and other foreign Mohammedans from the towns, who have as much intention of going to Mecca as to the moon, there being, of course, absolutely no objection to a native who really wishes to visit Mecca collecting locally. This form of cheating is extremely lucrative, provided the culprit can escape detection, as most

Mohammedan natives not only believe that they acquire merit by helping a would-be pilgrim to realise his ambition, but would consider that if they did not give such assistance as they could afford they would be committing a serious sin.

One gentleman whom I had the pleasure of fining pretty severely, and of sending back to the place whence he came, was a self-styled convert from Sikhism. He came through from Jesselton and Tuaran on a journey to Kudat to collect funds, according to his own account, to enable him to perform the pilgrimage; but previous to his arrival I had been warned about him, and told that he had been forbidden to ask for alms on his journey. He came and reported himself to me, and said that he wished to stop the night with the Pathan cow-keeper who looked after the Government herd of cattle.

However, he had hardly been a couple of hours in the place when I was told that he had been begging. It appeared that after having obtained several contributions from Bajaus whom he met in the shops and elsewhere he had gone into the nearest village and climbed up into a house where there were only women at home, an action quite against Mohammedan custom, and an outrage which in some countries would probably entail the penalty of death. Here he had demanded *sedekah*, and had continued to press his demands although the women asked him to return when the owner of the house was at home, promising him a substantial sum. Finally they gave him what money they could, and he then began to grumble, saying that it was not fitting that so large a house should make so small a contribution. This was, of course, another offence, since alms, however small, should be received with gratitude.

Ramadan, the fasting month, is ushered in among the devout by an epidemic of spitting, for the orthodox will not swallow anything from sunset to sunrise, their own saliva included. This continuous fusilade of expectoration is rather apt to get on the nerves at first, especially as the performers seem to want to accomplish their object with the maximum amount of noise, possibly in order to show forth their piety.

Hari Raya (the Great Day), the first day of Shawal, the month succeeding Ramadan, and therefore the first day on which those who have been fasting may take food and drink during the day-time, is a general occasion for feasting and rejoicing. The finish of the fast at about six o'clock on the last day of Ramadan is ushered in with the firing of small cannon and Chinese crackers, the din and smell of gun-powder in particularly pious neighbourhoods being often appalling. No doubt fasting is a severe trial, as, although food is plentifully partaken of at night, not even water may be touched during the day-time, a serious deprivation in a hot country; and of course chewing *sireh* or smoking are equally forbidden.

Among those who do attempt to observe the fasting month some do not persevere till the end, and others, though I believe this is not frequently the case in the Tempassuk, take both food and drink by stealth, in order that they may acquire an undeserved reputation for piety.

The Bajau or Illanun mosque is usually a slight house-shaped building with a palm-leaf attap roof and side-walls reaching only half-way to the eaves. The walls are also of attaps, and one end of the building, which has a niche in the wall, faces towards Mecca. The faithful are called to prayers by beating a large single-ended drum with a long body, made from a section of hollow tree-trunk. The drum is often suspended in the building. Some of the villages of the Sulaman Inlet have mosques built over the water.

The officers of the mosque are the Imam or priest, the Khatib, who acts as reader, and the Bilal, who calls the faithful to prayers. The man who performs the rite of circumcision is known by the title of Mudin.

Undoubtedly both the Bajaus and Illanuns, being but lax Mohammedans, still cherish many superstitions, relics of an older form of religion, which would be denounced as heathen by more orthodox followers of the Prophet; but to my mind their religious ideas are interesting just so far as their Mohammedanism is bad, or perhaps better, so far as their earlier animistic beliefs survive. I must, however, plead guilty to having done but little work on this subject, as I had so many more subjects for investigation among the Dusuns, and so little leisure in which to make inquiry, that I thought it useless to spend my time in attempting to gather remnants of beliefs, many of which had received a Mohammedan veneer of respectability.

In several cases, when taking down folk-tales from Bajaus, I have been annoyed to find, after I had been writing for some time, that I was getting stories of the doings of the Prophet or some of his followers—narratives which, of course, were not native to the soil of Borneo. In fact I almost gave up trying to collect Bajau stories for this reason, and I am afraid I somewhat hurt the feelings of a Bajau who was frequently at my house in company with a Dusun friend of mine owing to the marked preference I gave to the tales of the latter.

One of the chief non-Mohammedan rites practised by the Bajaus, and also by the Dusuns, is the yearly launching of small rafts or boats with offerings on them, in order to bear away from the village troublesome spirits which are supposed to have assembled on the raft to partake of the offerings. Similar rafts are made use of in the Malay Peninsula, and are generally called *anchak lanchong*; but here, I believe, they are now chiefly set adrift in times of sickness.

The practice of medicine among the Bajaus is a good deal mixed up with magical performances, while texts from the Koran, either written on paper or repeated, and much less orthodox recitations are used as charms, but I had not the time to dip deeply into the subject. Blowings with the mouth on the part affected are also employed to relieve pain by the old men who are reputed to be skilled in medicine.

Small flags, generally of white cotton stuff, are sometimes to be seen hung outside houses where someone is lying ill: they are possibly placed there with the intention of keeping away evil spirits.

I was told of one rather peculiar remedy which is sometimes employed when a child is thin and has a poor appetite. Should the parents hear that a crocodile has been caught near any of the neighbouring villages, the child is taken to the spot and its hand placed in the dead animal's mouth. The idea is that, as the crocodile is extremely voracious, a good appetite will be induced in anyone whose hand is placed in contact with its mouth.

CHAPTER XXVIII

WEAPONS & WARFARE

AS I think I have mentioned elsewhere, both Illanuns and Bajaus are by nature truculent swashbucklers. Owing to their overbearing demeanour, rather than to their bravery—though they are sometimes distinguished by a sort of reckless daring—they easily imposed themselves as superiors on the generally timid and unwarlike pagans. Being essentially predatory tribes, the manufacture of implements of warfare has naturally attained some degree of development among them; and, with a few exceptions, such as the blow-pipe and the *gayang* or *parang ilang*, all the kinds of weapons to be found in the hands of the pagans are also in use among the Bajaus and Illanuns, who were either their makers, or at any rate the middlemen through whom they reached the hands of their neighbours.

Since the manufacture of weapons of war is now to all intents and purposes a lost art among the coastal peoples, it is rather difficult to ascertain with any certainty which of the present weapons were made locally, especially as many types have a fairly wide distribution. Besides this, the Tempassuk district seems to be on the border-line between two cultures, southern and western and northern and eastern, the former being propagated from Brunei, the latter from the Sulu Islands and Mindanao.

Thus some of the weapons in use, such as the Malay kris proper, and probably the "Crusader" sword, or *pedang*, were introduced from Brunei; while the long Illanun sword, the *kompilan*, with its curiously carved and flattened handle, and its blade, narrow near the hilt, but broad and heavy at the point, came from Mindanao, the place of origin of the Illanuns themselves. Types of handle and blade somewhat similar to that of the *kompilan* are, however, found in islands farther to the east, notably Celebes and Timor. (See *British Museum Handbook to the Ethnographical Collections*, p. 94, (*b*) and (*c*).)

The kind of sword or dagger locally termed kris, but called *sundang* or *serundang* by the Malays of the Peninsula and of Sumatra (which, if we are to accept them as authorities, is not a kris at all, the Malayan kris being used only as a stabbing and thrusting weapon), and the *sundang* for cutting, slashing and stabbing, present rather a difficult problem as to their place of origin. Specimens of this type of weapon are fairly commonly to be found in the Malay States of the Peninsula and I believe in Sumatra also, while they are probably the weapons most in use among the coastal peoples of our two districts and according to report are derived from the Sulus. (See *British Museum Handbook to the Ethnographical Collections*, p. 95, where a specimen from Sulu is figured.) Possibly the *sundang* may have been introduced into the Peninsula and Sumatra by the pirates and traders who annually visited these waters from Borneo and Mindanao.

Another weapon which bids fair to rival the kris (*sundang*) in popularity is the *pida* or *barong*, also a Sulu weapon.

The companion of the *kompilan* or the long Illanun sword is a peculiar type of shield called *klasug*. This stands about four feet high, is about one foot six inches broad, and has a peculiarly shaped boss. As far as I have been able to ascertain—for specimens are difficult to obtain nowadays—the Bajau shield was generally circular and made of wood, but I believe that more rarely rattan shields like those of the up-country Dusuns were to be found among the tribe. No doubt, however, weapons and shields of almost any type made in this part of Borneo, or in those neighbouring countries with which there was much intercourse, were in use among the lowlanders, both Mohammedans and pagans, since I have had a *klasug* brought for sale to me by a Dusun and a *kompilan* by a Bajau.

True krises of the Malay or Javanese types seem to be uncommon, and are usually much prized. The value of a Sulu kris (*sundang*) is estimated partly on the workmanship of the blade, but much more on the material from which the hilt is made. Weapons of this type, with quite good blades and wooden hilts, can be picked up very cheaply; but a specimen with a fine blade, silver mountings and a large ivory handle will command anything up to seventy dollars or more. The art of damascening the blades of weapons, which formerly flourished in Sumatra, Java and the Malay States, seems never to have been developed in the part of Borneo with which I am acquainted; and with the exception of the blades of a few weapons (mostly Malay type krises) which were obviously of foreign origin, I never remember having seen this method of ornamentation employed.

The Bajaus and Illanuns appear to have formerly used brass chain-mail coats and some kind of brass helmet, which was called *atub-atub* and very possibly copied from those worn by the Arabs. I made many endeavours to obtain a specimen of each of these articles, but always without success. As far as I could ascertain, some European on a plantation near Kudat had formerly offered such high prices for them that the local stock, never very large, was quite exhausted. Padded and quilted coats ornamented with embroidered texts in Arabic characters, which probably had a talismanic use, were also sometimes worn under the coat of mail.

Spears of various types, which may be used either for stabbing or throwing, are largely used at the present day in hunting. When not in use their heads are protected by a wooden sheath, the two portions of which are bound together with rattan cane. I was lucky enough to obtain a rare kind of spear which was described to me as being only used by chiefs. Its peculiarity lies in the fact that about a foot in the middle of the shaft is covered with the long and delicate feathers of some kind of bird, but it is also decorated just below the blade with a beautifully worked silver mount.

I believe that the use of this weapon was ceremonial, and that it was carried before a chief as a sign of rank, just as the short spears ornamented on the shaft with bunches of dyed vegetable fibre and known as *tombak benderang* are to the present day borne before Malay Sultans on occasions of state.

Brass cannon, chiefly of the varieties known as *lela* and *rantuka*, are still to be found stored away in many Bajau and Illanun houses, especially those of men of importance. The majority of these weapons were cast either in Brunei or Sulu. Little toy cannon of the same metal are also sometimes met with. These were, I believe, and possibly still are, used for firing blank charges on festive occasions, as, for instance, at the end of the Ramadan fast.

The weapons of the Bajaus and Illanuns were utilised partly against the neighbouring pagan tribes, whom they seem to have oppressed very badly; partly against native or even European shipping; and, as I have mentioned elsewhere, the Illanuns were feared as far away as the coasts of the Malay Peninsula. The Bajaus' reputation as sea-robbers was only second to that of the Illanuns', the word "Bajau" being almost synonymous with pirate.

Abdullah, a Malay *munshi* (teacher) who lived at Singapore and was somewhat of a protégé of Raffles and other of the earliest administrators of that settlement, paid a visit to the east coast of the Peninsula, and in his *Pĕlayaran Abdullah* ("Abdullah's Voyage"), which he wrote in 1852, he gives us some idea of the fear inspired by the Illanuns in Pahang, Trengganu and Kelantan; indeed he fell in with a pirate prahu, apparently Illanun, at the mouth of the Kelantan river, but was fortunate enough to escape molestation on account of his having business with the raja.

He draws a picture for us of the pirate chief standing up in the prahu, a throwing-spear grasped in his hand, "his moustache on one side trained over his ear, on the other wound on his neck." He also remarks that the rover's followers were dark-skinned and sturdy, but gives us no description of the craft he owned.

Some details about the Illanun and Bajau pirates are given in the *Papers relating to Piracy (Borneo) presented to the House of Commons by Command of her Majesty, April 1850*, and in *Piracy (Borneo). Copies of Extracts of any Dispatches relating to the Suppression of Piracy off the coast of Borneo.* One of the most interesting references to the Illanuns which I have come across in looking through these is to be found in the extracts from the *Historical Notices upon the Piracies committed in the East Indian Archipelago*, by Jhr. J. P. Cornets de Grott, Secretary-General to the Minister for the Colonies (Dutch), of which the original French and an English translation are given.

Speaking of the Illanuns, he says: "The pirates of Magindano or Illanoun, one of the Philippine Isles, commonly called Magindanais and Lanounais, incessantly annoy the Isle of Bintang, and the islands in the vicinity of the latitude of Linga, as well as those situated between Borneo and the Peninsula of Malacca—namely, Poeloe Auwer, Siantan, Boengoeran, Poeloe Tingi, Poeloe Laut and Tammelan.

"In the middle of the month of April they generally quit their retreats, and proceed along the eastern and western coasts of Borneo, on the side of the Banka and Billiton Strait, where they arrive about the commencement of May. Their fleet is separated into small divisions, which hasten to commit their depredations upon the eastern coast of Sumatra, as far as Reteh, in the waters of Linga and Bintang, and amid the groups of islets which reach as far as Cape Romania. Towards the month of June the pirates generally unite together at Poeloe Tingi, where they seize many of the vessels belonging to Pahang, Trenganoe, Kembodja, and

Kelambang in the Peninsula of Malacca. In September and October they quit these latitudes in order to retire to their haunts. During their return they still find time enough for plundering the coasts of the Isles of Siantan, Poeloe Laut and Tammelan.

"The largest kind of prahus are defended by double nettings, and have from 50 to 80 men on board. They have two rows of oars, each of 30, and are armed at the head with 2 powerful guns of from 6 to 8, besides 6 or 8 *lilla* or swivels."

In another place he says: "Under the name of Lanouns, we include the pirates of Magindano, Suloo, and some places in the neighbourhood of Borneo, as Tuwara, Tumbassa, Mangkabo.

"No fewer than 100 vessels are fitted out at Magindano and Suloo, 50 at Tuwara, 20 at Tumbassa and 20 at Mangkabo [*i.e.* Tuaran, Tempassuk, Mengkabong]; 5 or 6 are actually sent out from Sumroka to Borneo, properly so called [*i.e.* the territories of the state of Brunei], near Tanjong Datoe."

A few other quotations from correspondence to be found in these papers may also be of interest:—

"Subsequent to the departure of her Majesty's ship *Samarang* from Bruné in the month of October 1844, one of the first measures of the Raja Muda Hassim, on assuming the reins of Government, was an intimation to Sheriff Hausman of Malludu [or Marudu] and to the Illanuns of Tempassuk of his treaty with her Majesty's Government for the suppression of piracy, warning them to desist, and ordering them on no account to visit or to trade with Bruné whilst they continued to pirate."

[MR BROOKE *to the* EARL OF ABERDEEN

SINGAPORE, 31*st March* 1845.]

"The pirates on the coast of Borneo may be classed into those who make long voyages in large heavy-armed prahus, such as the Illanuns, Balanigni, etc., and the lighter Dyak fleets which make short but destructive excursions in swift prahus. . . .

"The next pirate horde we meet with is a mixed community of *Illanuns* and *Bajows* (or sea gipsies), located at Tempassuk, a few miles up a small river [possibly the Pindasan]. They are not formidable in number, and their depredations are chiefly committed on the Spanish territory. They might readily be dispersed and driven back to their own country, and the Dusuns or villagers (as the name signifies) might be protected and encouraged."

(MEMORANDUM *with the above*)

The Bornean pirates were largely put down in the years 1844 to 1849 by Sir E. Belcher in command of H.M.S. *Samarang* and Captain the Hon. H. Keppel in command of the *Dido*, but in the *Return of Bounties paid for the Capture and Destruction of Pirates* in the same papers there is an entry of Illanun pirates, subjects of the Sultan of Sūlu, being captured off Trengganu by H.M.S. *Wolf* as early as 1839, while the taking of Malay pirates, some of whom may have been Illanuns, is recorded as early as 1837. Keppel was afterwards Admiral, and till his death a Director of the British North Borneo Company. He gave his name to Province Keppel. Much good work in suppressing piracy was also done by the Dutch, but this was chiefly elsewhere than on the north-west coast of Borneo.

In 1846 vigorous action was taken against the pirates in the Tempassuk, as is set forth in the journal of Captain Mundy (*Events in Borneo, Celebes, and Labuan*), who was in charge of the *Iris*, which together with the *Agincourt*, the *Hazard*, the *Phlegethon*, the *Spiteful*, the *Dædalus*, the *Ringdove* and the *Royalist* took part in the expedition, Rear-Admiral Sir Thomas Cochrane, who had hoisted his flag on the *Agincourt*, being in command. This fleet, after dealing with the Dyak pirates in Sarawak and capturing the city of

Brunei, the Sultan of which had murdered all those of his relations who were friendly to the British, proceeded along what is now the coast of British North Borneo, and anchored near Gaya Island, at the mouth of the Mengkabong river, and at Ambong, at which place they found that the flourishing village, visited and described by Sir Edward Belcher only two months before, had been reduced to ashes by Illanun pirates in revenge for the help the inhabitants had afforded to the British by selling them cattle and provisions.

On 30th July the squadron had arrived at Ambong. On the 31st, on rounding a promontory, a large prahu, which Mr Brooke, who was with the expedition, immediately recognised from its peculiar build to be a war-boat of the Illanuns, was seen pulling at top speed towards the Tempassuk river, and chase was given. To quote Captain Mundy's own words:

"The *Phlegethon* soon got between him and the shore, three boats were sent after him, and possession taken without resistance, for formidable as those pirates are, from their number and ferocity, no wonder they were appalled at the sight of the squadron now before them. The boat was sixty feet long, and carried one long twelve-pounder, and two brass six-pound swivels. She was rigged for sixty oars, with regular boarding nettings, but had only twenty men and the captain on board, the stern-sheets being occupied by a large bier, on which was placed a massive teak coffin, handsomely ornamented. When the chief was brought prisoner on the quarter-deck, and asked to what nation he belonged, and why he was so crowded with arms (she was full of *kampelans*—*i.e.* large double-handed swords—spears and krises), he said at once:

"'I am an Illanun and a pirate chief. I sailed from hence with four other vessels on a cruise. One of the officers died, and with a portion of my crew I am now bringing him to his home for decent burial.'

"On being asked if the officer died a natural death, he replied: 'Yes.'

"Orders were then given to open the coffin, when lo! there lay the remains of a body evidently slain in battle, or after a desperate struggle, but a few days before. A large sabre-cut extended across the forehead, and the chest and thighs were also desperately maimed. The pirate chief now became so enraged at this exposure that he boldly stated he had told a lie, and admitted that they had had an engagement with some of the Balanini war-boats, which they had driven off, but an officer being killed, he was, according to their custom, brought back for interment. It was about this time that a Spaniard, who had been released from slavery by Sir Thomas Cochrane on his visit to Bruné last year, and was now on board the *Phlegethon*, recognised among the crew the man who had made him prisoner, and had murdered the master of the Spanish vessel to which he belonged, while resisting the pirates' attack: shortly afterwards on examining the prahu, two other Spaniards came forward, declaring that they had been taken off the Manilla coast, and had since been compelled to labour as slaves on board the pirate prahus."

Captain Mundy then goes on to tell how, on an attempt being made to handcuff the Illanun chief, he, followed by all his people, jumped overboard, and attempted to gain the shore by swimming. They were, however, cut off and captured, and when brought aboard again were put in irons.

On the same day the Admiral and Mr Brooke, "protected by the armed boats of the *Agincourt*," went ashore and interviewed Sa Tabok, the Illanun raja. They reproached him for having broken the arrangements entered into the year before, and for attacking "the peaceful town of Ambong." He was finally given twenty-four hours to consider, being warned that if at the end of that time he and his chiefs did not come to the *Agincourt* and give ample guarantees for their future good conduct, his village would be attacked and destroyed. Sa Tabok admitted that he had broken his promises, but he would not say whether he would come to the *Agincourt* and give the pledges required.

On the next day, no signs of submission being shown, Captain M'Quhae of the *Dædalus*, with a force of two hundred and fifty seamen and marines, was "sent into the river, with orders to destroy the war boats and canoes, unless the chiefs offered terms of submission." They, however, found the place deserted, so all the war canoes and the principal buildings were burned. While the burning was proceeding the Illanuns were seen in the distance "brandishing their spears in defiance, and the chiefs on horseback at the edge of the jungle slowly moving backwards and forwards watching the ruin of their stately dwellings." But I should scarcely call "stately" a word which could be applied to any Illanun building.

On the same day Captain Mundy was ordered to head another expedition to deal with the pirates of the Pandassan (Pindasan) river, "ten miles to the north-east of the Tempassuk," arrangements being made for the visit to be paid on the following day (2nd August). Starting at daylight in the *Phlegethon* (a steamer belonging to the Honourable East India Company), in which the commander-in-chief had hoisted the flag, and with the gun-boats of the *Iris* and *Ringdove* in tow, the expedition anchored off the mouth of the Pindasan river, a notorious haunt of the pirates, at eight A.M.

The expeditionary forces consisted of one hundred and fifty seamen and marines, "exclusive of the Javanese crew under Mr Ross." Pindasan town or village was reached in safety, and was found to have been evacuated by the inhabitants, who, however, had not had time to carry off their "furniture." After sentries had been posted, Captain Mundy, the Admiral—who had joined the party at Pindasan—Lieutenant Vansittart and a body-guard penetrated some way into the surrounding country, and exchanged shots with the enemy, a few of whom were killed during their retreat to the hilly ground.

The idea had been that the Pindasan expedition should join hands with the forces on the Tempassuk river under Captain M'Quhae, but the ground being in a very bad state, owing to heavy rains, this plan was abandoned; so after burning every house in the town and destroying the war-boats in course of construction, one of which was a craft "fifty feet in length and beautifully built," the expedition returned to the *Phlegethon* and the same day the vessel returned to the mouth of the Tempassuk river and joined her consorts.

On 3rd August the captured pirates were transferred to the *Ringdove* for passage to Manilla, where they were to be given up to the Spanish Governor, and the squadron weighed anchor and proceeded to the northward. In the afternoon of the same day three pirate prahus were discovered trying to make good their escape, and were chased by the *Royalist's* boats, when after an engagement twenty of the pirates were killed and two of their prahus destroyed; there were no casualties among the *Royalist's* crew, owing to the pirates' bad aim, though the latter appear to have fought desperately.

After this the squadron passes for a time out of the districts with which we are concerned to visit the stronghold of Sheriff Osman in Marudu Bay (destroyed the year before), with a view to seeing whether that piratical Arab had returned and rebuilt his stockades. Returning from Marudu Bay, where they had found Sheriff Osman's fortifications still deserted, the Admiral set sail for China, accompanied by the *Dædalus*, *Ringdove* and *Royalist*.

Captain Mundy in the *Iris*, with the *Hazard* and *Phlegethon* also under his command, left for Ambong, anchoring on the same evening (7th August) at Batu Mandi and dispatching Lieutenant Little in charge of a party in a pinnace and a cutter on a further expedition up the

Pindasan river. Little was successful in burning an Illanun village and had a brush with the pirates on the return journey. He also captured and destroyed an Illanun vessel, whose crew escaped to the shore. The expedition rejoined the *Iris* and the rest of the squadron at Ambong, which they had reached on the evening of the 10th August.

From this place sail was made for Kimanis, and thence to the Membakut river to punish a pirate and marauder, one Haji Saman. Having met with some success in dealing with this gentleman, Captain Mundy visited Brunei to keep alive the fear which Raja Brooke had inspired in the Sultan during a visit that he had paid to the country a short time before.

Thence he again sailed for the Tempassuk district, calling in at Kimanis on the way, but was forced to make for Marudu Bay by a storm before he could visit "the piratical town of Sarang—only a few miles distant from the Bato Mande [Batu Mandi] rocks." Captain Mundy arrived in Marudu Bay on 1st September and on 9th September anchored off Ambong again, after nine days of very bad weather, during which he made three unsuccessful attempts to carry out the projected expedition against Sarang, being on each occasion obliged to run for safety by gales from the south-west quarter. Considerable fears were felt for the safety of the *Hazard*, which had become separated from her consort, the *Iris* (the *Phlegethon* with Raja Brooke on board had left for Sarawak some time previously). However, at daylight on 10th September the *Hazard* was seen in the offing and before noon she was safely anchored.

News was obtained at Ambong that the Illanuns of Sarang, who had been joined by the fugitives from Pindasan and Tempassuk, despairing of being able to offer a successful resistance, had removed their families and goods, "and gone across the country to the district of Tungku, on the eastern shores of Borneo," whence presumably they returned at a later date. Having thus attained the object of the expedition, in driving out the Illanuns, Captain Mundy sailed on other business to Kimanis and Brunei and did not again return to the Tempassuk district. He left Acheen Head, Sumatra, on 12th April 1847 and reached Spithead on 29th July of the same year.

I have so far said very little about the methods of land-fighting formerly in vogue among the Illanuns and Bajaus, but as I have already dragged out this chapter to an unconscionable length, through giving what extracts I could find dealing with the subject of Illanun piracy, I will only add that, in the majority of cases, fighting of this kind no doubt consisted of unorganised raids on the weaker tribes of the interior, the burning of the upland villages, the killing of the majority of the menfolk and the seizure of the women and children as slaves, who might either be reserved for the use of their Bajau and Illanun masters or profitably sold to the princes and chiefs of Brunei, Sulu and Mindanao.

CHAPTER XXIX

ANTIQUITIES

I AM inclined to think, with regard to antiquities, that it is quite possible that some interesting finds may be awaiting the excavator in British North Borneo, though I do not mean to suggest that any large buildings or buried cities will reward his labours. From what I have seen of the Tempassuk district I should say that relics of ancient occupation are by no means uncommon. Though unfortunately I had but little time to devote to the excavation of the legendary sites of ancient villages or graves, I managed to do a little work on one hill-top which was reported to have been occupied in former days by a Dusun village.

The most interesting collection of antiquities that I was able to make was one of stone implements. These, I believe, had not been reported previously from British North Borneo, though Dr Haddon had found one in Sarawak, and subsequently a fine collection of them was made by Dr Hose and presented to the Cambridge University Museum of Ethnography.

The three stone implements from Sarawak figured by Ling Roth were, I believe, reported previously to this discovery; but one of these, which is of palæolithic type, was obtained from a dealer, and is doubtfully Bornean, while of the two others, which were found by Mr Hart Everett, one is from a bed of river gravel and appears to be of palæolithic type, and the other, which was found in a cave, is a very rudely chipped object. All Dr Hose's specimens are of neolithic culture and are axe- or adze-heads.

Thinking that if stone implements had been found in

Sarawak there was no reason why they should not occur in British North Borneo, I began to make inquiries among the natives, aided by a catalogue of the National Museum of Antiquities of Scotland which I happened to have by me. This contained a large number of illustrations of Scottish stone implements, and I soon found that I was on the track of what I wanted, for the natives recognised the illustrations as being pictures of stones similar to those known to them as "thunder teeth" (*gigi guntor*). These, they said, were found at the roots of coco-nut and other trees which had been struck by lightning. Disregarding this statement, as natives will, if there be a legend that stone implements are thunderbolts, persuade themselves that they found one which they possess under a tree which has been struck, I made a few further inquiries, but without result.

One Sunday on going down to the Chinese shops as usual to see what up-country natives had come in, and to have a look at the cock-fighting, which was a weekly fixture on that day, I happened to see a Bajau draw out from his pocket something which I thought looked suspiciously like a stone implement, and rub the spurs of his fighting-cock with it. Calling up Kĕruak, the local Bajau chief, who happened to be in a shop close by, I asked him to get hold of the man and find out what sort of a stone he was using as a charm. On our taking the man on one side he very reluctantly produced a beautiful little axe-head made of a green stone, which looked very much like an inferior quality of jade. He told me that he did not like showing the stone to many people as it diminished its potency as a charm, and he absolutely refused to name a price for it.

After this I set two or three men to hunt for me, and one of them brought me a very fine specimen, of which I was able to get a model made; but here again the owner would not sell, although a very tempting price was offered. Subsequently when it became known in the villages that I was hunting for *gigi guntor*, and offering large prices, specimens began to be brought in for sale, some of the vendors saying that their father or grandfather had seen a tree struck by lightning and had dug under it for the thunder tooth until he found it, and others, in the case of newly found specimens, generally telling me fairly enough that they had picked them up when working in their padi-fields; that they had noticed them lying at the side of the track when riding along on their buffaloes; or had seen them sticking out of a bank of earth the old face of which had fallen away.

In all I managed to make a small collection of thirteen actual implements and two models, while I was lucky enough to find one small implement myself, which was lying on a bank of earth beside the bridle-path leading from Kotabelud to the steamer wharf in Usakan Bay.

The material of which three of the implements are made is a green nephrite; four are manufactured from a closely grained stone which is almost jet-black, and looks like some form of basalt, though the colour may be partly due to the specimens having been constantly rubbed and handled by the natives who found them; while other three, and among them that which I found myself, are of local claystone, so soft that it makes it difficult to understand how they can ever have been really used as cutting instruments. The remaining two are made, one of quartz and the other of some kind of sandstone.

Most of the implements may be classed as axe- or adze-heads of various types, but one of soft stone has a gouge-like form, and two implements and one model are very curious specimens, as they are axe-like in shape, but have a double-cutting (?) edge: what the use of these can have been it is very difficult to imagine.

All stone implements are highly prized as charms. They are put into the padi store to keep the padi in good condition; water in which they have been soaked is given to sick persons to drink; swords are rubbed with them in order to ensure their inflicting deadly wounds, and the spurs of fighting-cocks are similarly treated so that they may make deep wounds on the opposing bird.

Apart from stone implements proper, I found that flakes of reddish-coloured radiolarian chert were common on all the foot-hills around Kotabelud. These in most cases had the bulb of percussion well developed, though the whole flake was generally somewhat rough, chert not giving such a nice clean fracture as English flint. In addition to a large number of "flakes" I was lucky enough to find one typical "core." This red chert, which is known to the natives as *batu api* (fire-stone), is, in conjunction with a piece of steel, frequently used at the present day to strike a light. No attempt is made to dress the stone by chipping; either a piece of a convenient size is picked up from the ground, or, if none small enough can be found, a large stone is thrown against a boulder and the fragments collected, or pounded on a large boulder until it breaks in pieces.

I was inclined to believe, in spite of the modern theories of the formation of natural flakes and cores by lightning and other agencies, that these specimens are artifacts, one of the main reasons for my belief being the regular flaking of the "core." Against my contention, however, there is the fact that I have never seen a true implement made from red chert, but this is by no means to say that they do not occur.

Before describing the small excavations I made at Tudu, a hill overlooking Usakan Bay and the Illanun villages about Fort Alfred, I should like to say a little about reported finds of ancient objects in the Tempassuk district. I frequently heard stories of natives coming across old jars half buried on the tops of the grass-covered foot-hills about Kotabelud, notably near the bridle-path which leads to Tuaran, and there seems to be no reason to doubt the statements, though I have never seen a specimen which has been obtained in this way. These may be old burial jars, but from the descriptions given me they would seem to be too small to have been used for this purpose. Fragments of old celadon-ware are, however, not uncommonly to be met with around the bases of the foot-hills, and I have frequently picked them up myself.

One Bajau who knew that I was interested in ancient objects told me that he and a companion had once found an ornament of twisted gold—from his description I imagine it to have been a sort of torque—in his padi-field. They had cut it in two and had each sold his half to the local goldsmith at the price by weight of old gold. On application to the goldsmith he confirmed the Bajau's story, but told me that he had melted the pieces down and used them for making new ornaments.

Shortly before I left Borneo a report was brought to me that there was a rock not far from Kampong Piasau which bore the imprint of a gigantic foot, but as I was busy at the time I was unable to go and see whether it was a natural depression which happened somewhat to resemble a footprint or whether it was an artificial mark, such as I believe are sometimes found on rocks in Buddhist countries.

With regard to the village site on the hill called Tudu, which I have mentioned above, my intention was first called to the place by Orang Kaya Haji Arsat, the head Government chief of the Tempassuk. He told me that it was reported that the hill-top had been occupied in former days by a Dusun village—that is, in the times before the invasion of the Tempassuk by Bajaus and Illanuns—and that there was a legend about the destruction of the village by a hurricane; further, that men who had climbed the hill in recent years had found its top strewn with fragments of the cooking-pots used by the ancient occupants. On asking one of my Dusun friends about the matter, I found that the legend of Tudu was well known, and obtained the following story from him.

Long ago some men of Kampong Tudu were looking for

wood to make a fence, and while they were searching they came upon what appeared to be a great tree trunk, which was lying on the ground. They began to cut it with their working-knives, intending to make their fence from it, but to their surprise blood came from the cuts. So they decided to walk along to one end of the "trunk" and see what it was. When they came to the end they found that they had been cutting into a great snake, and that the end of the "trunk" was its head. They therefore made stakes and, driving them into the ground, bound the snake to them and killed it. They then flayed the skin from the body, and taking it and the meat home they made a great feast from its flesh. The skin of the snake they made into a great drum, and while they were drinking they beat the drum to try its sound, but for a long time it remained silent. At last, in the middle of the night, the drum began to sound of its own accord: "*Duk, Duk, Kagu; Duk, Duk, Kagu*" (*Kagu* is Bajau for hurricane or typhoon). Then came a great hurricane and swept away all the houses in the village: some of them were carried out to sea together with the people in them; others settled down at what is now Tempassuk village and other places, and from them arose the present settlements.

Being interested in the tale, and thinking that there was very probably some truth in the story of a village on the hill-top, as it would be an almost impregnable site in war-time, I arranged with the Orang Kaya to make the climb, and a few days later started from Kotabelud with three or four Dusun coolies armed with *changkuls* (a kind of Chinese hoe). At Fort Alfred I met the Orang Kaya, accompanied by an Illanun follower, and we started a very long and hot climb up the sides of the hill, which were covered with *lalang* (a rough grass).

On arrival at the top we at once saw that it would make a most admirable situation for a fort, as Tudu commands the whole of the surrounding country, and the hill-top is sufficiently flat to accommodate easily a decent-sized village, though water seemed to be scarce. The most prominent objects on the hill were two immense *memplum* or *impalum* trees which were in fruit at the time. These were obvious signs that there either had been a village on the hill, or that people had visited the hill-top in bygone days.

The next thing was to find a site for our excavations, and after searching for profitable ground for a short time by uprooting tussocks of *lalang* and inspecting the soil below them, I decided that one place, where the humus was very black, and where two or three pieces of rough pottery were found near the surface, was most probably ground on which a house had stood. In this opinion I was speedily confirmed, as on driving two intersecting trenches, about two and a half feet deep, at right angles across the site we came upon many fragments of rough pottery, broken bones of animals—chiefly pigs—and large numbers of sea-shells of species related to the clam and English cockle.

In addition to these we found four objects of much greater interest: one a water-rounded stone of granite with a diameter of about three and a half inches, which the Dusun coolies said would be probably used for smoothing the inside of cooking-pots during the process of manufacture; another an almost circular pebble of sandstone of slightly less diameter than the "potting-stone." This was flattened on either side and had an artificially made indentation in the centre of each flattened surface. Worked stones, sometimes completely perforated, sometimes with only two chiselled or drilled depressions, as in the above case, are frequently found in England associated with other articles of neolithic culture. Such stones were probably used as hammers, those with a hole having had a wooden handle pushed through them, and those with depressions only being held in the hand, the depressions affording a firm grip for the thumb and the index finger. It is possible that the bored stones may have been used as club-heads—*c.f.* the stone club-heads of New Guinea. I am inclined to think that the stone from Tudu may have been used for this purpose, as one edge is much chipped.

The remaining objects of interest were a couple of pieces of Chinese crackle-ware, one, which looked like a fragment of a small plate, being of the colour which is known as caledon, the other, which the natives seemed to think was a fragment of a *Gusi* jar, being greenish brown in colour, rather thick, with a very fine crackle. Unfortunately I had no time to excavate the place systematically, as it was with difficulty that I was able to devote even a day to the work. I may remark here that the Dusun coolies said that the fragments of rough pottery which we dug up were of different consistency to that now in use.

The only other ancient site I visited was far up-country on the bridle-path to the Interior. This place, which is some little way beyond the Singaran halting-bungalow (opposite Kiau), is an earthwork on the side of the hill, and as far as can now be seen consists of a trench about sixty feet long, with a corresponding mound on the valley side of it. The mound has been almost destroyed in making the bridle-path, but the trench is still fairly clearly defined.

The Dusuns tell the following legend about the place:—Once long ago there was a very tall man named Lamongoyan, who could cross a river at a single stride. He died on the top of the hill above this spot, and his people being unable to lift his body rolled it down to the grave they had dug, and buried him there. His head lies pointing inland and his feet towards the sea.

CHAPTER XXX

THE CHINESE IN BORNEO

THE statement is frequently made by residents in Borneo that the Dusuns are "half Chinese," and the same assertion is not uncommonly to be met with in books. Ling Roth, for instance, in his map of British North Borneo has printed in red letters across the whole coastal region of North-West Borneo from Brunei Bay to Marudu Bay, including the Tuaran and Tempassuk districts: "Mixed Chinese and Native Tribes" (*Natives of Sarawak and British North Borneo*, vol. i., and *The British North Borneo Herald*, 1st July 1914). Now definite statements of this kind should not be made unless there is very good evidence to show that they are true. I believe that the theory of the "half-Chinese" origin of these tribes first arose from a supposed reference made to the Chinese in certain Bornean names, and from legends of a former Chinese invasion of this part of the island.

As I had long been annoyed by the constant reiteration of these statements, which rested, to my thinking, on no sufficient basis of evidence, I wrote, some time ago, a letter to *The British North Borneo Herald*, setting out the arguments in favour of the Chinese theory, dealing with them as thoroughly as I could, and at the same time asking for any help from those interested in the subject which might tend to throw light upon the question and, if possible, settle it in one way or another. This letter of mine ran as follows:—

TAIPING, PERAK,
FEDERATED MALAY STATES,
4th June 1914.

SIR,—I am writing to you to ask whether any of your readers would be kind enough to help me in a small investigation which I am making as to the past history of British North Borneo.

In many accounts of Borneo it has been stated that there has been a large infusion of Chinese blood among the aborigines of the northern portions of the island, some writers even going so far as to say that the Dusuns are half Chinese. I am much inclined to think that their conclusions have been reached by a very slipshod process of reasoning, and that no large admixture has ever taken place. The following statements are, I believe, generally advanced in support of the theory, and I will endeavour to deal with them *seriatim*:—

(1) That the Dusuns use hats and ploughs similar to those of the Chinese.

(2) That the men of one Dusun tribe wear a pigtail.

(3) That the Dusuns look rather like Chinese.

(4) That there are accounts of Chinese embassies being sent to Brunei.

(5) That there is a legend of a Chinese expedition going in search of the jewel guarded by the dragon, which was supposed to live at the top of Mount Kinabalu; and that a party of Chinese, who were left behind, settled in the country.

(6) That old Chinese jars, beads and fragments of ancient Chinese pottery are common in Borneo.

(7) That several names of mountains, villages and rivers begin with *Kina*, and that this means "China" (Chinese).

(1*a*) Now with regard to the first statement, both the conical sun-hat and the same type of plough are used by the Malays, and I also believe by the Javanese and Siamese, whom I have never heard accused of being half Chinese. The plough and the sun-hat *may* have been adopted from the Chinese, but it seems to me extremely risky to say because one race, tribe or nation has borrowed from the culture of another with whom they have been in contact, that, therefore, there has been a fusion of blood. I have seen several most excellent copies of European straw hats made by the Dusuns, and going on the above assumption, if the wearing of these should become general, one might almost as well say that there was a large strain of European blood among the Dusuns. Or again, reasoning thus, why not say that the Chinese are half European, since Chinese bootmakers now turn out boots made in the European fashion?

(2*a*) The men of one Dusun tribe wear a pigtail. I have never seen this tribe, so I do not know if their pigtails resemble those of the Chinese. A pigtail is, however, one very convenient method of doing up long hair, and is, I believe, not confined to the Chinese. Moreover, even if it has been adopted from the Chinese, this does not necessarily mean that the Dusuns are half Chinese, though it would prove that there had been a strong Chinese influence in the country.

(3*a*) It is stated that the Dusuns look like Chinese, but I must say that I have never been able to see much similarity. I do not, however, contest the fact that there is a certain Mongolian element present among the Dusuns, as, I believe, there is among all the Indonesian peoples, this seeming to be fairly well proved by the occurrence of lank, straight hair, and occasionally of the typical Mongolian fold over the inner corner of the eye. What I do believe, however, is that the Mongolian element is not of comparatively modern—*i.e.* Chinese—origin, but that it was probably introduced before the Indonesian race left Southern Asia for its present home.

(4*a*) The accounts of Chinese writers, translations of which I have read, do not seem to indicate anything further than that embassies were sent to Brunei and *vice versa*, and that Chinese trading junks used to make regular voyages to barter the manufactures of China for the produce of the jungle, and probably, in South-Western Borneo, for gold and diamonds.

(5*a*) The story of the dragon seems to come to us from Chinese or Malay sources, and I have not heard of it among the Dusuns, though it may be known; nor have I ever heard the Dusuns of the Tempassuk claim descent from the Chinese. The legend, which has a distinctly apocryphal flavour about it, is mentioned by both Dalrymple and Earl, and the latter in referring to it says: "The Chinese suppose the Dyaks to be descended from a large body of their countrymen left by accident upon the island, but this opinion is entertained solely on the faith of a Chinese legend. [Pigafetta states that at the time of his visit there were 30,000 Chinese living in the town of Brunei, but his accounts of the place are probably much exaggerated.] If they can prove their paternity to the Dyaks, they must extend it to the whole race inhabiting the interior of the large islands of the Archipelago [*i.e.* Indonesians]." Evidently Earl did not consider that there was much probability of truth in the account.

(6*a*) Old Chinese jars and other objects are certainly common in Borneo, but I take it that this does not necessarily indicate anything further than that the Chinese have been trading with Borneo for many hundreds of years. There were, at the time of my residence in Borneo, about seventeen Chinese shops in the Tempassuk, and these were ample for the amount of trade in the district. Supposing in the old days—when foreign articles were probably much rarer in Borneo than they are at present, trade much less than to-day, and life much more insecure—that the same number of Chinese traders inhabited the district: are we to consider that they would leave any permanent trace on the native population? No. If there ever was any large Chinese population, it must have been employed in mining or agriculture, probably the former. But have we anything to prove that such a population ever existed in the Dusun country?

(7*a*) Now, sir, we come to the last statement, and it is with regard to this in particular that I wish to enlist your readers' help. The usual examples given of names which indicate the presence of the Chinese in Borneo are "Kinabalu" and "Kinabatangan." If *Kina* really does mean China or Chinese, this again by no means necessarily shows that the Chinese ever came to the country in large numbers as colonists. Who gave the mountain its name? Most likely the Dusuns, since they appear to be the oldest inhabitants of the country at the present day. Unfortunately I do not know Dusun, and so I cannot trace for myself the meaning of the word in that language, if a meaning exists other than that of "Chinese Widow Mountain." I have, however, long had my suspicions that the accepted explanation was not correct, and have thought that it was probably one of those rather clever, but badly mistaken derivations which Malay pundits are such adepts at manufacturing—*e.g.* Singapura, the City of the Lion; Sumatra, Semut Raya.

Recently I have come across another explanation of the name of the mountain, which I am inclined to think much more probable. Kinabalu, according to Dusun legendry, is the home of departed spirits, and Witti says that the spirits of the dead are supposed to bathe in the waters which rush from the gullies of the mountain and which are called "Tatsi di Nabalu." Hatton continually speaks of Nabalu, and not of Kinabalu, and in a recent article in *The Sarawak Gazette*, by Mr J. C. Moulton, the suggestion is put forward that Nabalu means the home of the dead—"Nabalu, the Dusun word, signifying resting-place of the dead." It is true enough that Kinabalu is supposed to *be* the resting-place of the dead, but does Nabalu *mean* home of the dead? Perhaps someone who is learned in Dusun can help me. It is worth noting, however, that the mountain is very frequently spoken of as Nabalu or Habalu, which appears rather as if the *Ki* were merely some form of prefix.

The name Kinabatangan presents more difficulties, as the central part of it looks very much like the Malay word *batang* (trunk or water-course), which is often attached to the names of rivers—*e.g.* Batang Lupar, Batang Pahang. How are we to read it, Ki-nabatang-an or Kina-batang-an? The supposition that *Ki*, *Kin* or *Kina* may be prefixes is, I think, rather strengthened by the following North Borneo names, which all begin with one or other of these syllables, while in some it would be difficult to say that there was any reference to China or Chinese:—

(1) Kinoram (a district near Marudu).
(2) Kinabalu (sometimes called Penelab, and Kampong in the Tempassuk district).
(3) Kinataki (a river in the Tempassuk district).
(4) Kinsiraban (the name of an up-country village).
(5) Kinokop (Pinokop or Tenokop, a river in the Tempassuk district).
(6) Kinharingan (or Kenaringan, the name of the Dusun creator).
(7) Kimanis (the name is said to be derived from Kayu Manis, but I should think that this is doubtful).

Perhaps the prefix is either *Ki*, *Kin* or *Kina*, according to the requirements of euphony.

I believe that there are several rather strong supporters of the Chinese population theory in the British North Borneo Service, and I should be very glad if they, and others, would give me any fresh facts either in support of, or in opposition to, the theory. Moreover, I should be particularly thankful for any information bearing on the derivation of the names in which reference to the Chinese is thought to occur. So far the subject has been but little dealt with in a critical manner, and it would be interesting if the matter could be thrashed out to a conclusion, be my views right or wrong. I am, sir, yours obediently,

IVOR H. N. EVANS.

To THE EDITOR,
The British North Borneo Herald,
SANDAKAN.

My queries and questionings resulted in four most interesting letters being received in answer. One of these, from Mr E. O. Rutter, then District Officer, North Keppel, appeared on pp. 136 and 137 of *The British North Borneo*

Herald of the year 1914; another, from Mr J. C. Moulton, Curator, Sarawak Museum, in *The British North Borneo Herald* of 3rd November of the same year; the other two —one from Mr E. H. Stephens of Padas Valley Estate, Beaufort, British North Borneo, and the other from the Rev. Father Duxneuney of the Roman Catholic Mission, Putatan—were addressed to me privately.

Mr Stephens' letter deals entirely with statements Nos. 1 and 7 of my letter. He informs me that the tribe of Dusuns who wear a queue are those of Bundu, on the coast of the Klias Peninsula. It is worn by young men, who cut it off on becoming fathers of families. He goes on to state that the tribe shows "undoubted traces of Chinese influence —*e.g.* their feast days coincide with the Chinese New Year, and other festivals"—and remarks that they seem to have a hazy tradition of a former Chinese connection. Furthermore, he remarks that since the Chinese have discarded the pigtail it is losing its popularity in Bundu. He thinks that, as these Dusuns live on the coast, the infusion of Chinese blood "is likely to have been both recent and local."

With regard to the meaning of the name Kinabalu he says: "Not being satisfied with the usually accepted derivation of the name Kinabalu, I have questioned Dusuns from districts in the vicinity and have been told that Nabalu does not mean 'home of the dead,' the spirit being said to '*mengalau Nabulu*,' *mengalau* apparently being a special word to describe the journeying of the spirit after death. With regard to the prefix *Ki* I can obtain no information." He sums up by saying that he thinks that the supporters of the Chinese theory will have great difficulty in proving how a Chinese population, which is by some writers considered to have left its mark on large sections of the present native population of Borneo, "vanished and left such flimsy evidence of its existence."

Mr Rutter's letter from *The British North Borneo Herald* I give below *in extenso*:

To The Editor,
British North Borneo Herald.

Tuaran,
British North Borneo,
31st July 1914.

Chinese Names in Borneo

Sir,—Your correspondent, Mr I. H. N. Evans, made some queries in your issue of 1st July as to the meaning of the prefix *Ki*, *Kin* and *Kina* found in names in British North Borneo. I do not believe that this prefix has anything to do with China or Chinese, and offer the following explanation:—

The prefix is almost invariably confined to names of gods, mountains and rivers, and I suggest that it is the Dusun and Murut word *aki*, meaning grandfather or ancestor; the original names were Aki Nabalu, Aki Nabatangan, Aki Langalangah, etc., and the *a* of *aki* has come to be dropped by ellipse: that this is not postulating too much may be shown by the example of the word Kinaringan (the name of the Dusun deity), which is also pronounced Akinaringan by the Dusuns. *Na* is itself a prefix which constantly occurs in the Dusun and Murut languages, sometimes denoting a past participle (= Malay *ber*), sometimes interrogatory (*nakito ku* = do you see?) and in other cases apparently for the sake of euphony.

The word *nabalu* in Dusun means widowed, without a partner (*balu* = widow or widower). The most striking thing about the mountain is its splendid isolation, and it is not beyond the ingenuity of a Dusun to give it some such name as "the Solitary Father," Aki Nabalu. I do not think that Nabalu means the home of departed spirits as suggested by Mr J. C. Moulton. It is true that the Dusuns believe that their spirits go to "Nabalu," but Nabalu is only the name of the place (or person) that receives them, just as Paradise and Hades do not in themselves mean resting-places of the dead, but are only names for those resting-places.

Take next Kilangalangah (a mountain in the Ulu

Labuk), where there is no euphonic *na*, and we have Aki Langalangah with the simple prefix *Ki*, the *a* as usual being dropped by ellipse. In Kinataki (a river which rises in Mount Kinabalu) the *aki* appears to be duplicated. The sense of *aki* is again well shown in Kinapunan (*punan* = Malay *pokoà* (*sic*), *lit.* tree, and hence fountain, source, origin), the name the Muruts of the Keningan district give their deity. The prefix is also to be met with in Kinasaluan, a tributary of the Talankai in the far interior, and in Kinantupong, a tributary of the Sugut: neither of these names is likely to be due to Chinese influence.

With regard to Kinabatangan, there is one great objection to the derivation Kina Batang, for to mean "the Chinese river" the adjective should follow the noun and the name should be Batang Kina. Batang (I believe) has the same significance in Dusun and in Murut as in Malay, and I suggest that the name is *aki-na-batangan*—the Father River, an appropriate term for a river with many tributaries or *anak sungei.*

That this theory of personification is not wholly fanciful may be shown by parallels among other nations. Compare Father Tiber, Father Thames, Father Zeus. I cannot recall an instance of a mountain being endowed with the name of father, but it does not need much imagination to suppose that a race who live under the shadow of a great mountain could believe that they were under its paternal and supernatural care. After all, Mount Kinabalu, glinting in the morning sunlight, is probably the most wonderful thing that an up-country Dusun has ever seen. Your obedient servant, (*Signed*) E. O. RUTTER.

Mr J. C. Moulton in his letter to *The British North Borneo Herald* makes the interesting suggestion that *Ki*, *Ka* or *K* in place-names, etc. (examples Kadamaian, Kalupis, Kiau, Klowat, Kappak, Kinataki, Kinabalu, Kaung, Kudat, Kaningau, Kimanis), may be the local equivalent of the

Sarawak *S* which is so commonly found as the first letter of names in that country (examples: Sadong, Samarahan, Segu, Simanggang, Sabu, Skrang, Sentah, etc., etc.). He thinks that *S* in place-names may be equivalent to the *Si* which is often used before names of persons of some standing. *Si* is possibly equivalent to the Malay *inche* = sir or Mr.

He asks Mr Rutter to make sure that *balu* is used for both widow and widower among the up-country Dusuns, remarking that "It is quite possible that Dusuns, especially those of the coasts, have now followed the Malays in using the word *balu* for both widow and widower." He suspects that closer inquiry among the hill Dusuns will reveal a different word for widower, as in Kayan, Kenyah, Kalabit and others of the more primitive languages. He further remarks that we cannot pass the anomaly "Grandfather-Widow" as a translation of the name Kinabalu, but this of course would only be the case if Mr Rutter were right in his supposition that *Ki* is equivalent to *Aki* (grandfather) and that *balu* only means widow and not widower.

He further says: "Although the balance of opinion appears to be adverse to that of Chinese influence we should not dismiss it too summarily, as Chinese intercourse with North Borneo has been fairly regular for about twelve centuries. There is little doubt that small colonies of Chinese have settled well in the interior from time to time.

"Spenser St John, writing in 1858, says: 'To show how extensively the Chinese formerly spread over the country I may notice that they had pepper plantations even up the Madihit as late as the remembrance of some of the oldest Murut!' The Madihit is a branch of the Limbang river, some seventy miles south of Brunei. Some three years ago I visited the actual place mentioned by St John, but no amount of inquiry showed that the natives of that part had ever heard of Chinese in their district. On the other hand, there can be little doubt that the natives of that part exhibit now some evidence of this former Chinese influence, probably many glaring proofs, if the traveller only knows the natives (and Chinese) well enough to distinguish between what are obviously non-Chinese and what are obviously foreign to that Borneo tribe (*sic*).

"It may be of interest to your first correspondent on this subject (vide *British North Borneo Herald*, p. 100) that I found a small rectangular wooden box in a Dusun house on Kinabalu, which was used by the owner as a pillow. The Dusuns appeared surprised to hear that it was identical in shape with that used by the Chinese for the same purpose. Of course it may easily have been copied from one purchased a generation or two back in a Chinese bazaar on the coast; on the other hand, there is just the possibility of it forming an interesting piece of evidence of a much older and more intimate Chinese influence.

"The question of whether 'Nabalu' actually *means* 'the resting-place of the dead' (see Mr Rutter's letter), or is only 'the name given to the place that receives them,' reminds us of the old problem, 'which appeared first, the egg that produced the hen, or the hen that laid the egg? . . ."

Now to take the letter from Father Duxneuney, which is by far the most interesting communication of those which I have received privately, or have been published as the result of my letter to the *Herald*, since I believe that he has solved once and for all the question of Bornean names in which it has so far been customary to consider there is a reference to the Chinese.

Father Duxneuney has lived among the Dusuns of Putatan as a missionary for many years, since 1893, and as he, apart from his official labours, takes great interest in all matters concerning native belief and customs, his opinion should carry great weight.

I will take first that part of his letter which deals with the question of Bornean names which are thought to refer to the Chinese. He remarks that the Dusuns of Putatan always call that majestic mountain, which is supposed by them to receive the spirits of the dead, Nabahu or Nabalu (see also remarks in my letter to the *Herald*), and that when he first went to that place nobody understood the word Kinabalu. He also tells me that at Putatan l and h are interchangeable—*e.g.* "here we say *hamin* (house), a few villages higher up it becomes *lamin.*" This is well worth noting, as it has an important bearing on what follows in his letter.

He goes on to say that when a person dies the body is washed and then taken out of the room and laid on the verandah. Here a kind of hut is built over the corpse, which is covered with very old and costly cloths. "This hut in called *bahu*—house of the dead." The cloths themselves are also termed *bahu*, and Father Duxneuney remarks that *bahu* thus comes to get a secondary meaning of "pertaining to the dead."

He divides up the word Kinabalu in this fashion, *Ki-na-balu* (or *bahu*). With regard to the *na*, he agrees with Mr Rutter in saying that it is a common Dusun prefix often denoting past time, or rather denoting an action as past but still existing. *Ki*, he says, is an abbreviation of the Dusun *kiwâo* = it is, it was, there is. He thus roughly translates Kinabalu as follows:—"There is a place or home pertaining to the dead." To illustrate the use of the two prefixes *Ki* and *na* in conjunction he gives these examples:

(1) *Matai* (I die), *kapalazan* (death, subst.), *ki-na-palazan* (the continuation of the death of a person). "For instance," says Father Duxneuney, "for one dies now to-day, one says *napatai* (he died); but to say that his death occurred a week ago we use *Kinapalazan dan san minggo iyohu.*"

(2) *Memehobàng* (to bury), *hobongan* (a burial), *kohobongan* (a burial ground). "If I want to mention a burial of some time ago—long past—I have to twist my tongue to *kinapomohobangan* (*ki* here means 'there is'

—*-na* denotes the past time—*pomohobong*=to be made buried) is the passive from *memehobang* to bury."

Father Duxneuney considers that Kinabatangan is the Malay word *batang* "Dusunised"; thus, I suppose, *Ki-na-batang-an* may be roughly translated the place where there is (and was from times past) a *batang-an* or main river.

He furthermore gives much interesting information with regard to the Chinese in Borneo. This summarised is as follows:—The plough was formerly not used by the lowland Dusuns (Kadasan) of Putatan, and there are still natives alive who can remember when all land was prepared by hand. Hats of any kind are little worn, the head-cloth being the covering most in use. The hats are worn by the women at harvest, and on the occasion of a marriage a conical hat which is worn by the boy (bridegroom) is taken off his head by the priestess and placed on that of the bride. These hats are manufactured by the hill people. Jars, gongs and guns were mostly introduced from Brunei and thus, "if Chinese, came only indirectly to the native."

Father Duxneuney, however, tells me the Chinese had a great (commercial) influence amongst the natives in former times, before Labuan and North Borneo "came under Britain's commerce." He says that when he first came to Putatan (1893) there were only a few Chinamen in the interior. If I understand his letter rightly, these went up to trade from their shops at the Government post. He remarks that the whole trade of the country was in Chinese hands (this is still true of all retail trade throughout the country). "Everything I had," he says, "from a glass tumbler to a British North Borneo dollar, from a piece of cloth to my newspaper, *The Tablet*, was in their eyes made in China.

"How great was the influence which the Chinese had as *traders* is illustrated by the following incident which happened here only last year. A little native girl, about twelve years old, and a schoolmate were looking at an illustrated Bible history—they were unconscious that I was near. I heard one of them remark about a picture of Adam and Eve driven out of Paradise: 'It is rather bad that they go without clothing—only some leaves.' The twelve-year-old lady answered: 'Yes, but at that time there were no Chinamen.' She was quite serious, and evidently thought: no Chinaman, no shop to buy clothes at."

Father Duxneuney points out that the Putatan Dusuns have a legend that one of the hills in the district was originally near Kinabalu (Nabahu), but moved thence to its present position. He thinks that this may perhaps be taken as evidence that the Putatan Dusuns originally came down from the hill country around Kinabalu.

Though admitting, as I do, that the Chinese have long had great influence in Borneo as traders, he propounds the following problems for solution by those who believe that there was formerly such a large resident Chinese population in Borneo that many of the native tribes, and especially the Dusuns, are half Chinese:—

(1) "*Language.*—There is not the least similarity between Dusun and Chinese. Old Chinamen who have lived in the country for twenty years or more and have married Dusun wives never acquire the Dusun language—not to say master it. [A Chinaman who goes to a foreign country when he is already grown up seems seldom to master the native language. The China-born Chinese of the Straits and Borneo rarely acquire any fluency in speaking Malay, and when they do, invariably mispronounce very badly. Native-born Chinese of Borneo and the Straits acquire the language of the country without difficulty.] The latter has a very intricate grammar (something like Greek) and an enormous vocabulary. There is no trace in the Dusun language of Chinese influence."

(2) "Why is there no trace of any written language? By

the born trading instinct of the supposed progenitors of the Dusun one would expect that at least numerals would have been transmitted to their offspring."

(3) "No traces of reverence for ancestors or parents are found among the Dusuns, worship or reverence of this kind being essentially a Chinese characteristic."

(4) There seems to be no mention of the Chinese in native legendry.

I think that I have now dealt fairly with the greater part of the correspondence which appeared in *The British North Borneo Herald* in answer to my original letter. On re-visiting Borneo in 1915 I resolved to try and investigate the matter further in the Tempassuk, proceeding chiefly on the lines suggested by Father Duxneuney.

Mr Rutter stated in his letter to the *Herald* that *balu* means widow or widower in Dusun (presumably in the dialect of Tuaran or of the Tempassuk). I therefore put questions to Gumpus of Tambatuan, in the Tempassuk district, asking him what he would call a man whose wife was dead, and a woman whose husband was dead, being careful to avoid the use of the Malay word *balu*. He gave me the two words *opus* and *na-poud* (the latter apparently a past participle (?) widowed), which he said were applied either to a widow or a widower. A Tuaran native similarly questioned gave me *na-poud* only.

The Dusuns of Tuaran seem to speak of the mountain more frequently as Pengaluan (the name Pengaluan is, I find, mentioned by Whitehead) than as Nabalu, but this is obviously a noun of the same derivation (formed as in ordinary Malay), the *b* being dropped for the sake of euphony (*balu*, *pen-* or *peng-balu-an*, Pengaluan). Similarly the special word which Mr Stephens says is used of the ghosts ascending Nabalu, which he gives as *mengalau*, but which is in the Tempassuk pronounced *mengalu*, obviously also comes from the same source, the *b* again being dropped owing to the difficulty of saying *meng-balu*.

BAJAU VILLAGE AT MENGKABONG, TUARAN DISTRICT.

Many of the houses can be reached only by boat ; some have planks thrown across to dry land. Adjacent houses are often connected by narrow gangways. Though these make a picturesque scene their inhabitants are poverty:stricken and wretched to a degree. Their main occupations are fishing and salt-making, coupled with insufficient cultivation of rice.

Direct questioning of a Tuaran Dusun as to whether any objects used at burials or lyings-in-state had the term *balu* applied, procured the information that the *Gusi* jar which was sometimes placed near a corpse was called *pen-a-baluk* (the *k* was pronounced very distinctly). A Dusun of the Interior (a Tambunan man) told me that *balu* meant newly buried, and he and a Piasau (Tempassuk) man both gave me to understand that Pengaluan and Nabalu (or Kinabalu) *mean* the place where the dead go to.

With regard to the *na* in Nabalu (or Ki-na-balu), I obtained several more place-names in which this syllable occurs; in the case of one, Penabalu or Kinabalu, which I have already mentioned in my letter to *The British North Borneo Herald*, I was told that the name was derived from the fact that there was (or used to be) some sort of a hole or cave near the village which had both an entrance and an exit, and through this a river flowed. *Na-labu*, I understand from my Dusun informant, might be roughly translated "it goes through"; a man, for instance, being asked if a hole went right through from one side of a bank to the other, if it did, would reply: "*Na-labu*."

Let us now consider the evidence which goes to show that, in general, so-called proofs of the half-Chinese origin of the Dusuns are of the flimsiest.

With regard to the ploughs, hats, pillows, etc., used by the Dusuns, we may disregard them as proofs of a Chinese origin for the reasons set forth in my letter.

(2) The Mongolian characteristics found among the Dusuns are common to all Indonesian peoples to a greater or lesser extent, and were probably chiefly acquired before they left the coasts of Asia.

(3) It seems that *Ki-na* does not mean Chinese, *na* being a prefix signifying action past but still existing, which is common in place-names, and *Ki*, derived from Kiwāo, meaning "there is" (Father Duxneuney). It is worthy of note, however, that the Dusuns and some other tribes in speaking

T

Malay *do* talk of *Orang Kina* (Chinese), instead of *Orang China*, which is the proper pronunciation, since they seem to have difficulty in pronouncing *Ch*, turning it generally either into *K* or *S*—e.g. *siramin* for *chermin*, *sampur* for *champur*. No doubt the coincidence that certain Dusun place-names begin with *Ki-na* and that *Orang China* was pronounced *Orang Kina* was eagerly seized on by Malay (or other) pundits, ignorant of the language of the country, but desirous of making derivation for place-names, and connecting them with romantic stories.

One subject which I have not yet dealt with calls, perhaps, for some attention, and that is the question of an admixture of Chinese with the Dusuns of the Klias Peninsula. I have not been able to investigate the matter for myself, but Mr Wooley, Commissioner of Lands, tells me that locally there has undoubtedly been a mixture a couple of generations back or more, and that many natives claim a Chinese father or grandfather.

Granted that this is so, it cannot be taken as a proof of the assertion with regard to the Dusuns in general. The mixture appears to be purely local, and the locality is on the sea-coast. There is, of course, no barrier of custom or prejudice preventing Chinese from intermarrying with Dusuns, and given a sufficient number of Chinese settlers, a mixed race would be sure to arise; but I do not grant that we have any proof of there ever being a large Chinese population in the Tuaran or Tempassuk districts, or in the Interior. The supposed admixture of Chinese with natives, which is said to have given rise to the Dusuns, must, if it ever took place (which I do not believe), have occurred very much more than two or three generations ago, that being the period given by Mr Wooley for the Chinese-Dusun intermixture in and around the Klias Peninsula.

CHAPTER XXXI

DIARY OF A JOURNEY TO MOUNT KINABALU

JULY 4TH.—Went on board the s.s. *Sandakan* of the Straits Steamship Company at 7 A.M., and left Singapore at about 8 A.M. Not many passengers on board, and nobody that I knew when I was in Borneo before.

JULY 5TH.—Weather good and a nice fresh breeze. Passed between the Natuna Islands.

JULY 6TH.—Nothing in particular to record.

JULY 7TH.—Arrived at Miri in Sarawak, where there are oil wells. Went off to the shore in the Oil Company's launch shortly after arrival with E., one of the passengers; got permission from the Company's manager to take a walk round their property. There are numerous wells, and some of the derricks on the surrounding hills can be seen from the anchorage. A pipe-line runs out to sea, from the end of which steamers are loaded. Climbed to the top of the hill with E. and one of the Oil Company's employees, who was kind enough to show us round.

Took a few photographs of the wells and also of some Semanggang Dyak men. The Semanggang river is a tributary of the Batang Lupar. A number of these people have recently been imported to clear away grass and undergrowth. They were wearing large sun-hats, short breeches of European-made blue material, and in some cases figured sleeveless coats of native-woven cloth, the ground colour of which was black, while the patterns were in white. They wore earrings of various types, and had some very nicely decorated bamboo boxes, used for holding tobacco. One man had a large silver button inserted in the upper edge of either ear, and the pair were joined together by a string of fine beads, which hung loosely under his chin.

Tattoo marks of the kind known to the Sea Dyaks as *kelingai* ornamented many of the men's forearms; star-like tattoo patterns were to be seen on the inner sides of the calves of their legs, and also V-shaped blocks of patterns on their throats. As, however, we had to hurry back to the launch, I had but little time to make observations. Left Miri at about 4 P.M.

JULY 8TH.—Arrived at Labuan Island shortly after day-break. Mount Kinabalu on the mainland was plainly visible. Labuan is said to be about ninety miles from the mountain. Went on shore before breakfast. Not much change to note since I was here last, except that the coal mines are no longer working. The little town is as clean and bright, and the island as pretty, as ever. Hunted for the Malay shop where I formerly bought some old silver-ware, but the owner seems to have removed to Brunei. Some modern Brunei brass-ware was on sale in one *kedai*, and I purchased a small figure of a dragon, while two other passengers bought a large brass *sireh*-stand and a *parang ilang* (Dyak sword) respectively.

Back to the ship for breakfast, and then went ashore again. Several Kadayan (?) women in the town, one with large silver buttons in the sleeves of her coat. All wore black lace head-coverings and short black jackets, and had open carrying-baskets on their backs. Returned to steamer and watched some Malays very cleverly spearing garfish, which were passing up and down near the lighter from which the *Sandakan* was loading coal.

Went ashore again with E. at about 3 P.M. with the intention of reaching a Kadayan village, but we took a wrong turning and finally arrived in a Tutong settlement. Nothing was particularly worthy of note there, as the people are Mohammedans and very civilised, but the house walls, made of mid-ribs of palm leaves, laid horizontally, were interesting, and we also saw a nice carrying-basket ornamented with patterns. Returned to the wharf at six o'clock via the old colliery railway. All night at Labuan.

July 9th.—Left Labuan at daylight, and after great trouble in coming alongside the wharf, owing to an old pile causing an obstruction, I landed at Jesselton just before 4 p.m. Hurried off to the Treasury to get some money, of which I had run short, and luckily found it open. Back again to the *Sandakan* for dinner. Heard from various people that some of the Marudu Bay and Tempassuk natives have recently given trouble. They seem to have been Bajaus, Illanuns and Dusuns. A number of the insurgents were killed or captured near Pindasan, but things are now quiet, the trouble having occurred a couple of months ago. Owing to the restlessness of some of the Tempassuk people, the District Officer, North Keppel, has temporarily removed from Tuaran to Kotabelud. The junior officer is now stationed at Tuaran.

Other news was that Haji Arsat (the head chief in the Tempassuk) has lately been given the title of Orang Kaya Kaya instead of Orang Kaya, which was his style in my time, and has been made Supernumerary Assistant Officer with 3rd Class Magistrate's powers; also that the Kotabelud house, formerly built under my supervision, had been burned down through a fire which started in one of the bathrooms.

Jesselton has changed a good deal since I was here last. A large amount of ground has been reclaimed, a reservoir constructed, the wharf improved and new buildings put up. Electric-light plant has been installed, and will soon be working, while ice-making machinery is on order from England. There seem to have been several Government chiefs in the recent disturbances; but I do not know which, if any, of my Tempassuk friends were mixed up in the affair. The leader of the enterprise was one Kulindad, Marudu district Dusun. Made arrangements at the Treasury for drawing money.

July 10th.—Up to the Resident's office at 9.30 a.m. and talked over my plans with him. Telephoned to old Sergeant Genang at Tuaran and asked him to try and get me either my old Chinese cook or my former "boy"

(Omboi). Genang says that he thinks the cook has gone to Jesselton. Omboi is at Tuaran and will probably come if I want him. Arranged to call up Genang at 3 P.M. for further information. Down to the wharf to get baggage off the *Sandakan*. M., who is in charge of the customs, kindly put my baggage through for me without any trouble, and further helped me by sending off one of his men to Gaya Island to try and arrange with some of the Orang Bernadan—*i.e.* Tawi Tawi Islanders, who are settled there—for a prahu to take me to the mouth of the Tempassuk river, for I have decided to go as far as I can by sea. Back from the steamer to the Rest House with E., who was my guest to lunch.

Rang up Genang at Tuaran, who told me that Omboi was with him in the office. Asked him to let Omboi speak to me and made arrangements that he should start on foot for Jesselton to-morrow (distance said to be about twenty-four miles). Customs boatman came in saying that he has not been able to get a boat in Jesselton, but suggested that he should go to the market as early as possible to-morrow morning and get hold of some of the Bernadans when they come in with their fish. Out with E. to take some photographs of the town. *Sandakan* left for Kudat at about 6 P.M.

JULY 11TH.—Out buying provisions in the morning. Omboi arrived at about 3.30 P.M. and the customs boatmen brought in some Bernadans a little later. These men, a crew of three, will take me in their boat to the Tempassuk for five dollars per man. Went to the club at 5 P.M., where I did not meet many people that I knew, and thence to the Resident's to dinner. My old District Officer is with him, and I was very pleased to meet him again. This was a lucky chance, as he is now Resident of the Interior, and has come down for a few days after having a rough time in the Murut country, where there has been some pretty big fighting. Took a wrong turn on the hill in the dark on the way back from the Resident's, and, after wandering about for a long time, found a Chinaman's hut. Knocked up the occupant and got him to guide me to some place that I knew. Finally emerged on the railway not far from the hospital.

July 12th.—Bernadan men in early with their boat, a strongly built tripod-masted prahu called a *lipah-lipah.* After finishing up various business got on board at twelve o'clock and started for the Tempassuk, calling in at the customs on the way to get a pass. Sailed on with a favourable wind past the mouths of the Inanan and Menggatal rivers. Anchored for a while off the Kuala Tuaran at dark owing to a storm from ahead, which was apparently coming on. However, it never reached us, and, the wind being again favourable, we sailed, and arrived at Kuala Abai some time before daylight. This the boatmen, who did not know the coast well, tried to persuade me was the mouth of the Tempassuk river, but I, seeing hills near the shore, told them that it could not be as there are no hills at the mouth of the Tempassuk. We therefore anchored till daybreak, and as soon as it was light found that I was right, and saw several boats coming out of the mouth of the Tempassuk, some distance ahead of us.

July 13th.—Made for the entrance of the river, passing several large boats (*prahu pakerangan*), whose occupants were engaged in fishing with seine nets. One of my crew on entering the river threw a couple of handfuls of rice into the water as an offering to the spirit of the stream. This he told me he had vowed to do should we arrive at our destination without trouble or mishap. We had a tedious and very hot journey up-river to Haji Arsat's house at Fort Alfred, sailing being impossible, and the boatmen tired. Haji Arsat at home to meet me. Had a long talk with him and learned the following news:—

(1) That a new tax of twenty-five cents per annum is to be laid on all coco-nut-trees from which toddy is collected.

(2) That a tax is also to be put on *tapai* (rice wine). (Difficult to collect!)

(3) That a veterinary surgeon now visits the Tempassuk.

(4) That forced labour has been abolished, even with regard to the upkeep of bridle-paths.

(5) That the rates of wages for coolies have been slightly raised.

(6) That a Dutchman and a Swiss are going prospecting for oil to Saiap (on a spur of Mount Kinabalu).

(7) That the recent trouble arose partly from the demarcation of lands with a view to collecting quit-rent.

(8) That the Dato Temenggong (a very old chief) is dead.

Arranged to leave for Kotabelud the next day, the baggage going by buffaloes, and to call in at Tamu Timbang, it being market day, on the way.

JULY 14TH.—To Tamu Timbang by boat with Haji Arsat. Many Bajaus there, but only a few Dusuns. Met various old acquaintances, and among them Saleh, my former clerk. Went round the market, but did not buy anything. On from the market to the shops, where I met Keruak (a Bajau headman)—he has been ill, and does not look fit even now —and Sirinan (a Dusun friend of mine), who, I thought, seemed glad to see me. Up to the office, into which I peeped—much the same as in my time. Met several police who were formerly under me.

From the office to Arsat's Kotabelud house near the river, where I was to stay until I went up-country. Had a long talk with Sirinan. Much delay in getting food, as only three buffaloes turned up at Fort Alfred to take my baggage in the morning, though six were ordered; however, the missing three with the rest of my stuff arrived before dark. Sat up till late talking with Arsat. The District Officer is at Pindasan settling up affairs after the trouble, but will return in a day or two; so I shall wait to see him.

JULY 15TH.—Up early, to the office with Arsat and then down to the shops, where I bought a fine old silver belt-clasp, an old brass (Brunei) kettle and some other articles.

JULY 16TH —Around the shops. Picked up some

IN A RICE FIELD NEAR TAMBATUAN.

A little Dusun boy left in charge of articles deposited by his parents. The large carrying basket is used for holding padi or tubers; upon it rests a spear with blade sheathed. The smaller basket is used for small personal belongings when going on a journey.

SOME DUSUN MUSICAL INSTRUMENTS.

These instruments are ordinarily played together. They consist of a set of dulcimer gongs, a drum, a flute, a nose-flute (one nostril is stopped with leaves when playing it), and two stringed instruments of bamboo, played by women.

weapons and a small brass cannon in the pawnshop, and a shell-bracelet from a Bajau man. Up the hill with Sirinan to have a look at the burnt remains of my old house. Arsat off to Siraban on business. This village has now moved down to the flat land. There being a market to-day (Tamu Darat) many people have gone off to it.

JULY 17TH.—B., the District Officer, returned from Pindasan. He was kind enongh to send out a couple of police to beat up coolies for me. Lunch and dinner with B. He has, as pets, two young Orang-utans and a *wah-wah* monkey. Bought a cow for fifteen dollars from the Dato Meradan, had it killed and divided up, and portions given to the District Officer, the clerk, the police, the Chinese shopkeepers and the local headmen. Made arrangements for starting up-country to-morrow.

JULY 18TH.—Late in leaving Kotabelud, owing to the coolies not being up to time. (Our destination Tamu Darat, as I am in no hurry, and prefer to take things easily.) Passing Siraban, Perasan and Piasau, and following the bridle-path, we left the villages of Rangalau and Lasau behind us on the right, and Gaur, situated on a hill on the other side of the river, on the left. Thence past Pinasang (on the right). Below the village the flat lands on either side of the path have, this year, been ploughed for the planting of dry padi (*kendinga*).

Our party consists of myself, Gimbad (a Dusun of some influence in Tempassuk village), Omboi (my boy), Tinggi (a Tuaran Dusun policeman), and fifteen Dusun coolies (Piasau and Tempassuk men). I allowed the coolies to get ahead, so as to have things ready on my arrival, and followed with Gimbad.

Near Pinasang some Dusuns were hunting with dogs in a strip of jungle, which is separated from the bridle-path by a piece of undulating land covered with rough *lalang*-grass. Just as we became aware of this, owing to the barking of the dogs, a large wild pig (a sow) broke covert and halted for a moment on a slight knoll. Seeing us, she ran ahead, crossed the bridle-path in front of us, and rushed down a hill into the river. Gimbad, immediately he saw her heading for the river, drew his *parang* and dashed off in pursuit. He followed her into the stream and wounded her in the back above the hind-quarters. She then turned on him and he wounded her in the snout. Finding that she was getting the worst of it, she started to swim away again, only to be wounded a second time in the back. After this Gimbad gave up the chase, and I watched the sow gain the opposite bank, wearily climb it, and disappear into some brushwood on the edge of a strip of jungle. By this time some of the hunters had come up, and they crossed the river, which was at that place only waist-deep, taking a dog with them. They also vanished into the brushwood, but in about three or four minutes they reappeared, dragging with them the pig's carcass. She had been too exhausted from loss of blood to go far, and a spear had given her the *coup de grâce.*

From this place on to the Tamu Darat ground without further adventure. To-morrow we are to try and make Kabaiau, and I hope to set out earlier than I did to-day, as the walk was rather trying, owing to our starting late, and thus catching the full heat of the sun, for the bridle-path as far as Tamu Darat is almost without shade.

19TH JULY.—From Tamu Darat ground to Kabaiau *opis* (halting-hut)—the word is derived from "office." Met a number of Tamis (Ulu Tuaran) coming down to trade hats, *sireh*, etc., and also another lot of Dusuns from Kaung Ulu. A probably stolen cow or buffalo had been killed on the bridle-path a few days ago, as witness a heap of dung and leafy branches put down in an attempt to cover the blood-stains. This was below Ghinambur Narinang village. Passed the villages of Bongul, Sempodan, Kabaiau, Lengkobang and Paka on the far side of the river and Ghinambur Maku-Paku, Ghinambur Baiaiat, Ghinambur Narinang and Lapan Tabobun on our side. Kabaiau *opis* and its neighbourhood in a very dirty state owing to up-country Dusuns stopping in it on the way to Tamu.

July 20th.—From Kabaiau to Tambatuan: some very fine views of Nabalu by the way. Left the bridle-path opposite Tambatuan village, and climbed down the hill-side through crops of *kaladi* to the wet-padi fields in the valley, where we found several women at work.

The Tambatuan villagers do not use the plough in preparing these *ranau*-fields for planting. The grass is cut short, and water is then let in from the river until the roots die. The ground is rather uneven, and there are some slight attempts at terracing. Forded the river—*i.e.* the Tempassuk or Kadamaian.

Gumpus (the headman of Tambatuan), who had been warned of my arrival by the coolies, was awaiting me, and came over to help me across. Thence up the long and steep hill to Tambatuan village, rain coming on before we reached our destination. After a rest and some food I paid off my coolies and Gimbad. Gumpus and crowds of villagers in at night. All went into fits of laughter on being shown their faces in my magnifying shaving-glass. Bought a good many specimens. To my disgust a Dusun dog stole a large and newly opened tinned tongue. As many pigs about as ever. Some sickness (dysentery?) here, and also, I hear, at Kiau.

July 21st.—Developing photographs and buying specimens. Crowds of Dusuns in. A fashion in tattooing has set in here since my last visit, four years ago, due, I am given to understand, to a Dyak policeman having stopped in the village for some time. The patterns to be seen are, therefore, chiefly debased forms of Sea Dyak designs and are not truly native to the country. Gumpus has quite covered himself with these pictures. We are living in a spare house of his, in which he stores his gongs, of which he is very proud. Rain all day long.

July 22nd.—This day and to-morrow, Gumpus says, are Dusun tabu-days, no work being allowed to be done in the fields. Purchased a goat and had it killed for the benefit of the villagers. Out with Gumpus for a stroll round the village. Bought a large number of ethnographical specimens, some of them very fine. I shall make my long stay here, and only put in a night or so at Kaung and Kiau. Continual rain from noon until long after dark. I go to bed very tired every night, as I scarcely have a minute's rest all day owing to the crowds of people who come to see me, talk, and sell things. They start arriving at six o'clock in the morning and the last of them leave me at about 10.30 or 11 P.M. However, I am very much pleased with things in general, and have no wish to check them. My only complaint is that there is so much to do, and so little time to do it in. Usual chorus of pigs under the house at night. Tinggi, the Tuaran Dusun policeman, seems quite a good fellow. Gumpus looks after me like a father.

JULY 23RD.—Did not set foot outside all day long as I spent the first part of it in developing photographs, and then with Gumpus's help set to work to catalogue some of the things I have collected. Dusuns in with butterflies to sell. Usual rain in the afternoon.

JULY 24TH.—Having given out that I would pay one cent for every butterfly brought to me in good condition, and two cents for large species, I have been overwhelmed by the amount of work the Dusuns have made for me. So many insects have been caught that I have had to throw away dozens of the commoner kinds. I have stopped buying ethnographical specimens, as I think that I have got nearly everything needful, and I shall run short of cash before getting back to supplies at Kotabelud unless I am careful. Went out in the early morning with Gumpus to take photographs of Mount Nunkok and of Kinabalu, also of two human skulls hung up outside a padi store.

JULY 25TH.—A dull day with a high wind, probably the forerunner of a drought, of which the Dusuns will be very glad, as they are waiting to burn their clearings. Took some photographs. Spent some time with Gumpus talking about omen-birds and the meanings of the names of various villages.

JULY 26TH.—Finished off naming and cataloguing specimens, Gumpus assisting me. Did some photographic work. This again is a Dusun tabu-day with regard to field-work.

JULY 27TH.—This day of the month is called *Limbas* by the Dusuns. Work is allowable on wet-padi fields, but not on hill clearings. Gumpus, therefore, off to his *ranau* (wet-padi) fields. Developed some more photographs and took a stroll round the village. Found a spear set up in front of one house for the purpose of guarding against the spirits of disease. Got Omboi and Tinggi to tell me something of Tuaran burial and marriage customs. I was amused to watch a Dusun pig laboriously searching for, and collecting, the fallen leaves of coco-nut palms, which she made into a nest for her young.

JULY 28TH.—Another Dusun tabu-day. Did some photographic work. Amused myself and the villagers by getting up some races for boys and girls, giving prizes of a few cents to the winners. Musical entertainment (gongs and drums) by Gumpus and other Dusuns at night.

JULY 29TH.—Left Tambatuan for Kaung. One of the Tambatuan boys, who is mentally deficient, followed Gumpus and myself, who had started after the coolies. He was making a great fuss because his mother, one of my coolies, was leaving him. Gumpus called to him to go back, but he only went a little way, and then followed us again. I told Gumpus to call him to us and explain that it was all right and that his mother would be back to-morrow. However, he would not come, but kept just in sight of us through the bushes on the hill-side below the village, and, when we had crossed the Kadamaian and were scaling the hill on the opposite side to reach the bridle-path, he was still to be heard lamenting by the river-side, where he had been joined by some other children.

We had an abominable journey to Kaung, with floods of rain nearly the whole time, and were, of course, drenched through and through. I was shivering with the cold and wet, but Gumpus did not seem much disturbed. Managed somehow or other to get to Kaung *opis*, where I found the coolies, Tinggi and Omboi had arrived safely; the latter, however, had nearly given in on the road and had occasionally to be pushed along by the coolies. However, we now seem fairly well recovered, and I hope that there will be no ill effects. Paid off six coolies. Several Kaung men came over to see me. Bought some specimens from them. The river is in flood, but in spite of this several of the Kaung people crossed it, though others went round by a bamboo bridge which they have made a little way up-stream from the village.

July 30th.—Sent a messenger to Kiau to ask Ompo (an old friend of mine) to come and see me. I have decided not to go to his village, as the track is in a very bad state, and it is doubtful if I should do as much in the way of collecting specimens there as I can here, since Kiau is, comparatively speaking, frequently visited by Europeans, who are intent on climbing Nabalu. Ompo arrived at about 5 p.m. He seems very friendly and quite fit. Small toddy (*bahr*) party at night. Bought a number of ethnographical specimens. Settled to leave here the day after to-morrow. River still in flood after yesterday's rain, but fordable for local Dusuns. In the morning I crossed by the bridge to Kaung village, taking with me Gumpus, Tinggi and Omboi. Took some photographs, including the bridge, shoot fish-traps, village guardian-stones, head-house (containing two skulls in a basket), etc., etc.

July 31st.—Went over to Kaung with Ompo, Tinggi, Gumpus and Omboi, crossing by the river, which has now gone down. Climbed to the upper part of the village, which I had not visited before. Another head-house there, the human skulls, contained in a basket, being mixed with several of those of the Orang-Utan. There are two head-houses in the lower village, each containing a couple of skulls, but one of them has fallen down. Took more photographs and bought a number of specimens. Ompo returned to Kiau this evening.

AUGUST 1ST.—Left Kaung for Gumpus's *ranau sulap*—*i.e.* watching-hut on the wet-padi fields—below Tambatuan village and arrived there. Not a troublesome journey when done in dry weather, as to-day. Since there has been no rain for the last few days, Gumpus and some of the Tambatuan men want to burn off their clearings to-morrow, and the former has asked me to continue my journey on the day after. This I have consented to do, with the proviso that I pay no wages for to-morrow. In this hut there is hanging up, under the thatch, a small bamboo trough, which was used as a receptacle for last year's rice soul (*membaraian*), and close to it, and stuck into the thatch, are two small bamboo knives with which the rice soul was reaped. I have asked Gumpus to let me have all these. A few of the Kiau people, and one Tambatuan man, being afraid that it may rain to-morrow, have burned their clearings to-day, but I doubt if they have been very successful, as the wood is not yet sufficiently dry after the heavy rains of a few days ago.

AUGUST 2ND.—At Gumpus's *sulap*. Extensive burnings of felled jungle to-day. One burnt on the hill near us excellent. Several Dusuns, chiefly Kaung Ulu men, passed by on their way to Tamu Timbang. Gumpus, who has burned his clearing, but not very successfully, came in towards evening, bringing with him a bamboo of rice wine. He says that he will have five days' work collecting the unburnt wood on his clearing for a second firing. I noticed that a single tree has been left unfelled in a clearing near us, and thinking it probable that there might be some superstitious reason for this, asked a Dusun why it had not been cut down. He replied that it was left as a perching-place for the birds, as, if there was no tree left for them in the clearing, they might curse the crop. Sand-flies and horse-flies here in plenty, and sleep difficult.

August 3rd.—Left Gumpus's *ranau sulap* for Kabaiau (about four miles away) and arrived there. To-morrow I hope to reach Ghinambur Narinang, so as to take raft from there to Kotabelud on the day following. I am sending off a couple of lightly laden coolies early to-morrow to tell the Narinang people to make the raft. On the way to Kotabelud I intend to call in at Tamu Darat, the day after to-morrow being market day. During the early part of to-day all the country towards Tamu Darat was obscured by clouds of smoke, as the Dusuns there are burning off their clearings, being afraid that rain is coming.

August 4th.—From Kabaiau to Ghinambur Laut. Stopped at Ghinambur Narinang by the way to inquire if there was a possibility of getting a raft, having sent off two coolies early as I purposed yesterday. Found that there were no bamboos in the neighbourhood and that it was therefore impossible to construct one. Journey as far as Narinang not unpleasant, but from Narinang to Ghinambur Laut the path was rough and the sun hot. On arrival I heard that several rafts belonging to the Kabaiau people are moored at the mouth of the Penataran river, and that their makers are coming down to Tamu Darat on them to-morrow.

The Ghinambur *opis* is now in ruins. The village, though not visible from the bridle-path, is only a few chains distant on the other side of a small strip of jungle. Put up in a rather small Dusun house. Everybody here (and elsewhere) very much exercised about the new twenty-five-cent tax on coco-nut-trees used for obtaining *bahr*. Got some excellent oranges, which I did not know grew lower down the Tempassuk valley than Kiau and Tambatuan, and also several durians. (The orange-tree seedlings seem to have been obtained from Kiau.)

August 5th.—Left Ghinambur Laut for Tamu Darat and arrived there. A very small market to-day, as the up-country Dusuns are busy working on their clearings. The Swiss oil-man turned up in the Tamu. He is on his way to

In Kaung "Ulu," a Typical Up-Country Dusun Village of the Tempassuk District.

On the left is a house in course of construction. "House-horns," found on many Dusun dwellings, can be seen at the apex of the roof in the centre.

Kabaiau. Haji Arsat, Keruak, Bagu, Sirinan, ex-sergeant Lakui and other old friends of mine at market. Left the Tamu by rafts, Gumpus and Omboi on one, I on another. Arrived at Kotabelud in the afternoon. The District Officer away in Jesselton.

AUGUST 6TH.—Nothing particular doing. Drew some money and paid off my coolies. Sangin (a Bajau, and an old friend) came in towards evening from Kagurhan, to which place he has removed from Kotabelud. Had a chat with him and told him to let me see some brass-ware, which he wants to sell to-morrow. Sirinan also in for a talk, bringing with him a very nicely made model of a Dusun plough. Bought an old Chinese jar and a stone implement from a Bajau, and a couple of large and fine sun-hats, made by the Tamis (Ulu Tuaran) people, in the shops. We are putting up in a newly erected bungalow on the top of Kotabelud hill, which is situated between the fort and the site of my old house.

AUGUST 7TH.—Arranged with Sangin to buy some of his brass-ware. Repacking Dusun collections with Omboi.

AUGUST 8TH.—Sangin came in with his brass-ware and the Illanun loom (with half-completed cloth) which I asked him to get for me. Arranged with Sirinan to go to Kampong Tempassuk to-morrow to try and excavate the reputed site of an old village.

AUGUST 9TH.—Left Kotabelud with Sirinan at about 8 A.M. Crossed the river at Gunding and, from there, walked to Gimbad's house at Tempassuk. On nearing the village we came to his irrigation canal, quite a big affair. I noticed that in one place its banks were considerably higher than elsewhere, and immediately suspected that this was the place where he said his canal had cut through an old house site. On Gimbad joining us, I found that I was correct in my surmise. The banks of the canal at this place were strewn with bits of coarse and thick pottery, different from that made by the Dusuns at the present day.

Gimbad and Sirinan picked up several yellow glass or

paste beads, like those which the Dusuns still value; but we saw no fragments of Chinese pottery. We also found two stones (naturally rounded by river action) which had evidently been selected because of their shape for some purpose or other. Possibly they were used for potting stones, but they are much larger than the pebbles employed for that purpose by the modern Dusuns. After trying the soil here and there with the *changkol*, and seemingly exhausting the possibilities of the site, we repaired to Gimbad's house, where he produced another bead (blue), which he had found while making his canal, and a fairly large, flattish piece of brass ornamented with some rudely cast patterns. This and the bead I purchased.

Another interesting object found on the same site was also produced, but the man who owned it refused to part with it. This was a well-shaped little hone or cleaning-stone with a hole bored in it at one end to enable it to be suspended from a cord. Its length was about five inches and its breadth about seven-eighths of an inch, while it may have been one-third of an inch in thickness. The stone of which it was composed was greenish brown, fine-grained and fairly hard. Leaving Tempassuk, where we had been regaled with a meal of rice and small boiled fish (both dried and fresh) and with rice cooked with Indian corn, all washed down by a plentiful supply of *bahr*, we made for Bunsud's house at Tamboulian, but unluckily found him out.

However, his lieutenant Lipatan welcomed and entertained us. From Tamboulian we made our way to Piasau, where we called in at Ransab's, but he also was out. Left Sirinan in the village (his own), and returned to Kotabelud with the coolie that I had taken with me in the morning to help in excavating.

August 10th.—Bought rather a nice old brass betel-box in one of the Chinese shops. I was sitting talking with Sirinan and a Bajau in the evening outside our hut when a small snake glided past, close to Sirinan, going in the direction of the house. Its colour was black, and I suspected that it was a cobra, as they are common on the grassy hills round Kotabelud. In this I turned out to be correct, for it puffed out quite a large hood when Omboi and the Bajau set to work to dispatch it with sticks.

AUGUST 11TH.—Bought a large Illanun sword and a *Trīdacna* shell-bracelet from Kalud, and a long, Illanun type, shield (*klasug*) from Sirinan. The latter went off to Usakan to superintend some repairs to the wooden jetty, which was always giving trouble in my time. Went down to meet Haji Arsat at the shops in the evening, and made a few purchases. Lipatan and another Dusun in the *bahr* (toddy) at about midday.

AUGUST 12TH.—To Tamu Timbang in the early morning, where I took a few photographs of the market. No fish to be obtained, as Omboi and I were late in getting there and everything had been bought up by the Chinese, and by the Bajaus, who were preparing for their Hari Raya festival, which, in most villages, is to be celebrated to-morrow. Bought a sun-hat of a type I wanted in the market and also a newly cast Illanun horse-bit (brass). Sampled some Bajau *penjarom* cakes and then home.

One Bernadan (Tawi Tawi) *dapong* (large, double outrigger boat) turned up to the market, which is held by the river-side, and I have arranged, through Haji Arsat, who was also at the Tamu, for three of these craft to await me at Tamu Timbang ground on Sunday, with a view to sailing for Mengkabong on Monday morning. The hair of the Orang Bernadans' children, two of whom were on board, has quite a red tinge, due, I suppose, to constant exposure to sea breezes and salt water.

The Bernadans that I have seen so far are of a lower type than the Bajaus; their skin colour is dark through constant exposure, and their eyes are small, roving and glittering: forehead low and features animalian.

On arrival at Kotabelud I found Sangin waiting for me, and paid him for the specimens that I took from him the other day. Bought a stone implement of a rare type from a

Bajau, who also brought in a very nice old green crackle-ware Chinese dish for which he asked ten dollars. I offered two dollars, but this was refused, but I subsequently got it for three dollars. Bengali, Gimbad and two other Tempassuk Dusuns in with a present of *bahr*, which we consumed between us. Numerous flights of green pigeon passed under the house after tea.

I was sitting outside watching these when Dr H., the oil expert, came by on his way to Haji Arsat's house, having just come in from Saiap, where he had gone (via Melangkap) from Kabaiau. I showed him the stone implement bought to-day and he seemed surprised, saying that there was a nephrite (the mineral of which the implement is made) hill in the neighbourhood of Tempassuk village. We are to visit this on Friday to see if we can find signs of the stone having been worked. I also mentioned the radiolarian chert flakes, which are to be found on Kotabelud hill, and we are to search for some of these to-morrow.

AUGUST 13TH.—Out with Dr H. to the end of Kotabelud hill in search of chert flakes, of which we found several. From there to the shops to buy Illanun cloths, and then to Koruak's village to take photographs of Hari Raya festivities. The District Officer returned to-day and came round to see me towards evening. Dinner with the District Officer.

AUGUST 14TH.—Down to Haji Arsat's house to see Dr H., who is foot-sore from his journey up-country. Thence to the shops to pay some bills, and then to Diki's Kampong at Perasan to take photographs of the Aari Raya celebrations.

AUGUST 15TH.—Rather a bad attack of fever. Gimbad, Sirinan, Lipatan, Bengali and other Dusuns came in to see me, bringing *bahr* with them, but I was not fit enough to talk very much to them.

AUGUST 16TH.—Still fever. The Bernadans' boats have not yet come in. Left for Haji Arsat's house at Fort Alfred and arrived there feeling very much done up. Our three boats in towards evening.

August 17th.—Still fever. Left Arsat's house at about 3 p.m. Omboi and I in one boat, heavy baggage in the other two. Anchored off Ambong at night.

August 18th.—Winds contrary and going therefore slow. Landed once to get firewood and once for water. Anchored for the night at the mouth of the Mengkabong river.

August 19th.—Up the Mengkabong river to Mengkabong village. Omboi off to Tuaran to see his wife. I, being still unwell and weak from not eating, did not go, though I should have liked to have done so. Took a number of photographs of the village. Rain all afternoon. Left towards night for Jesselton and anchored till daybreak under an island within sight of that place.

August 20th.—Sailed into Jesselton, gave up pass at the customs office and landed close to the Rest House.

August 21st.—Repacking specimens. Visited one or two people whom I knew formerly.

August 22nd.—To dinner at W.'s to see his excellent collection of brass-ware.

August 24th.—Left Jesselton for Papar by the eight o'clock train. The railway between Jesselton and Papar passes partly through mangrove swamps, partly along the seashore and partly through padi-fields owned by Dusuns and Bajaus. Arrived at Papar, made my way to the pawn-shop, always the first place I visit in a settlement, and picked up some nice pieces of brass-ware. In another Chinese shop I purchased a locally made Dusun sun-hat decorated with fine patterns, and a very heavy and beautifully worked brass betel-casket of a type of which I had long wanted to get an example. Many of the Dusuns here have become Christians, there being a Roman Catholic mission station in the vicinity, others are converts to Islam.

Externally, in their manners, I did not think that they compared favourably with their less civilised brothers, but perhaps the improvement is internal only, and thus not visible on the surface. Land in Papar seems to be at a premium, and the little township presents quite a busy appearance. The Chinese here grow vegetables for Jesselton market; otherwise I do not know how they live, unless it is by taking in one another's washing. The new bridge over the Papar river is *the* great engineering work of Borneo.

Met M. in the Rest House, where I went to get a drink. He and I came out on the same boat to Borneo together as cadets. He very kindly gave me tiffin and sent his boy with me to a Dusun house to see some old jars, among which, however, there were no true *Gusis*. The return train to Jesselton was over two hours late, but did eventually arrive. The scenery along the line is rather fine in places, especially where the railway runs near the coast. Both Dusuns and Bajaus seem to be late in planting their padi, they still being at work ploughing and harrowing in some places.

AUGUST 25TH.—Finished packing. Said good-bye to the Resident and to some other people. Went on board the s.s. *Selangor* at about 4 P.M. Heavy rain all day. The boat will not sail till 3 P.M. to-morrow, though the advertised time is 5 P.M. to-day.

AUGUST 26TH.—Left Jesselton. Anchored till daylight off some small island.

AUGUST 27TH.—Weighed anchor at about 5 A.M. for Labuan and arrived at about half-past ten. Decided not to stop in Labuan (as I had intended to do). Omboi had, therefore, to be sent back to Tuaran. Luckily I found a launch which was about to leave for Weston on the mainland; so, putting him on board, I gave him directions for reaching Jesselton via Beaufort.

AUGUST 28TH.—Arrived at Miri early in the morning, but only stopped to take off mails.

AUGUST 29TH.—Beautiful weather. Passed some islands (? the Natunas) at 12 A.M.

AUGUST 30TH.—Arrived at Singapore.

APPENDICES

APPENDIX A.

DERIVATIONS OF SOME TEMPASSUK PLACE- AND VILLAGE-NAMES, AS GIVEN ME BY NATIVES

(1) Bengkahak	(a village)		from *bengkahak*, a crow.
(2) Paka	,,		,, *paka*, *lalang*, grass.
(3) Kinsaroban or Kinsiraban	,,		,, *sarob*, to burn.
(4) Lengkobang	,,		,, *kubang*, a pass between hills.
(5) Bundu	,,		,, *bundu*, a kind of mango fruit.
(6) Tambulian	,,	possibly	,, *uli* or *muli*, to go home.
(7) Tambatuan	,,	,,	,, *tambatuan*, a kind of grass or bamboo.
(8) Penalabu	,,	,,	,, *nalabu*, a hole which goes through.
(9) Senimpodan	,,		,, *senimpod*, to swallow. There is a legend that a child was once swallowed at this place by a kind of fish called *balus*.
(10) Piasau	,,		,, *piasau*, a coco-nut-tree.
(11) Tiong	,,		,, *tiong*, a deep pool.
(12) Rangalau	,,		,, *rangalau*, a kind of tree and fruit.
(13) Nahabah	,,	possibly	,, *na-habah*, fallen (of a tree): *i.e.* the village would thus be the place of the fallen trees.
(14) Tempassuk (river and village)			Said to be so called from a whirlpool which the Bajaus made in the river by means of magic.

APPENDIX B.

MEASUREMENTS OF "ORANG DUSUN" (1915)

Serial No.	Head Length	Head Breadth	Cephalic Index	Remarks		
1	188 mm.	138 mm.	73·4	Up-country	Dusun of Tambatuan	Tempassuk District
2	183 ,,	144 ,,	78·6	,,	,,	,,
3	196 ,,	139 ,,	70·9	,,	,,	,,
4	178 ,,	134 ,,	75·2	,,	,,	,,
5	186 ,,	142 ,,	76·3	,,	,,	,,
6	180 ,,	134 ,,	74·4	,,	,,	,,
7	201 ,,	148 ,,	73·5	,,	,,	,,
8	188 ,,	147 ,,	78·1	,,	,,	,,
9	192 ,,	142 ,,	73·9	,,	,,	,,
10	178 ,,	143 ,,	80·3	,,	,,	,,
11	181 ,,	137 ,,	75·6	,,	,,	,,
12	188 ,,	144 ,,	76·5	,,	,,	,,
13	188 ,,	141 ,,	75·0	,,	Kaung	,,
14	182 ,,	141 ,,	77·4	,,	,,	,,
15	177 ,,	138 ,,	77·9	,,	,,	,,
16	183 ,,	143 ,,	78·1	,,	,,	,,
17	180 ,,	142 ,,	78·8	,,	,,	,,
18	181 ,,	143 ,,	79·0	,,	Tuaran	Tuaran District
19	191 ,,	142 ,,	74·3	,,	,,	,,

APPENDIX C.

THE MALAY LANGUAGE AS SPOKEN IN NORTH-WEST BORNEO

Malay, not being the mother tongue of this part of Borneo, although it is the *lingua franca*, as might be expected, is spoken extremely badly. Various words are used which are unknown in the Malay of the Peninsula. Possibly they may occur in the native languages, or in the patois of the Bruneis, who naturally speak a Malay dialect. Some of these words are given below:

(1) *Bubut*, to pursue (*hambat* or *kejar* of the Peninsula Malays).
(2) *Tagi*, to dun a man who is in debt.

(3) *Kelalei*, to recognise.
(4) *Gagau*, to be busy, to be worried by having too much work to do.
(5) *Balousir*, to run (used of either men or horses).
(6) *Bangkar*, a raft (*rakit* in the Malay Peninsula).
(7) *Siring*, edge—*i.e.* of a river, a box, etc. (*tepi* in the Malay Peninsula).
(8) *Kaban*, a box.

I have remarked elsewhere on the difficulty the Dusuns seem to have in pronouncing *ch*, and the way they have of turning it into *s* or *k*.

Other peculiarities are that a final *k* is pronounced clearly, and not half swallowed (glottal cheek), until it sounds like a mixture between an *h* and a *k*, as in the Peninsula, and that in some words in which there are *r*'s and *l*'s these letters become curiously transposed. Thus the ordinary Malay words *seluar* (trousers) become *serual*, *lapar* (hungry) *rapal*, *luar* (outside) *rual*, etc.

Abbreviations are not so commonly used as in the Peninsula, where *tidak mou* (don't want) usually becomes *ta'mou* and *tid' ada* (there is not) *t'ada.*

The word *dengan*, which in the Malay Peninsula frequently means *with* (*sahya potong dengan parang*, I cut it with a *parang*), in the mouths of the Dusuns becomes *jangan* (*sahya potong jangan parang*).

Map for "Among Primitive Peoples in Borneo."

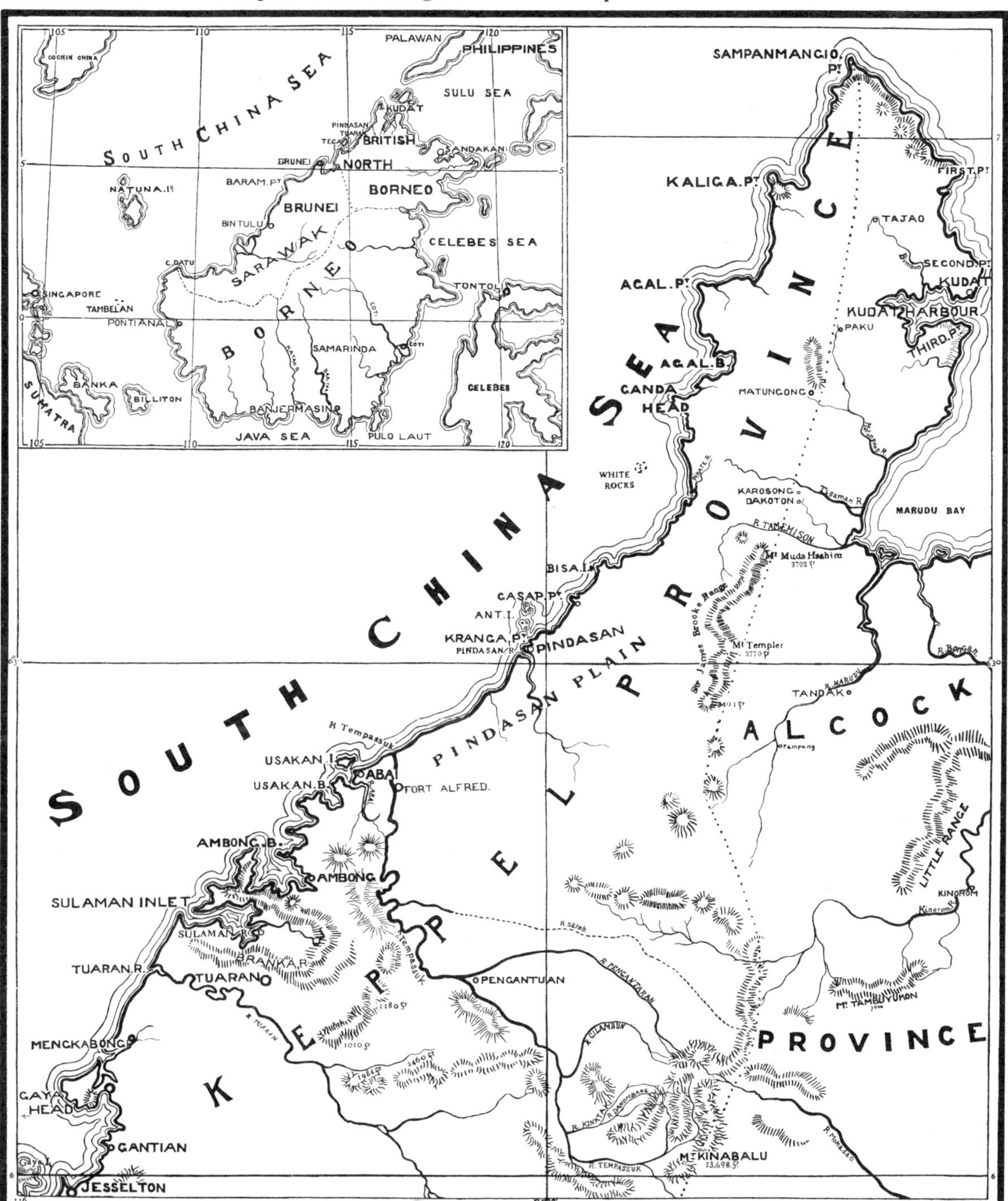

SCALE = 1 : 396,000.

INDEX

Printed in Great Britain by the Riverside Press Limited
Edinburgh
1922